Dietrich W. R. Paulus
Joachim Hornegger

Pattern Recognition and Image Processing in C++

vieweg

Verlag Vieweg, P.O. Box 5829, D-65048 Wiesbaden

Printed and bound by Hubert & Co., Göttingen
Printed on acid-free paper
Printed in Germany

ISBN 3-528-05491-3

Ralf Jungclaus
Modeling of Dynamic Object Systems

Christoph W. Keßler
Automatic Parallelization

Jürgen M. Schneider
Protocol-Engineering

Dietrich W. R. Paulus/Joachim Hornegger
**Pattern Recognition and
Image Processing in C++**

Dejan S. Milojicic
Load Distribution

Franz Kurfeß
Parallelism in Logic

Elmar Eder
Relative Complexities of First Order Calculi

Reinhard Gotzhein
Open Distributed Systems

Vieweg

Part II Object–Oriented Pattern Analysis 109

Part III Pattern Recognition Algorithms 237

Part IV Appendix

For Dorothea, Belinda, and Dominik

Preface

Parts of this text were used for several years by students in a one–term undergraduate course in computer science. The students had to prepare projects in small groups (2–4 students).[1]

This book emphasizes practical experience with image processing. It offers a comprehensive study of

- image processing and image analysis,
- basics of speech processing,
- object–oriented programming,
- software design,
- and programming in C++.

The book is divided into four parts.

In the first part we introduce image processing, image analysis, programming tools, and the basics of C++.

In the second part we describe object–oriented programming in general and the possible applications of object–oriented concepts in C++. Several applications of object–oriented programming for image processing are discussed as well. The new features of C++ are introduced entirely through the use of examples. We cover the proper representation of the data that is a result of pattern analysis as well.

The third part describes a complete system for image segmentation. Some of the material covered refers to the exercises found in the first and second parts: this verifies our belief that an image segmentation system of programs can be developed while simultaneously acquainting others to C++. We combine the data representation described in the second part with the algorithms that use and manipulate them here in the third part.

In part four — the appendix — program listings of those required sources for an image analysis system kernel are given which can not be compiled from

---

[1]The projects are included here as exercises. Further course materials (slides in Postscript or TEX as well as all programming examples) are available upon request (see page 332 for details).

the examples. This part completes the instructions and exercises given in the second and third parts of the book.

While working through the book and exercises, the reader will have read some of the text in part III twice: once, to fill the structures in the second part with actual data, and once more, to apply his newly acquired knowledge of object–oriented programming to pattern analysis.

The introduction of the C++ programming language is done in an informal way (as in chapters 2,4,6,8, and 10–17). We do not specify all the language details.[2] However, everything the reader needs is described in sufficient detail to cover most applications of image analysis programs. Only a basic knowledge of a higher programming language is required. For example, we do not specify the meaning of "variable", "function" etc. We assume that the readers of our book are interested in both pattern recognition and C++.

C++ is, by itself, *not* an object–oriented programming language. It needs further tools such as class libraries. We use the nihcl class library that is found in the public domain. A brief introduction is given in chapter 14. The source code listed in chapter C is a subset of a larger object–oriented image processing package called ἵππος [Pau92b]. The various ways to acquire these sources are listed at the beginning of appendix C.

The input of images or signals and the output to screen or sound devices are not treated here. These strictly hardware–dependent issues have to be solved differently on every computer. Some locations of sources of image display programs using the windowed environment X11 are also listed in section C.3. The chapters on edge detection and contour following (21 and 22) use figures and text which were taken from [Brü90] — with permission of the author.

This book teaches

not only C++ but *real object–oriented* programming

and

algorithms for image and speech processing

---

[2]Footnotes provide references for those who want to know the details.

Part I

"We must begin inquiring whether the distinction between what can and what cannot be seen in the pictures by 'merely looking at them' is entirely clear. (...) Does merely looking, then, mean looking without the use of any instrument? This seems a little unfair to the man who needs glasses to tell a painting from a hippopotamus."
Nelson Goodman, [Goo69]

The goal of this section is to provide the basic background knowledge required for the more sophisticated applications in those that follow. Details are left to footnotes and to the references. Only those subjects relevant for part II and III are mentioned.

In this part of the book we will introduce three different topics:

- Principles of pattern recognition and their applications to image and speech processing,
- Mathematical techniques for image and speech processing,
- The conventional part of the C++ programming language with simple applications to image and speech processing,
- Software engineering principles and tools in Unix, C++, and pattern recognition applications.

The authors wish to express their special thanks to all those who helped to make this book. First of all, Prof. Dr. H. Niemann, the head of our department, for his constant advice and support. Furthermore, R. Beß, J. Denzler, and A. Winzen helped to keep PUMA (the common system, Sect. 3.9) running. Dr. E. Nöth and Dr. Th. Kuhn helped with the speech processing sections. Dr. H. Brünig provided pictures and text from his PhD thesis. F. Tropschuh proofread a first version of the text.

Our special thanks are to Carey Butler who carefully revised our text and did his best to improve our English and style. All remaining errors are our fault and we apologize for them.

4

1 Pattern Recognition

In this chapter we will briefly introduce the basic ideas and the models used in the field of pattern recognition. We exclude biological aspects and treat only the mathematical and technical aspects of perception. This is done in a very informal way, since it is not within the scope of this book to present a rigorous discussion of pattern recognition theory. We put our main emphasis on explaining image and speech processing concepts. The research problems treated are motivated by practical examples. After a brief introduction to the applications of pattern recognition, a sketched mathematical description of patterns, problem domain, and environment is given. Since modern computer systems need digital data, we will also discuss the central problem on how continuous, observable signals can be transformed into digital signals.

A more technical description can be found in the literature (e.g. in [Pra78].)

1.1 Images and Sound

The basic input data to any pattern recognition system are recorded in the form of digitized signals. These digitized signals are then processed by the system. Images as well as speech are typical examples of input data and represent the most important areas in the research and application of pattern recognition.

Digital images and speech signals are very common in today's computer and audio–visual equipment. Digital high–definition video is becoming a huge market. Almost all personal computers now have video and audio capabilities and publishing programs now enable the mixing of digital images with text. PC users are familiar with the JPEG and MPEG standards which are often used for image transmission. Image data formats (like TIFF e.g. [Poy92]) are compatible across hardware borders. Special hardware for video conferences using personal computers and standard computer communication networks are being sold now as well. Several types of media are used in conjunction with each other: text, speech, pictures, movies, etc. The combination of these many media sources and uses is called *multimedia*.

Digital signals can be *synthesized* by a computer based upon a description given to it; sound can be generated by a synthesizer or a voice generator and images are created by *computer graphics*. Natural signals are *recorded* by special devices; sound is captured by microphones and images are recorded by cameras.

The treatment of these signals is called *signal processing*. If a computer tries to "understand" what a natural signal "means", then we call this process pattern recognition and analysis . The terms "image processing" and "speech processing" are used as general terms for signal processing and the analysis of images and sound. The relation between graphics and image analysis is shown in Figure 1.1. In this book, we cover the recognition of image and speech processing: this may be different from algorithms that treat visualization or sound generation.

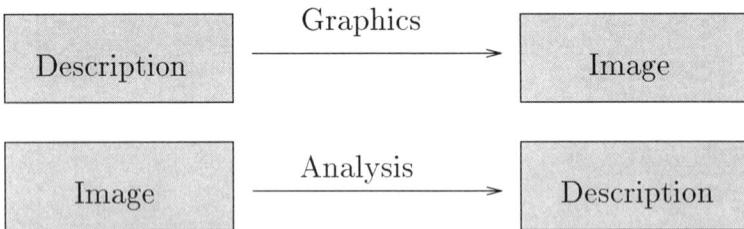

Figure 1.1   Graphics and analysis

1.2   Applications of Pattern Recognition

Applications of pattern recognition can be found in several areas. For instance, industry, medicine and the military make extensive use of pattern recognition techniques. Image processing of satellite images, automatic and computer aided medical diagnosis based on X–ray or MR–images, robot control using visual information, and autonomous vehicles serve as common examples. Other applications are automatic address reading systems or the development of an electronic appointment diary, where the interface is a system for handwritten character recognition. Optical readers are commonly used in banks or shopping centers.

Acoustic communication with computers, dialogue systems, and speaker recognition are potential applications of speech processing. In the future we will have car telephones with which you can dial out using just your voice.

Other applications may be found, for example, in seismic processing where the input signal comes from a seismic sensor. Other signals are processed in medicine like sounds of the heart or signals from the brain (which have more similarity to speech processing than to images).

1.3 Environment, Problem Domain, and Patterns

Human beings use their eyes, ears, skin, and taste as sensors to perceive their environment. These sensors provide our brain with the stimulation necessary for perception. Technically speaking, we model the environment as a large number of variables, or dimensions, whose values cover a specific range that can be recorded by sensors like CCD–cameras or a microphone. Dimensions will not be considered, if they are not measurable by sensors.

Algorithmic approaches to pattern recognition problems require the presentation of a mathematical framework and a formalization of each problem domain being examined. We now briefly provide a general mathematical approach to pattern recognition [Nie90a].

We describe the environment U by the following set

$$U = \{\mathbf{b^r}(\mathbf{x})|r = 1, 2, \ldots\}, \tag{1.1}$$

using vector functions $\mathbf{b^r}(\mathbf{x})$. The dimension of the $\mathbf{b}^r$ may be different for every r. The components are by definition real numbers.

Examples:

- $b^1(x, y)$: sea–level (x = geogr. degrees longitude, y = geogr. degrees latitude)

- $b^2(x, y, z)$: temperature, (x,y,z) position in 3D space

- $b^3(x, y, z, t)$: wind–force / wind–direction (vector!) at a certain time t

The aim of pattern recognition is not the description of the *complete* environment. Instead, we limit ourselves to special application domains or parts of the environment, the so called **problem domain** Ω:

$$U \supset \Omega = \{\mathbf{f}^r(\mathbf{x})|r = 1, 2, \ldots\} \tag{1.2}$$

The dimensions of $\mathbf{f}$ and $\mathbf{x}$ are now fixed and adjusted for each application. Examples are color still images, movies (image sequence), and speech:

- Color image (three color channels R(ed) = 1, G(reen) = 2, B(lue) = 3): $f_r(x, y)$, $f_g(x, y)$, $f_b(x, y)$.

- TV image sequence (time dependent): $f_r(x, y, t)$, $f_g(x, y, t)$, $f_b(x, y, t)$.

- Speech signal: $f(t)$.

Elements of the task domain Ω are called **patterns** $\mathbf{f}^r(\mathbf{x})$ and represented as multivariate vector–functions.

$$\mathbf{f}^r(\mathbf{x}) = \begin{pmatrix} f_1^r(x_1, x_2, \ldots, x_n) \\ f_2^r(x_1, x_2, \ldots, x_n) \\ \ldots \\ f_m^r(x_1, x_2, \ldots, x_n) \end{pmatrix} \tag{1.3}$$

1.4   Characterization of Pattern Recognition

H. Niemann characterizes the field of pattern recognition in [Nie90a]p.4, as follows:

> "Pattern recognition deals with the mathematical and technical aspects of automatic derivation of logical pictures of facts. At the present state of the art this comprises classification of simple patterns as well as analysis and understanding of complex patterns."

In general, the patterns we are working with can be divided up into different categories. On the left in Figure 1.2 an example is presented for a simple pattern. In contrast, the other two images show more complex patterns.

Figure 1.2 On the left a simple pattern, the remaining examples represent complex patterns.

During the *analysis* process, an *individual* symbolic description is computed for each pattern. This description may be different for any two patterns. In pattern classification, a fixed label (namely the class index) is assigned to every pattern. Formal details are given in chapter 5.

If simple patterns are given, our primary interest is in classifying the complete image into one class. A typical example is the recognition of written characters. The decomposition of images and a symbolic description of the observed scene appear during the analysis of a complex scene. A simple classification of a complex pattern is obviously impossible since this will not be sufficient for a complete description of the scene. For instance, satellite images can be decomposed into the regions "forest", "street", "water", and "town" before a subsequent processing step begins.

1.5 Recording of Speech Signals

Before we describe how digital signals are computed from continuous ones, we will briefly describe some basics of the recording of speech signals and images. Speech signals are usually recorded using microphones. The quality of a recording device can be measured partially by the signal to noise ratio (see section 7.8).

A diaphragm is made to be stimulated by impulses in the frequency range from 10–25000 Hz. The diaphragm's physical movement is then converted to an electrical signal. Unfortunately, due to the mechanical parts in the transmission, the device does not respond to all frequencies equally. A typical speech signal recorded with a microphone is shown in Figure 1.3.

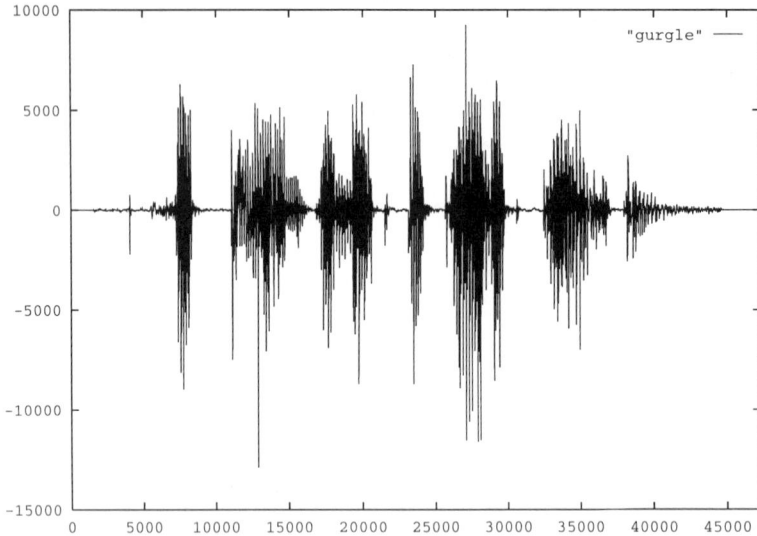

Figure 1.3   Part of the utterance "The pan galactic gurgle blaster".

1.6   Video Cameras and Projections

Many image processing systems use gray–level images as input data for their recognition and analysis algorithms. These images can be recorded by a video camera or similar sensors which project a three-dimensional scene onto a two-dimensional plane. We will consider two different kinds of projections here which are commonly used for modeling the real projection onto a CCD–chip.

The most realistic way CCD–cameras capture images is using perspective projection. This kind of projection is also the way that images are projected onto the human eye. The simplest model of a camera with perspective projection is the so called *pin hole camera* (Figure 1.4). Figure 1.5 and Figure 1.6 show the principles of perspective and orthogonal[1] projection in two dimensions. For mathematical simplicity, weak perspective projection is often used as an approximation to the perspective projection, which is a scaled perspective projection (see below).

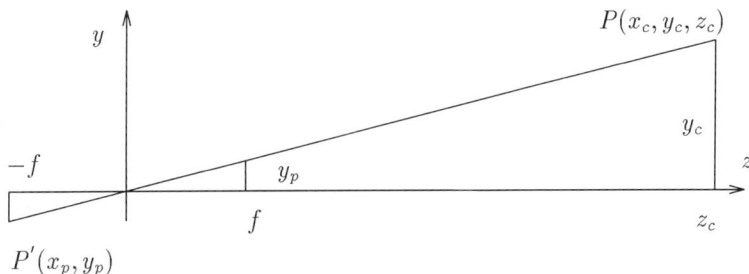

Figure 1.4 The pinhole camera model

In the pinhole camera model, we have a focal point lying behind an image plane. Three-dimensional points are projected onto points in an image plane in such a way that the lines starting from the focal point to the 3–D scene points intersect the image plane; this indicates the locations of the projected points. The resulting image coordinates (x_p, y_p) can be written in terms of the camera focal length f and the three-dimensional object coordinates (x_c, y_c, z_c) in the following manner:

$$x_p = \frac{f\,x_c}{z_c} \qquad y_p = \frac{f\,y_c}{z_c}, \qquad (1.4)$$

where z_c represents the depth of the observed 3–D point. The so called "Scaled Orthographic Projection" (or "Weak Projection") provides an approximation to perspective projection. Scene points are simply projected orthogonally from the observed three-dimensional scene onto the image plane. The projected point of the 3–D point (x_c, y_c, z_c) is therefore (x_c, y_c). In perspective projection, the size of the object in the image plane varies for different distances,

---

[1] Also called "orthographic" projection

so the resulting orthographic projection image has to be scaled by a factor, for simulating the changes in perceived size. Nevertheless, weak perspective projection does not capture perspective distortion.

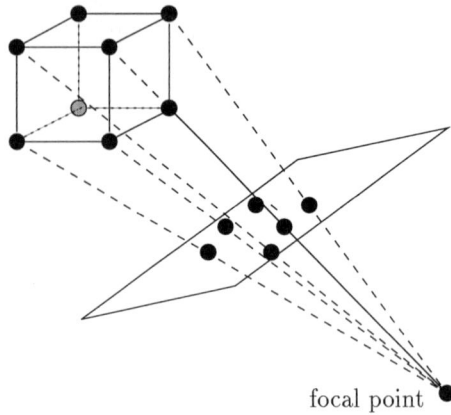

focal point

Figure 1.5 Perspective projection

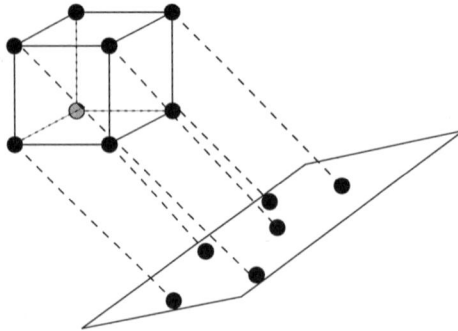

Figure 1.6 Orthographic projection

1.7 From Continuous to Digital Signals

The vectors (1.1) and (1.3) represent continuous signals. However, today's computer systems usually process digital data with finite precision. Therefore, we have to convert analog to digital signals by so–called A/D converters. Figure 1.7 shows an example of a color image converted to three discrete matrices and a transition of an analog speech signal to its digital version.

In everyday life, we watch movies at the cinema, which are composed of sequences of discrete images (25 images per second). Our brain does not recognize the discrete structure; we observe continuous sequences. This illustrates the aim of the so called *sampling theorem*. It seems to be sufficient to take a special number of discrete states for the reconstruction, i.e. interpolation, of a continuous signal.

For an obvious distinction between analog and digital signals it is necessary to introduce the following notation. For continuous signals we use $f(x, y)$ for two-dimensional and $f(t)$ for one-dimensional signals. For the discrete signals we make use of indices, i.e. f_{ij} resp. f_t.

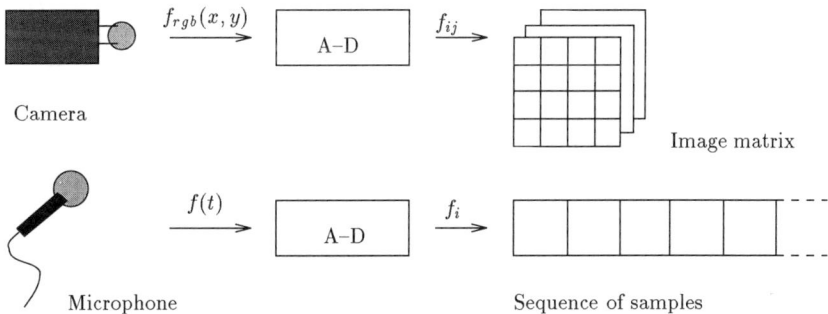

Figure 1.7 A/D-conversion for pattern recognition. The continuous signals $f(x, y)$ resp. $f(t)$ will be converted to the discrete f_{ij} resp. f_t.

The conversion of continuous to digital signals is characterized by two parameters:

1. The *sampling rate*, which follows immediately from the sampling theorem.

2. The *quantization* of the signal value, which is responsible for the quality
   of the sampled signal.

The quality of signals is measured by the *signal–to–noise–ratio* measured in
dB. The sampling theorem states that after the transition of an analog signal
to a digital version of a band limited signal with the limited frequency ω_G, the
original signal can be exactly interpolated by a discrete sum, if the sampling
period was lower or equal to $1/(2\omega_G)$. The error of this quantization has to
be zero. We will see more about this topic in Sect. 16.1.

Of course for real signals, like natural speech, the band limitation is not
generally satisfied. But band limitation can be forced artificially using band
pass filters. If the sampling rate is too small, *aliasing* occurs.

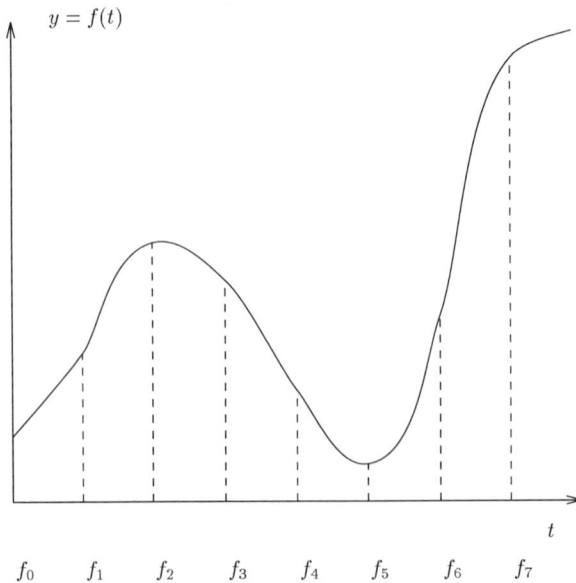

$y = f(t)$

$f_0 \qquad f_1 \qquad f_2 \qquad f_3 \qquad f_4 \qquad f_5 \qquad f_6 \qquad f_7$

Figure 1.8 Sampling of a continuous 1–D signal

The quantization aligns the range (R) of the continuous function to the digital range $(0, \ldots, N)$. The digital values result from the number of used bits
in the binary representation of the discrete range. This situation is graphically sketched in Figure 1.8 and Figure 1.9. The sampling rate is the width

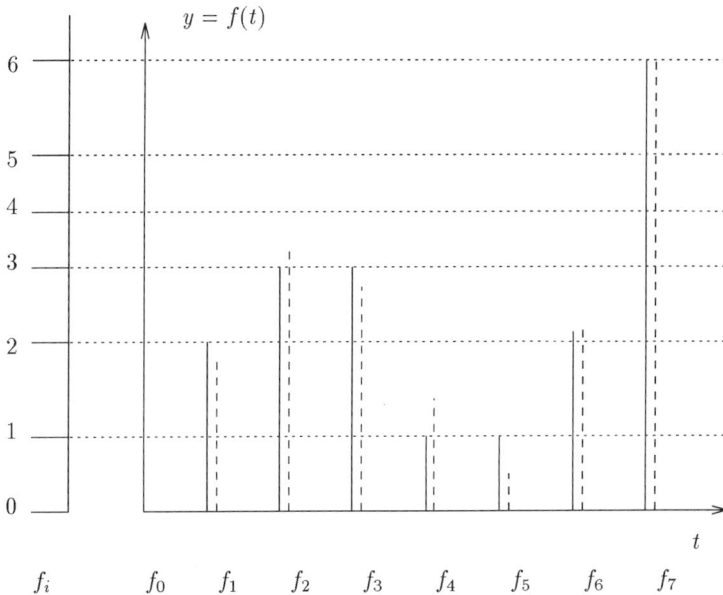

Figure 1.9 Quantization: dashed line: sampling value, solid line: discrete value; on the left: discrete range

of intervals on the time axis (Figure 1.8). The quantizations are the discrete steps on the y–axis and are determined by the characteristics of quantization (Figure 1.9). The characteristics can be expressed by the so called *characteristic line*, which obviously does not have to be linear. Nevertheless, linear characteristics are satisfactory for practical purposes. The error of quantization can be computed using the distance between the continuous and discrete function values, e.g. the euclidian distance. A more comprehensive discussion of the sampling theorem can be found e.g. in [Nie90a, Nie83].

1.8   Sampling Theorem in Practice

For practical applications in image processing, quantization and sampling rate are usually non–parametric; the technical equipment, like CCD–chips or the resolution of a monitor, have fixed values for these parameters which cannot be modified by users.

For simplicity, we assume only linear quantization characteristics in the following chapters. The processed images will be gray level images, i.e. they have just one channel.

The movie example introduced above is also suitable for showing the necessity of the sampling theorem and the connection between the sampling period and the limited frequency. Assume in a movie, which shows 25 discrete images a second, you observe a wheel rotating with the frequency f. Everyone of us has observed the phenomenon: Depending on the speed of a car, the wheels rotate forward or backward. The explanation is a trivial one using the sampling theorem. Only when the frequency f of the wheel is smaller than or equal to $25/2$, then it is possible to reproduce the continuous rotation of the wheel; if the frequency f is greater than the sampling rate of $25/2$, the continuous signals cannot be reconstructed. In those cases it is possible that the wheels seem to rotate backwards.

In the field of speech recognition nonlinear quantization has noticeably improved the recognition quality; in many cases, logarithmic quantization is done as well.

1.9   Visualization and Sound Generation

For visualization and acoustic control we also need a conversion from digital to analog signals. This D/A–conversion is shown in Figure 1.10. Theoretically, the sampling theorem guarantees a faultless reconstruction of the continuous signal.

Typical problems occur if the signal is visualized with another size than the original recording. In this case, care has to be taken that the sampling theorem is not violated.

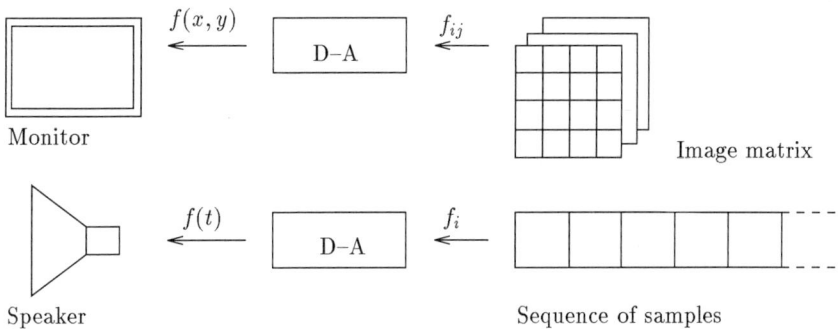

Figure 1.10 D/A–Conversion for visualization and acoustic control. The discrete values f_{ij} resp. f_t. are converted to analog signals $f(x, y)$ resp. $f(t)$.

Exercises

1. Verbally describe the pictures in Figure 1.2. How would a individual symbolic description of them look?

2. Suggest possible numerical and syntactical features for the objects and scenes shown in Figure 1.2.

3. Which problems will arise with respect to the sampling theorem if a digital image has to be resized (shrunken or expanded)?

4. Let Ω be a discrete task domain of size n. How many different ways exist to define a k class partition on this set?

5. Which sampling rate is needed for a signal with a limited frequency of 10 kHz?

6. What happens if in perspective projection the focal length is very large? What do we get in the limit?

7. Describe the effects of the sampling theorem on your audio, TV, and video equipment. Does the CD player obey the rules of the sampling theorem?

2   From C to C++

This chapter presents a brief introduction to programming in C++; we treat C++ as an extension of C [Ker78]. It will enable readers to write very simple programs.[1] As stated in the introduction, the description of the language does not cover all the details. The syntax definitions are incomplete with respect to the language definition; they are complete, however, in the sense that they contain all the applications which can be found in this book. For those who are not familiar with C, the very basic properties of C (and therewith also of C++) are described in Appendix A. Sect. 2.2 and 2.3 can be skipped by those who already know C. Sect. 2.5 and 2.6 describe standard formatted input and output which is part of the C programming language and available in C++ as well.

2.1   Syntax Notation

The C programming language has become very popular and is used in many pattern processing systems. More recently, attention has shifted towards object–oriented programming. C++ is the natural choice for those who want to do object–oriented programming and have a C background or want to re–use their existing C program sources. Most ANSI–C programs will compile with the C++–compiler, i.e. they *are* themselves C++–programs. C programs differ from the current C++ language mostly in the declaration syntax and — of course — do not contain all the object–oriented features.

Some kind of notation has to be used when a new syntax for a programming language is to be introduced. We use the following simple syntactical conventions:

- syntactic structures in square brackets are optional,

---

[1] ... as long as they don't ask too much about what's going on...

- alternatives are separated by a bar "|",

- an * indicates arbitrary repetition (including omission),

- a + indicates at least one repetition,

- terminal strings (i.e. those strings which will literally appear in the source code) are typed in `teletype` and are underlined.

An example including several of these features is shown in the syntax of floating point numbers.

Syntax:

$snumber := \underline{0} \mid \underline{1} \mid \underline{2} \mid \underline{3} \mid \underline{4} \mid \underline{5} \mid \underline{6} \mid \underline{7} \mid \underline{8} \mid \underline{9}$

$int\_number := snumber^+$

$real\_number := int\_number^+ \; [\underline{.}] \; int\_number^* \mid int\_number^* \; [\underline{.}] \; int\_number^+$

When an intuitive description is simpler than a formal definition, we either mix the style or use a verbal description only. The following is an example of a syntax definition for comments in C++.

Syntax: $\underline{//}$ *any text until end of line*

A complete formal definition of the C++–language can be found in [Str91a].

2.2 Principle of C++ Compilation

The source code of C++–programs — and similarly of C programs — are translated by a compiler.[2] By convention, C source files have the extension .c and the C++ files end in .C. Initially, sources are preprocessed by a program called cpp. [3] In this step all lines beginning with the symbol # are evaluated. Except for comments, no information other than preprocessor directives may be present on these lines.

---

[2]In contrast to interpreted languages.

[3]Some non–Unix systems may call it differently or work without it. The principle of compilation is however the same. Usually, C and preprocessed by a program called cpp. C++ compilers share this preprocessor.

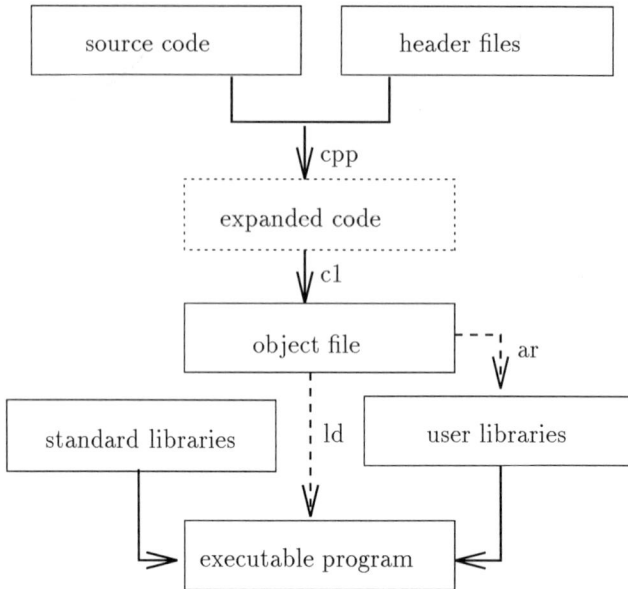

Figure 2.1 From source code to executable programs

First, we consider the lines starting with `#include` followed by a filename as `<system-file>` or as `"personal-file"`. In both cases, a temporary file is generated by the compiler, where the corresponding system– and personal files are explicitly inserted (dotted box in Figure 2.1). By convention, included files usually have the extension ".h": they are called *header–files*. The path entries of the compiler are searched for the files included by `#include <file>`. When `#include "file"` is used, the compiler searches for the file in the current directory first before looking in the default compiler path.

Most of the files searched for by `<file.h>` are part of the environment for the compiler or operating system. They may be found at a common place for all users of the system. Private files `"file.h"` will often be used by only one user.

The temporary file produced is then compiled successively by one or more programs contained in the compiler. Usually, two compiler passes produce an object module, which has the extension `.o`. Executables are then created by a linker which resolves external symbols from the system libraries and adds the interface to the operating system. Alternatively, the object module may be added to create or modify a library. Figure 2.1 shows the data flow of the compile process: compiled modules may be either linked to the executable file directly or archived in a library (usually with extension .a). [4]

2.3 Function Calls and Arguments

We now present a brief introduction to functions and their arguments. In doing so, we concern ourselves solely with how to deal with constant arguments and function call syntax; the remaining details about functions are given later (section 4.3). Here is a very simple example of a program. It consists of a main function (always called main) and a preprocessor directive (#include). The code is syntactically correct both in C and C++.

```
#include <stdio.h>        /* preprocessor include directive */

main()                    /* definition of function: main */
{                         /* begin block */
    puts("hello\n");      /* function call of puts with
                             constant argument */
    exit(0);              /* exit gracefully */
}                         /* end block */
```
①

The imported file stdio.h allows the inclusion of common input and output functions (I/O) by inserting their declarations into the source code. [5] The imported file is placed within the compiler environment and is inserted in the program by the preprocessor.

---

[4]If dynamic linkage is used (so called "shared libraries"), the resolution of external symbols from the libraries happens at program runtime.

[5]Of course, streams in C++ are safer and nicer (Sect. 14.5). But for teaching purposes we explain standard function calls rather than introducing cout << without proper preparation.

Input and output functions are not part of the language definition of C++. They are made available from standard libraries via function calls. The function call `puts` stands for *put string* and prints its argument on the screen; the program, when executed, will produce the output "hello". The compiler "knows" about this function because it is declared in the file `stdio.h`. A call to the function `exit` with argument 0 ends the execution and flushes all open files. By convention, the argument 0 indicates proper program termination, whereas any other value would indicate some sort of error condition.

Note that a function can be called by just giving its name. The arguments that are passed to the function must be enclosed in parentheses. Here, we see a function with only one argument: later, we will use functions with several arguments separated by commas and sometimes even functions with a variable number of arguments.

Actually, `main` is also a function. The program above *defines* the function main; the other functions referred to are only called and are defined somewhere else. Their definitions are attached to the executable by linking it with the system libraries (see Figure 2.2).

2.4   Declaration and Definition of Variables

Each identifier has to be declared before it can be used. The *declaration* merely introduces the name and its associated attributes to the compiler. The *definition* of a variable, however, requests a storage location for the value as well; the definition also serves as a declaration.

- In C, variables have to be declared and defined at the beginning of each block (see also Table A.2). C++ allows this nearly everywhere.[6] The declaration is valid inside the current block.

- If identifiers are declared outside of functions, they are *global* and are valid in every function following the declaration. Global variables should be used very carefully. Good programmers avoid global variables!

---

[6]In the following chapters we will note occasional exceptions, where declarations are not allowed.

Simple variables can be defined and initialized at the same time. The initialization's validity will not be checked by all compilers (i.e., uninitialized variables will not always produce a compiler warning). Some compilers initialize variables with default values, some others do not. These compiler dependencies should be avoided since they do not ensure portability of the software and show bad programming style.

The basic syntax of the variable definition is as follows:

Syntax: ▌ [const] *Type* [ptr] *var1* [= *val*] [, [ptr] *var2* [= *val*]]* ;

This means that we first specify the type of an identifier, and optionally, *something* which will be introduced later (called `ptr` here) followed by the identifier's name. Optionally, we may then list any additional identifiers. Any of the variables in the list may be initialized to the value given after the "=" sign. It is recommended that all variables are initialized immediately along with the definition.

```
int i;                      // definition of i uninitialized!!
long l = 3, 12 = -4L;       // definition and initialization
char * str0 = "abc";        // string variables are char *
char * str1 = "cde", * str2 = "ax", c = 'a';
const int ci = 3;
```
(2)

Example 2 shows some definitions and declarations. Strings are denoted by `char *` and can be assigned a constant value; the `*` is repeated for the subsequent definitions; the `*` corresponds to the `ptr` in the above program fragment. Strings are explained in detail in section 6.5. In the last line, `str1` and `str2` are strings, whereas `c` is a single character. Constant values — such as the variable `ci` in the example — can be declared as such and have to initialized immediately.

2.5   Unix–File Access via Standard Functions

Most (useful) programs need some sort of input and output. As was already stated, the C–language was developed together with the Unix operating system. Input and output were originally separated from the language definition. However, most programmers use the standard interface provided in the stdio.h header file.

The Unix naming conventions and the basic philosophy for file and terminal I/O were used when C was ported to other operating systems (even to MS-DOS). We may thus talk about files as if we all were using Unix.

Unix offers — as one of its remarkable features — a uniform file concept which includes directories and devices in a homogeneous way. Access of files in C is done by function calls. C++ encapsulates the I/O by streams and are treated in section 14.5. The stdio–interface is however still available in C++ allowing existing C routines to be reused. Three channels in Unix which are always ready for input and output; they are referred to as a FILE*:[7]

- stdout: this is the destination for regular output, (output may be delayed due to buffering)

- stdin: this is the primary source for input (e.g. from the keyboard),

- stderr: errors should be printed here; they will be printed instantly.

New output and input channels are opened by a function call to fopen with two string arguments: the first is the file name and the second is the access mode ("w" for write and "r" for read). Existing files will be destroyed by the use of "w"! The function fclose closes a channel which was opened by fopen; the argument is the FILE* (see Example 3).

```
const char * terminal = "/dev/tty";    // constant string
FILE * tty = fopen(terminal,"w");      // open console output
fclose(tty);                           // close the stream
```
③

---

[7]What type is a FILE? What does the * mean? As I told you, don't worry!

2.6   Formatted Input and Output

The name of the function "printf" stands for "formatted print" and prints to
the current standard output device (stdout). It provides a general facility for
the conversion of data to text. The declaration of these functions is included
in the file stdio.h. The number of arguments to these functions is dependent
on the first argument, which is used to format the text. In this string, there
may be several substrings beginning with a percent sign (%) and are treated
specially. All the other characters are printed as given (see Example 4).

```
int i = 3;              /* define and initialize variable i */
printf("Text\n");       /* will print the string */
printf("i = %d\n", i);  /* will print i = 3 */                     (4)
```

The characters immediately following the percent sign determine the format
of the text and the type of the required arguments (Table 2.1). The actual
arguments corresponding to those specified in that string are listed next. For
every percent sign, except for %%, there is one argument.[8] Further options
exist for the format string which are less commonly used.

%x	output of integral value hexadecimal
%d	output of integral value decimal
%ld	output of long–value decimal
%c	output of character
%s	output of string
%%	output of %
%f	output of double or float value as integer plus fraction
%e	output of double or float value scientific notation

Table 2.1   Format control for printf

---

[8]Except for the %* not mentioned in the table (see for example [Str91a]p. 357).

```
int i = 30;   float f = 1.3;
printf("%d students were marked %f\n", i, f);
printf("%s%c %f %%\n", "that i", 's', 33.0);
```
⑤

The percent sign can be followed by a numerical value specifying the length of
the output text. This value precedes the character of the specified type. The
output length of integers and strings can be given as integer values. Negative
values for width means left adjustment. Floats and doubles are formatted
using float values. The number before the decimal point specifies the overall
width and the value after the decimal point stands for the number of decimal
places.

```
printf("%5d students were marked %3.1f\n", i, f);
printf("%-20s %7.2f %%\n", "that is ", 33.0);
```
⑥

The additional argument of the function "fprintf" specifies the output file. A
function call to fprintf(stdout,...) and printf(...) is equivalent.

```
fprintf(stdout,"%5d students were marked %3.1f \n", i, f);
fprintf(stderr,"Fatal Error %d\n", errno);
```
⑦

2.7 Main Program

The function main has to be defined once in each complete C or C++ program.
The function represents the main part of the program (see also example 1).
Usually, it is defined with two arguments called argc and argv. Theses variables contain the arguments given by the operating system interface (e.g. the
command line processor). The variable argc contains the number of arguments; argv provides the locations of the argument strings (see section 6.9

for more details). The first value is the name of the program (as it is known to the operating system); it is referred to as argv[0].

```
#include <stdio.h>          /* will not C++ compile without it! */
main(int argc, char ** argv)
{
     int i = argc;
     char * progname = argv[0];
     FILE * out = fopen("/dev/tty", "w");
     fprintf(out,"Program name \"%s\" %d args\n", progname, i - 1)
     exit(0);
}
```
⑧

In Example 8, the variable i is defined and initialized to the number of arguments. A string variable progname will be assigned the name of the program. An output file is opened with a fixed name (a device in Unix). The program name and the number of arguments are printed to this file which is then closed automatically before the end of execution of the program by the call to the exit routine. Note that \" in the format string of the fprintf function call prints ". It is however good practice to close all open files explicitly.

2.8   Preprocessor Directives

The preprocessor (section 2.2) can define and replace simple macros. The program source line

| Syntax: | #define name [value] |

defines a macro name which is equivalent to value which may also be empty. The preprocessor substitutes each occurrence of name in the source code by the value value. C++ also provides constant variables for this purpose (see section 2.4).

A macro may also have arguments enclosed in parentheses which follow immediately after its name definition. When the macro name is encountered during preprocessing, the arguments are substituted during the preprocessor's expansion process. An example is shown in Example 9. The program fragment will print 1 2 3.

```
#define EMPTY
#define ONE 1
#define NEXT(a) a+1

printf("%d %d %d", ONE, NEXT(ONE), NEXT(2));
```
⑨

Macros are mostly obsolete in C++ and can in many cases be replaced by constant variables. For conditional compilation, which is introduced now, they are however still required, as well as for macros which use a type name (such as an int) as argument.

2.9   Conditional Compilation

One might wonder what an empty macro definition in the previous section would be good for. One application is to include and exclude parts of the source text in the files depending upon the definition of a macro.

```
#define X
#define A 2
#ifdef X1
   printf("X defined\n");
#elif A<3
   printf("X undefined A < %d\n",A);  /* ** */
#else
   printf("X undefined %d\n", A);
#endif
```
⑩

In Example 10, only the source line marked ** is passed from the preprocessor to the compiler, i.e. only this line is put in the intermediate file by cpp. As

`#include <file.h>`	include system file
`#if expression`	conditional based on expression
`#ifdef name`	conditional based on existence of macro
`#ifndef name`	negation of `#ifdef`
`#else`	part of if–then–else–endif
`#elif expression`	short for if then else if ...
`#endif`	end of part starting with `#if..`
`#undef name`	reverse a definition

Table 2.2 Preprocessor directives

can be seen from this example, simple arithmetic expressions are also possible and can be evaluated by cpp.

Macro definitions may also be set from the command line when invoking the compiler. In this case, several different flavors of a program can be generated without changing the source code. The frequently used preprocessor directives are summarized in Table 2.2. The `#if..` parts may be nested. Macro definitions may be extended over several lines; if the last[9] character in the line is a backslash, this character will be ignored and the next line will be glued to the current line.

Exercises

1. Write a program that prints your address including the date and place of your birth and your profession into a file named "my_address". Try different ways of formatting the output!

2. Arguments can be passed from the command line to a program as program execution begins. The variable `argv` contains all parameters given on the command line when the program was called. The ith argument can be retrieved by `argv[i]`. Standard functions are provided for converting strings to integers or floats such as `atoi` and `atof` respectively.

---

[9]Really the last (!), no blanks or tabs may follow this character!

The following line assigns the converted first argument string to the variable i:

```
int i= atoi(argv[1]);  // assign return value of call
```

Write a program that prints its number of arguments and interprets the first argument as an integer i. Also print the ith argument.

3. What happens if you provide an illegal value of i at run–time, (e.g. you provide the argument line "4 a b")?[10] Will the system warn you?

4. What is the shortest complete C++–program?

5. Try to understand the following C–program:

```
char*s="char*s=%c%s%c;main(){printf(s,34,s,34);}";
main(){printf(s,34,s,34);}
```
⑪

Run the program and send the output to a file! Can you invent something similar?

Why is it a C program and not a C++–program?

6. *Syntactic Macros*
It is tempting for a Pascal programmer to write a program as in Example 12 and 13.

```
#define BEGIN {
#define END }
#define IF if(
#define THEN )
#define ELSE  else
```
⑫

---

[10]remove the file **core** if you create one!

```
main ()
BEGIN
     int i = 1;
     IF i < 0
     THEN BEGIN i = 0; END
     ELSE i = 1;
END
```

(13)

This is, however, bad programming style for C++ and C. In particular, some tools like the "C–beautifier" cb will not work with this code.

Rewrite this program to standard C++. Pascal programers also note the if—else syntax; there is no then!

3 Software Development

In this chapter we introduce the basic principles of software development with a special emphasis on pattern recognition programs. Basic concepts of documentation and program design are also explained.

3.1 Software for Pattern Recognition

Digital images, represented as matrices of fixed size, are the basic data for computer vision. Usually, gray–level images have 256^2 or 512^2 pixels with 256 different gray–levels, i.e. each image contains, respectively, 64 KBytes and 256 KBytes of data. For color images, such as RGB–images with three color channels, three dimensional arrays are needed for representing an image. The number of two dimensional arrays needed for color images depends on the number of color channels. For motion analysis an image sequence of 25 images per second has to be processed. If we use 512^2 color images, a second of the image stream would need 18.75 MBytes.

Speech recognition algorithms are based on a *sequence* of sample values. When considered as a certain interval of time, these sequences can be interpreted as vectors. Very often, the sample frequency of speech signals is 16 kHz with a quantization of 12 or 16 Bits. Consequently, the amount of information per second is 23.4 and 31.25 KBytes, respectively.

This shows the amount of data pattern recognition algorithms have to process. Implementations of pattern recognition systems are huge programs with many lines of source code. Even if the system described in this book seems to be small, it will rapidly grow in size if it is applied to real world problems. It is therefore essential that the rules of good software production are strictly obeyed in the projects of this course.

Large systems must have a sufficient amount of documentation over its behavior to be useful for other users. To facilitate further improvements, the code should have been extensively commented by its implementors. The structure of such systems must be modular and this modularity should be based upon recent developments in the field of software–engineering. Each programmer contributes a small part of the complete system, which should use all implemented modules. It is crucial to guarantee compatibility between modules, documentation, and comments as well.

3.2   Principles of Software Development

Figure 3.1 shows the classical cycle of software development. Recent research in the field of software-engineering such as CASE (*C*omputer *A*ided *S*oftware *E*ngineering, [Fis88]) differs from this established approach. CASE–tools make it possible to generate code automatically during the planning–and design phases. Additionally, automatic code generation influences its own documentation.

The program development in Part I uses the traditional approach (Figure 3.1). With the analysis of the problem, we also start with the documentation of the software (box 0). The documentation is finished within the final version of the code (box 10).

Syntactical errors in the source code are taken into consideration in box 7–9. In box 9, the syntax check of the source code is done, for instance, by the compiler. If errors are found, we proceed with box 8. More serious problems, e.g. logical mistakes, make a complete revision necessary, symbolized in box 5.

In the first phase of a project a computer is not needed. In the planning phase (box 5–6), the computer can be used for supporting the work because there are software tools available for generating structograms or flow diagrams. The test phase of the program is generally done in a development environment using *debugging* tools.

The principle of *stepwise refinement* can be seen in box 4 and box 6.

Object–oriented programming is associated with the keywords "class", "object", and "inheritance" and will be discussed with more detail in chapter 9. Several changes in the classical development cycle and the terminology were introduced in the course of object–oriented programming and talked about in Chapter 9 as well.

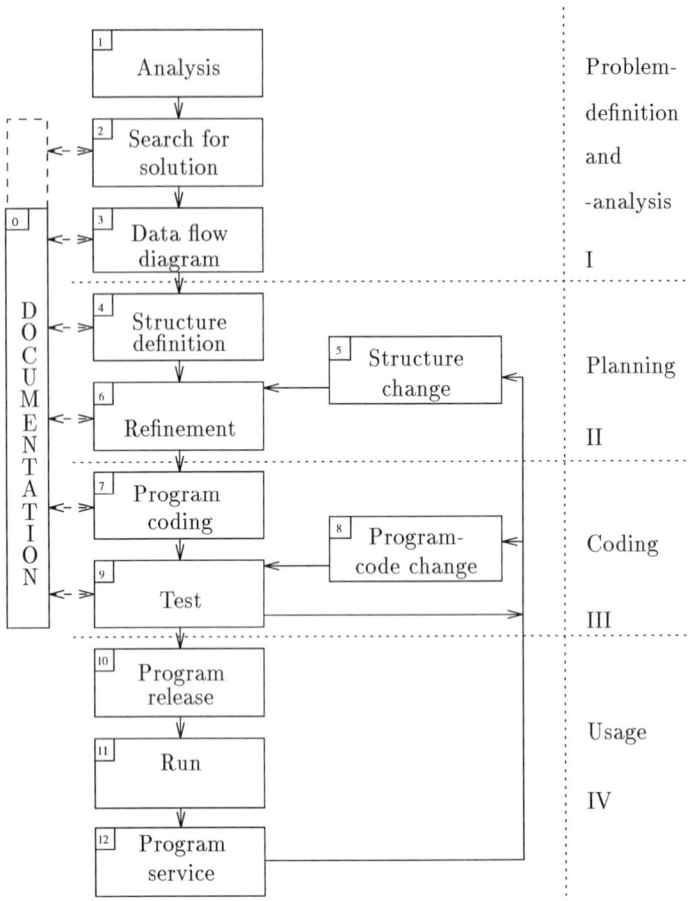

Figure 3.1 Classical cycle of software development

3.3   Modular and Structured Programming

Obeying the principles of modular programming, we generally split program
source code into several parts. Most often implementation code is considered

separately from the interfaces that will influence it. In C/C++, header files are used to share common interfaces between different modules.

Unfortunately, C++ does not enforce that the sharing of variables and data is controlled by a clean interface definition. However, global variables used by several modules create dependencies which are often hard to understand and lead to "spaghetti–code".

The flow of information naturally follows the statements in the source code. Unconditional jumps are bad practice. Function calls return to the statement following the calling statement. They modify only what is specified in the function definition. Modifications of global variables should be the exception ("side effects") and should be well documented.

We state the following rules:

- no gotos

- no side effects of function calls

- no global variables

The target of modularizing programs is guided by well defined interfaces (in C/C++: the use of header files). The principle of local changes states that as long as the interfaces are not involved in those changes, the changes have no (undesirable) influence on other modules. Well defined dependencies for source code fragments and interchangeability of modules are primary goals of modularization.

3.4   Comments and Program Layout

Comments in source code are neglected by many software engineers. Nevertheless, good and sufficient comments of source code aid in the reuse and maintenance of software.

Programs should at least contain components covering the following:

- description of the module (description of the file, revision number, state of the project, name of the author, etc.)

- description of the functions, their arguments, and their semantics,

- description of the main part of the program including the options of the command line.

Mnemonic identifiers for variables and files and comprehensible comments should be taken as a matter of course; it supports and facilitates documentation and the chance of producing reusable software.

Proper indentation of code lines makes the code a lot more readable. Usually, statements in the same block of code are lined up vertically. New blocks are indented by one tabulator position.[1]

C++ assists commenting with its comments which can be added to the end of each line (see page 19). It is highly recommended to add terse and descriptive notes to each code line.

3.5   Documentation

The components of usable documentation are textual descriptions of the semantics of a program as well as the abstract structure of the modules and interfaces.

The flow of control can be visualized by structograms. Be careful to avoid the use of C syntax within graphical visualizations of algorithms. The primitives of structograms are blocks which can be nested or stacked on each other. A sequence of statement can be depicted as in Figure 3.2.

```
statement
...
statement
```

Figure 3.2   Structogram element for sequential execution

Three types of loops are shown in Figure 3.3. The FOR loop is used for iteration, the WHILE loop checks the condition before the loop is entered,

---

[1]For C and C++ there exist two styles for indentation. Most Unix systems provide the program **cb** which is a C–Beautifier . See the manual of this program for the description of the styles.

and the UNTIL loop checks it at the end, i.e. the loop is executed at least once in a UNTIL loop.

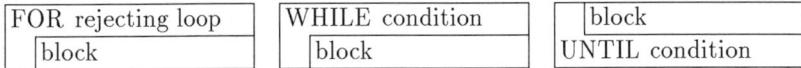

| FOR rejecting loop | | WHILE condition | | block |
| block | | block | | UNTIL condition |

Figure 3.3 Three types of loops

The graphical presentation of a branching in the flow of control shown in Figure 3.4 is not the standard form, but available in the strukto–TEX–style.There also exist also an element for more than two branches which is not shown here.

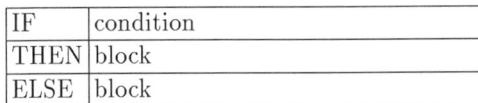

IF	condition
THEN	block
ELSE	block

Figure 3.4 Conditional execution

Algorithms designed with the use of structograms will almost automatically result in well structured code.

Data flow can be documented with data flow diagrams. Especially in object–oriented systems, special care has to be taken on the documentation of data structures. Entity–Relation Diagrams (ER) which are common in data base design can be used. Modern object–oriented software development provides extensions of these ideas (Sect. 9.1).

3.6   Teamwork

The design and implementation of huge software systems like image analysis or speech processing can not be finished by a single person. Successful teamwork requires common sense on the following items:

First of all, it is necessary to coordinate and plan the project. The complete problem should be partitioned into approximately independent parts. The interfaces of each partition should be defined. For implementation purposes, modules and classes are suitable concepts for information hiding. If more than one person will change the files, version and access control should be implemented. This guarantees that no conflicts will occur – for example that two partners edit one and the same file. Furthermore, all changes and their authors should be taken down.

3.7   Efficiency

Efficient programming is often forgotten by computer programmers. It is, however, very important for image and speech processing. Especially for real time processing of images and speech, the huge data rates require efficient code. Efficiency has to be a major design goal for image and speech analysis programs but should almost never interfere with structured and clean programming. If necessary, "dirty tricks" have to be well commented and have only local influence on the program. [Sch90] gives some examples of efficiency considerations for segmented programs.

The test phase of a program (box 9 in Figure 3.1) reveals inefficient parts of a program which have to be changed. High modularity helps to keep the required updates local. On modern computer processors, the costs of calling a function and passing arguments to it are small and performed in few processor cycles. When the function called computes more than just a trivial expression, the relative computation time of the function body is high compared to the time needed for calling and returning. No reduction of the efficiency is thus to be expected if programs split the code in many small functions, which are in turn easier to be tuned up. C++ additionally provides functional syntax even for trivial computations, which can be executed *without* loss of efficiency (Sect. 8.8).

3.8   Tools for Software Development with Unix

Unix is more than just an operating system kernel; it includes several tools for program development. The operating system itself provides access facilities for teamwork. Unix groups can be built who share rights on individual files or directories. Locking mechanisms are present in newer versions of Unix to avoid conflicts.

For software development, the following features and commands are useful for software production, especially in a team with shared resources:

- groups (ask your system administrator)

- newgrp (change your current group in system V based unix)

- umask (can be set to grant access to a group by default)

The following tools are useful for every programmer. They should be used in any project, no matter whether in a team or working alone.

- make a program maintenance tool. make will do all the required actions after a change in the program source code.

- rcs a revision control system. rcs will record your changes and in addition grant or deny access to source files shared by several users. Various related tools exist.

In appendix B. we briefly describe these common Unix tools.[2]

3.9   PUMA

Program development and experiments in the field of pattern recognition are costly and time consuming. For simplifying this process a programming environment PUMA[3] was designed and developed [Pau92b]. PUMA is machine

---

[2]They are also available for MS–DOS

[3]**Programmier-Umgebung für die Muster–Analyse** — in English: a programming environment for pattern analysis

independent; consequently, experiments and programs can be implemented without considering special hardware constraints. Special mechanisms, like the automatic generation of documentation, support the implementation of the software engineering guide discussed above. The principles and tools shown in the previous sections are used in PUMA. The system is used as a pool for common functions, classes, and programs for image and speech analysis.

PUMA includes (**AN IM**age **A**na**L**ysis **S**ystem) ANIMALS (see chapter 17). The implemented classes are named with „hippos" (**HI**erarchy of **P**icture **P**rocessing **O**bject**S**), from now on written with Greek letters ἵππος (pronounce as: „hippos") [Pau92b]. In ANIMALS we define common command line interfaces. Different programs doing similar things look similar to the user.

In this book we present a subset of the ἵππος–interface. It is tailored to simple applications but fully compatible with the larger system. The algorithms in Part III are implemented in ANIMALS. The functions and classes can serve as an example for modularity.

Implementation as well as data storage of a system should be machine–independent. In this system — and in Part II of the book — we show how this can be implemented.

We experienced that program documentation which is kept in separate files from the source code almost never reflects the actual status of the project. Therefore we put all the documentation into the source and header files, as close as possible to the implementation. Consistency of documentation with the actual programs was enhanced considerably. An implementation of this idea is left as exercise 5.

Exercises

1. Write a `Makefile` which compiles the C++ program `my_program.C`, adds the object file to the library, and generates an executable program `test` using the library.

2. Decide and discuss which commands are useful or nonsense. Try them on your machine!

```
> co -l test.C,v
> co -l test.C
> ci Makefile
> chmod ugo-rwx *
> chmod -x /bin/chmod
> chmod +w test.C,v
> make love
> got a light?
```

(14)

3. Huge programs are divided up in modules and the C++ source code can be found in different directories.

   Assume we have the following directories:

   `filters, segmentation, models, classification.`

   Each subdirectory contains C++ code and a Makefile for compilation, building libraries and executable programs. Write a Makefile in the actual directory which automatically updates the complete program system by calling make world.

4. Check the rcs manual and find out which of the information in the module header of a program (Sect. 3.4) can be added automatically.

5. Write an awk script which extracts the module head from program and header files and creates a readable layout from this information. Include general information about the program, its usage, and its purpose.

   If necessary, mark this information appropriately, e.g. by DOC_BEG text DOC_END, to help extraction with awk.

   Add this command script to the makefile and program in exercise 1.

4 Expressions, Statements, Functions

In this chapter we briefly introduce the expressions and statements used to change the values of variables. The flow of control can also be altered by the use of control structures which will be introduced. Modular programming and simple user–defined functions conclude the explanations.

4.1 Instructions and Expressions

For short, int, float, long, and double the binary operators +,-,*,/ have their usual intuitive semantics. The operator precedence is identical to the rules of mathematics and parentheses are used for grouping as well. Exponentiation does not exist as an operator. Mathematical operations are also admissible for variables of type char. Characters are converted to integers in C and treated as tiny integers in C++. Range checking and the overflow of integers are not detected by the system at runtime so if data–types are mixed in an expression, an automatic adjustment of types is performed.[1] This process is known as *implicit conversion* . Automatic type conversion is a complicated topic. We recommend, therefore, to use explicit conversion whenever in doubt. The C++–syntax for type conversion is simple and looks like a function call:

| Syntax: | *type (expression)* |

Alternatively, the C–syntax can still be used (and in some cases must be used):[2]

---

[1]There exist different rules for the conversion in C and C++, due to the fact that in C, for example, there is no char–valued expression.

[2]The C–version of the cast must be used when the type cast to is not simple type name, e.g. in (byte **) ptr.

Syntax: $(\text{ type })\ expression$

Conversion from `float` or `double` to integer types truncates to the appropriate range. When rounding is required, add 0.5 to the `float` value.

Instructions are terminated with semicolons. The assignment operator is "=". Integer division is performed with "/" when the operands are integers; the modulus operation is "%".

```
int i = 3 * 5;              /* value: 15  */
float f = 0.7 + 3;          /* value: 3.7 */
int j = int(f) * ( i + 2 ); /* value: 51  */
```
(15)

Example 15 shows three lines of code. In C++, declarations are statements and can be used at almost every place, where statements are admissible. The first line defines a variable `i` which is initialized by the expression 3 * 5. Then, the value 3.7 is assigned to the floating point variable `f`; in the expression, the integer 3 is first converted to a floating point number. The third line shows the use of an explicit type conversion; the value of `f` is truncated to 3. Decrement and increment operators can be used only with variables of integer type.

The statements of the type `Var` *op*= `Value` are abbreviations of an expression followed by an assignment; they are logically equivalent to `Var` = `Var` *op* `Value`. These statements are valid for all numerical variables. By the way, it is these very same operators which give programs in C and C++ their typical appearance (Table 4.1), especially in C++ where user defined functions can be attached to these symbols (Sect. 7.10).

A sequence of statements can be combined to a single statement by the use of curly brackets ("{" and "}"). A sequence of expressions separated by commas are regarded as one expression which evaluates to the last expression.

In contrast to C, C++ has character and floating point valued expressions. In C, every expression involving a `float` will be converted to `double`; characters will be converted to integers. In some cases, this will result in different behavior of C and C++ programs.[3]

---

[3]Try to find examples and verify your ideas with your compilers!

Operator	Explanation	Example
++	pre– or postincrement	++i; i++;
--	pre– or postdecrement	--i; i--;
+=	increment and assignment	i += 4;
-=	decrement and assignment	i -= 4;
*=	multiplication and assignment	i *= 4;
/=	division and assignment	i /= 4;
%=	modulo operation and assignment	i %= 3;

Table 4.1   Arithmetic operators

4.2   Logical Values and Conditionals

Neither C nor C++ supply the data–type `boolean`: instead, integral values can be used as truth values. The value 0 stands for `FALSE`, everything else is interpreted as `TRUE`. Operators for comparison are:

Syntax: *expr1* $\geq$ |$\geq$ |$\leq$ |$\leq$ |$\neq$ |$==$ *expr2*

The operator `==` checks whether two values are equal. A common mistake is to confuse the assignment operator `=` and the equality operator `==`. Inequality can be tested using `!=`. The operator `<` (`>` `>=` `<=`) checks whether the expression on the left is smaller (greater, greater or equal, smaller or equal) than the expression on the right side.

Logical values — i.e. integral expressions — can be combined by operations as listed in Table 4.2. The precedence of operators is complicated and a common source for errors. We suggest the use of parentheses to make the wanted precedence obvious.

Often it is necessary to control a program through the use of validity tests with boolean expressions. Normally, statements are executed in the sequence given in the program. Expressions are evaluated from left to right. Conditional execution as well as loops and function calls can alter this sequence. Unconditional jumps (`goto`) are almost never needed and considered bad programming style [Dij75]; C/C++ provide alternatives to the use of `goto` (Sect. 4.4).

Operator	Explanation	Example
&&	AND	`((i>1) && (i < 2))` ...
||	OR	`((i>1) || (i < -2))` ...
!	NOT	`((i>1) && (!(i < 2)))` ...

Table 4.2 Logical operators

Conditional execution can be done using the `if` statement:

Syntax:	<u>if</u> (*expression*) *statement1* [<u>else</u> *statement2*]

Statement1 is executed if the expression evaluates to an integral value other than 0. Otherwise if the `else` clause is present, *statement2* is executed. Nesting of conditional statements is possible. As in Pascal, the "else" is assumed to belong to the next possible "if". Example 16 shows this situation.

```
if (i > 2)                    // if #1
    if ((i == 5) || (j < 3))  // if #2
      j = 4;
    else                      // belongs to if #1
      j = 8;                                        (16)
```

Of course, the statements in the conditional branches can be blocks (see Example 17). Also note the typical indentation style for `if` and `else` cascades in the following example (see also section 3.4) which puts the last `else` under the previous `else`. Cascades of if–else–if–else etc. thereby can be aligned.

```
if (i > 2)        j = 3;
else if ((i == 5) || (j < 3))    // if cascade
     j = 4;
else {                           // here we use a block
     j = 8;
     i = 2;
}                                // we line up the block
```
(17)

4.3 Function Definition

Modular programs split the code into functions and procedures which group a series of statements or expressions together. Functions are used in expressions and may return a value; procedure calls are considered statements in their own right. Their actions can be controlled by *parameters* called *arguments* for functions.

The void key word prefixes a procedure[4] declaration in C++. A procedure definition in C++ looks like the following:

| Syntax: | void *identifier* ([*type argument*] [, *type argument*]*) *block* |

The block in the procedure definition is called the *body* of the function. A function may be called using its name followed by a possibly empty list of arguments included in parentheses. The arguments have to correspond in number and type to the list given in the declaration. These arguments are passed to the function and their values are substituted for the variables in the function body.[5] The control returns to the location following the call after termination of the function. This happens when the last statement of the function body is executed or upon encountering a return statement, as shown in Example 18.

---

[4]The term *procedure* is used here as in Pascal. Procedures are functions which do not return a value.

[5]At this point we know only about passing arguments by value. Later we will see other possible mechanisms (section 8.4).

```
void printij(int i,int j)              // definition
{                                      // function body
    if (i < 0) return;                 // conditional return
    printf("I is %d, J is %d\n", i, j); // print something
}                                      // return

main()                                 // main function
{                                      // body
    printij(1,2);                      // call other function
}                                      // return
```
(18)

Functions may have a return value. This already happened in Example 8 where the variable output was initialized with the return value from the call to fopen. The syntax for functions is as follows:

Syntax:

returntype identifier ([*type argument*] [*,type argument*]*) *block*

The execution of the function can be terminated at any point inside the function body with a return statement:

Syntax: return *expression*

whereby the expression has to be of the type given by the *returntype* in the function declaration. The use of functions is exemplified in Examples 19–20; this also shows how access is made to command line arguments. The (external) function atoi has one string argument[6] taken from the command line. It *returns* an integer value — namely the conversion of its string argument to a number.

---

[6]See also Example 8

```
int sign(int i)                 // sign function definition
{
    if (i < 0) return -1;       // case 1
    if (i == 0) return 0;       // case 2
    return 1;                   // otherwise
}
```
(19)

```
main(int argc, char ** argv)    // main function
{
    int j=argc+sign(atoi(argv[1])); // function call
}
```
(20)

If the return type is omitted from a function definition (as in the previous examples with the functions main), it is assumed for historical reasons to be of type int. If the use of a function is intended where no return value is needed, then the function should be declared as void; this will disallow its use in expressions. It is admissible for functions to call themselves, i.e., recursion is possible.

Since procedures are just special cases of functions — returning the type void — in the following we talk about functions and arguments only and omit the terms "procedure" and "parameters".

4.4 Loops

Three types of loops exist in C++ corresponding to the structograms in section 3.5. The syntax of the while and the do loops are as follows:

Syntax:

    1) <u>while</u> <u>*(expression)*</u> *statement*
    2) <u>do</u> *statement* <u>while</u> <u>(</u> *expression* <u>)</u>*;*

We call the *statement* in the loop the "loop body"; it may of course be a block containing several statements. In the while–loop the statement is executed as long as the expression evaluates to something other than 0. The do–loop terminates when the expression evaluates to 0; the loop body is executed at least once. Since both loops use the keyword while, it is crucial to use proper indentation (Example 21, see also section 3.4)

```
while ( i > 2) {
    printf("%d ", i);
    --i;
}
```

```
do {
    printf("%d ", i);
    --i;
} while (i > 0);
```
(21)

The third loop syntax is the for–loop, which is a special type of the while–loop:

Syntax: | for *(statement1; expression; statement2) statement3*

This is equivalent to a while loop

statement1; while (expression) { statement3; statement2; } .

The for–loop contains two assignments and one boolean expression. The first assignment initializes the loop variable, the second assignment can be used to change the loop variable, and if the boolean expression becomes false (i.e. zero), the loop terminates. Any of the statements may be empty.

Any loop can be terminated by a break statement. The continue statement skips the rest of the loop body and continues with the next iteration. These constructs help to avoid gotos. They are commonly used but in principle unstructured (no symbol exists in standard structograms, section 3.5). Example 22 shows these constructs.

```
for (int k = 0; k < 10; ++k) {
    int j = foo();                 // get some value
    if (j == -1) break;            // exit the hard way
    if (j == 0) continue;          // skip the following
    printf("%d ", i, j);           // otherwise: print
}
```

$$\boxed{22}$$

4.5   Declarations and Scope

As already noted, identifiers have to be declared prior to their use. Functions, for example, may be declared first and then defined later. In this way it becomes possible for two or more functions to call each other mutually (Example 23).

```
void a(int);                            // declaration
void b(int,int);                        // declaration
void a(int i)        { /* ... */ b(i,1); }   // definition
void b(int i,int j) { /* ... */ a(i);  }   // definition
```

$$\boxed{23}$$

The name of a variable becomes known to the compiler as soon as it compiles the declaration statement. Declarations inside a block are invisible from the outside but may be passed to further nested blocks via function calls. The value and the storage location of this variable is lost when the block is left. It will be reallocated upon entering the block where the declaration occurs.[7]

Declarations outside of any function are called *global*. These names are visible in any function following the declaration. It is considered bad programming style to use many global variables across different files.

As in many other programming languages, the name of a variable that has already been declared outside of a given block may be reused within this block for a completely different purpose. The closest declaration (with respect

---

[7]Depending on compiler implementations.

to scope) will be the one referenced to within the block. In Figure 4.1, we depict functions by two nested blocks; the first introduces the names of the arguments, the second corresponds to the function body. Inside a function, the argument names can overwrite global name bindings. Inside the function body, new declarations may then introduce new names. Declaration 1 will be known in Functions 1 and 2. Declaration 2 will be known only in Function 2. Local variable 1 will be visible only in Function 1. Local variable 2 will be visible only in Function 2. Example 24 shows how variable names can be overwritten in nested blocks and by function definitions.

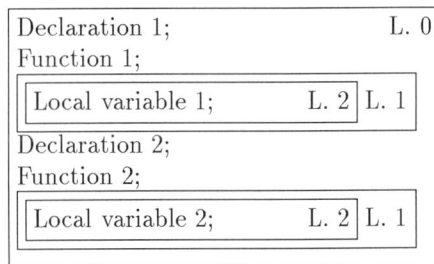

Declaration 1;		L. 0
Function 1;		
Local variable 1;	L. 2	L. 1
Declaration 2;		
Function 2;		
Local variable 2;	L. 2	L. 1

Figure 4.1 Declaration inside blocks

```
int i, l;                   // global variables (bad style!)
void foo(int i, int j, int k) // global i will be invisible
{
  int l;                    // will overwrite global l
  { int j; }                // will overwrite argument j
}                                                        (24)
```

If a local variable is tagged static, it will keep its value even if the program control passes out of the block (Example 25). When the block is entered again, the variable will be accessible with its old value. The name, however, is nevertheless invisible from the outside.

```
void foo()
{   static int counter = 0;                    // keep the value
    printf("foo was called for the %d-th time\n", ++counter);
}
```
(25)

4.6   Switches

Instead of cascading numerous levels of if else if else ..., a switch can
be used when all the conditionals depend on the same integral variable. The
value of this variable can be used to dispatch to several *constant* integral
values. These values are used as case labels. The execution of such a branch
can be terminated with a **break** statement. If the break is missing, the control
continues with the next statement. When this is desired it should always be
commented. Otherwise, it might look like one of many common programming
errors in C. A **default** case can be specified which is applied if none of the
switch values are matched.

| Syntax: |

switch (*expression*) { case *const-expr:** [default:] *statement** }

After the opening curly bracket of a switch, a declaration is possible. These
variables may not be initialized. Inside the switch, declarations are not allowed, except when they are inside a new block.

A function including a large switch is shown in Example 26. Note, that some
of the statements "fall into the next case", which is commented, as required.
We will use this example later on; then we be able to understand the meaning
of the error message in the default case of the switch.

```
void foo2(int c)      // function will modify global i and j
{   extern int i,j;   // GLOBAL VARIABLES
    switch(c) {
        case 1:  ++i;   // fall into next case
        case 0:  ++j;
             break;
        case 3:  --j;   // fall into next case
        case 2:  ++i;
             break;
        case 5:  --i;   // fall into next case
        case 4:  --j;
             break;
        case 7:  ++j;   // fall into next case
        case 6:  --i;
             break;
        default: fprintf(stderr,"Illegal direction (%d)\n",c);
    }
}
```
(26)

4.7   Linkage

A file acts as one unit to the linker (Sect. 2.2). All names defined on level L. 0 in Figure 4.1 which are not tagged static are known outside of the module. This is useful when several modules are to be linked together (see Figure 2.2).

We now inspect Example 27. The object module for M1 will contain the information that the symbol verbose will need and that symbol foo will provide. The object module for M0 provides the symbols verbose and main; it lacks the symbol foo. It is the job of the linker to resolve these references in order to provide M0 with what it requires.

```
/* M1.C */
#include <stdio.h>
extern int verbose;
void foo()
{
  if (verbose)
     printf("foo() called\n");
}
```

```
/* M0.C */
extern void foo();
int verbose;
main()
{
     verbose = 1;
     foo();
}
```
(27)

The symbol static is used for two different purposes. On level L. 0 it is used
for the linker and controls the visibility of the symbol outside the module; on
higher levels it is used for the compiler and controls the lifetime of a variable
and its value.

Some common problems with external linkage in C can be avoided in C++
which now has the feature of "type–safe–linkage" (Sect. 8.5).

4.8   Programming with Modules

A good strategy for programming with modules in C++ is the following. All
interfaces should be defined in header files. All local functions and variables
should be made static to avoid the interference of identical variable names.
Interfaces are included with the preprocessor directive #include. The main
module (main) does not export symbols; i.e. other modules do not depend on
this module. A larger example is shown in Examples 28–30.

```
/* M1.h */
extern void foo();
```

```
/* M2.h */
extern int verbose;
```
(28)

Example 28 shows two header files which are used as interface definitions.

```
/* M1.C */                      /* M2.C */
#include "M1.h"                 #include "M2.h"
#include "M2.h"                 int verbose = 0;
void foo()
{
  if (verbose)
      printf("foo() called\n");
}
```
(29)

Example 29 shows two source code files which use the interfaces in the header files.

```
/* M0.C */
#include "M1.h"
#include "M2.h"
main(int argc, char ** argv)    // nonsense example
{
    int verbose = (argc > 1);   // verbose used as boolean
    if (verbose) foo();         // conditional call
}
```
(30)

The main module in Example 30 uses the header files and defines the function main. In order to get a complete executable program, the linker has to combine the compiled modules from Example 29 with this main program.

If program source is split into several files, various dependencies will be created. The program make as introduced in section B.2 is most commonly used for the documentation and maintenance of these dependencies.

4.9   Control Structures

The syntactical units controlling the sequence of execution in the program
are called "control structures". Table 4.3 summarizes the existing control
structures of C and C++. The goto is in the table but should generally be
avoided in good programs.

Control Structure	Explanation	Example
if	conditional	`if (i == 0) ++i;`
else	conditional	`if (i == 0) ++i; else --i;`
while	while–loop	`while (i > 0) --i;`
do	do–loop	`do ++i ;  while (i < 10);`
for	for–loop	`for (i =0; i < 10; ++i) i*=2;`
break	exit loop	`while(1) if (++i > 0) break;`
continue	continue loop	`while(i > 0) if (--i > 4) continue;`
return	return from call	(see section 4.3)
switch	branching	(see section 4.6)
goto	jump	considered harmful! [Dij75]

Table 4.3   Control structures for C and C++

Example 31 demonstrates the use of control structures. The program will
generate a synthetic sinusoidal speech signal. The sample values are assumed
to be eight bit characters. The constant value for π is defined in math.h.

```
#include "math.h"
main(int argc, char ** argv)
{    // should check arguments
     double step = M_PI/ atoi(argv[1]);
     for (int j = 1; j <= 1024; ++j)
       printf("%c", char(256 * sin(j * step)));
     exit(0);
}
```
(31)

Exercises

1. Graphically show the dependencies of the files in Example 28.

2. Write and test a makefile for the Example 28. Include the dependencies for version control with RCS.

3. How can the `break` and `continue` statements be avoided? Transform the code in Example 22 into an equivalent program without break and continue and draw the structogram.

4. Compare the C++/C control structures with those present in other programming languages.

5 Classification and Pattern Analysis

Depending on the input data and the problem to be solved, there exist three major areas in pattern recognition and pattern analysis:

1. classification of simple patterns,

2. classification of complex patterns, and

3. analysis of complex patterns.

In the subsequent parts of this book we are going to emphasize our discussion on the third point above, even though we will briefly introduce all of them. A comprehensive discussion of these items is presented in e.g. [Nie83]. In this chapter we give an overview on the architecture of pattern recognition and analysis systems. We outline the relation of knowledge based pattern understanding systems to general problems of artificial intelligence.

5.1 Classification

As was shown in Sect. 1.4, the goal of pattern classification is to associate a class with the given input pattern. With respect to the classification process, the task domain (see Sect. 1.3) is partitioned into k disjunctive classes Ω_λ ($\lambda = 1, \ldots, k$), i.e. $\Omega_\mu \cap \Omega_\nu = \emptyset$ for $\nu \neq \mu$. The classification assigns each observed pattern exactly one class of this partition. Several applications suggest the insertion of a *reject class* Ω_0; for example for those applications where rejection will bring about lower costs than misclassification.

Some examples can illustrate the goal of classification:

1. classes $A - Z$ and "unknown" for character recognition,

2. forest, street, field, water for the automatic generation of maps using satellite images,

3. voiced fricative, voiced non-fricative, unvoiced phone, plosive for word recognition.

The classification algorithms can be divided up into two classes: syntactical classifiers and numerical ones. If the features of patterns are real numbers, vectors, sets or other structures on the field of reals, the resulting classification system will be a numerical one. Typically, statistical principles are used for the design of numerical classifiers for speech recognition purposes [Hua90]. Based on the geometric nature of objects, numerical classifiers in the field of image processing are often based on some distance measures [Mar82]. Basic statistical methods for pattern classification will be introduced in Chapter 7. Spectral features for speech classification are presented in Chapter 16.

Syntactical classification uses the results of parsing a syntactic description of the pattern using a formal language. Examples for syntactical image classification can be found in [Bun92]; syntactic classifiers for speech recognition are used in [Nie83].

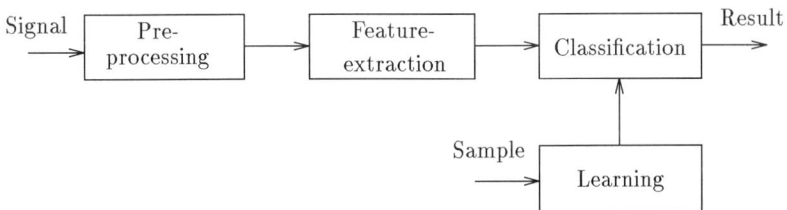

Figure 5.1   The architecture of a simple classification system [Nie83]

Figure 5.1 shows the modules of a classification system for simple patterns. The modules *preprocessing* and *feature extraction* are within the scope of this book and are outlined in Sect. 5.2 and 5.3. The classification module decides which class fits best to the computed features. Usually, a training set (sample) is used and the parameters of the classification process are adapted in the learning module. The modules for classification and learning are not considered in this book; they are described in detail in [Nie83].

5.2   Preprocessing

Before features can be extracted, the signal is *preprocessed*. Usually preprocessing operations are problem independent. Patterns are transformed into patterns, i.e. an image matrix into an image matrix or a speech signal into a speech signal.

The goal of preprocessing is to simplify the computation which will have to be done in later stages of the analysis. The signal may be enhanced, normalized, filtered, etc. in order to reach this goal. For example, smoothing of patterns represents a typical operation in the preprocessing stage (chapter 19). Smoothing will eventually reduce unnecessary details or noise and may thus speed up succeeding processing. Other examples of preprocessing operations are things such as filters or changes of the size of images or the duration of speech signals.

Another common preprocessing technique is the normalization of the input signals. Energy normalization, for example, would adjust the loudness of speech signals or the darkness of an image. Some normalization algorithms for images are described in Sect. 20.4. Size normalization of patterns or rotation of a given sub–pattern into a normal position is common e.g. in character recognition.[1]

5.3   Feature Extraction

In the classification process, features of a given pattern are extracted. For instance, numerical features can be vectors of real numbers or a set of vectors which characterize the class of a pattern. For speech signals one can use the zero crossings or Fourier descriptors (Chapter 16). The average gray level of a special region in an image can be significant in the classification of objects. Some simple statistical features are, for example, the average intensity in a local spatial neighborhood of a picture region or the variance in the temporal proximity of a speech sampling value.

In some applications it is better to use symbolic features instead of numerical ones. The process of feature extraction can be characterized as problem independent. Patterns are transformed into features; numerical values are

---

[1]This is not a trivial problem. Consider the sampling theorem!

computed in statistical feature extraction; the mean of gray levels for example. A symbolic representation of a feature is, for instance, the attribute "convex" of a specific surface patch.

The computed features are used decisively in the classification process. Symbolic features once extracted are fundamental for syntactical classifiers [Bun92]. The computation of these symbolic features for images is described in Part II and III of this book.

5.4 Analysis

Here we cover the analysis of complex pattern searches to obtain the individual description of an input pattern. In general, this requires a knowledge–based processing of the patterns, i.e. the system is based on knowledge within the range of the application. The first part of the analysis requires no application dependent knowledge. The general structure of this is shown in Figure 5.2. Preprocessing can be done problem independently. The parameter setting and selection of the appropriate preprocessing method may however be based on assumptions about the signal, i.e. on knowledge about the problem. The preprocessing operations correspond to those used for the classification of the simple patterns (Sect. 5.1).

Like preprocessing, image segmentation algorithms mostly require no knowledge about the objects in the scene. Speech can be segmented solely based on the information in the signal. The choice of the best suited algorithm and its parameters can be guided by knowledge.

In this book, we use preprocessing and segmentation of patterns solely for the purpose of pattern analysis. This corresponds to the lower two blocks in Figure 5.2. Model driven analysis (the upper two blocks in Figure 5.2) can be understood as a search and optimization process during which optimal correspondences between the knowledge about the given scene — represented as models in the knowledge base — and a segmented image are found.

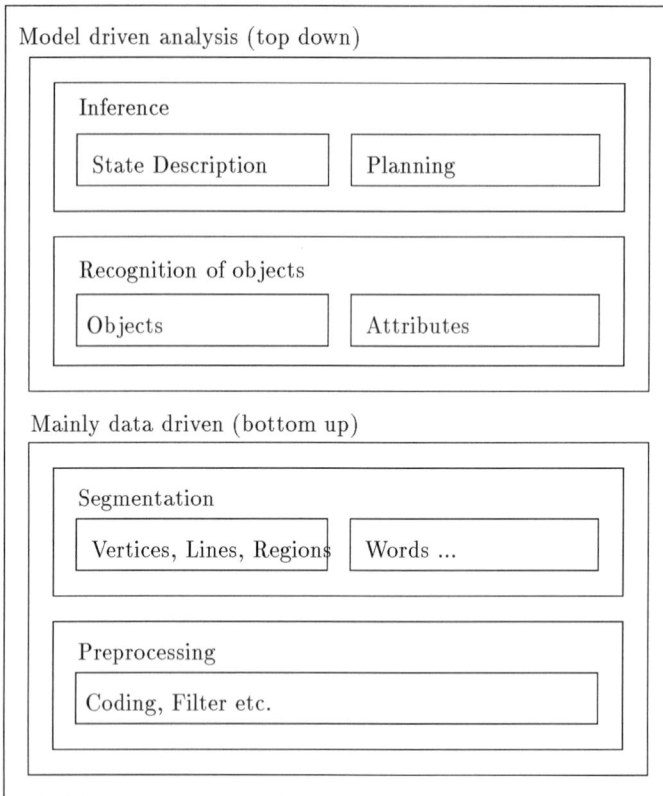

Figure 5.2 Structure of a knowledge based system for pattern analysis. The left part represents the image analysis process, the right one the speech analysis (from [Nie90b]).

5.5   Image Segmentation

The search for the characteristic and simple parts of patterns is called *segmentation*. It is frequently a data driven process where knowledge about the application domain is not required. In this book, we mainly cover these problem independent segmentation techniques. In a model driven approach, problem dependent knowledge for segmentation can be used. The resulting algorithms are then less general and are described only in the context of the specific problem domain.

Image segmentation can be based on homogeneities; namely, homogeneous regions that are detected in the image. Alternatively, discontinuities can be used for the detection of primitives. It is assumed that these correspond to contours in the real objects. Line based segmentation is the result of this way of looking at images. We will cover techniques for line segmentation in chapters 13, 21, and 22.

The resulting primitives of the segmentation are dependent upon the methods utilized. Some examples are lines, regions, or vertices: the latter being a result of the intersection of two or more lines. In the field of speech recognition the detection of single words is within the scope of segmentation as well.

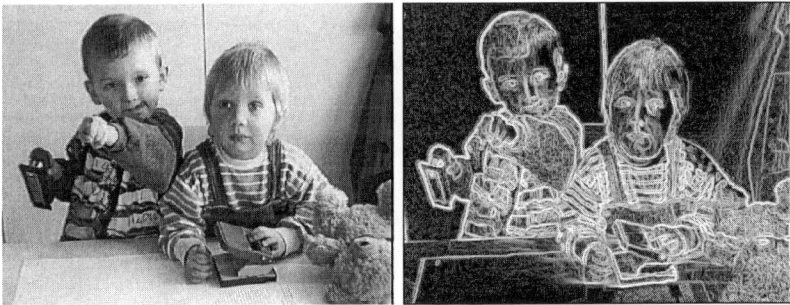

Figure 5.3 Image Segmentation 1: input and edge candidates

Indications are that simple geometric objects are an important part of human visual perception. Usually, the segmentation process is carried out in a series of computational steps. First the edge candidates are extracted from the image (Figure 5.3). These candidates are then linked to lines. The corners and intersections (vertices) are located and the lines are approximated by circular arcs or straight lines (Figure 5.4). All of these objects are represented and stored in a common interface for image segmentation called a *segmentation object* (Sect. 15.8). We will cover the representation of such data in Part II; in Part III we describe algorithms for the computation of such data.

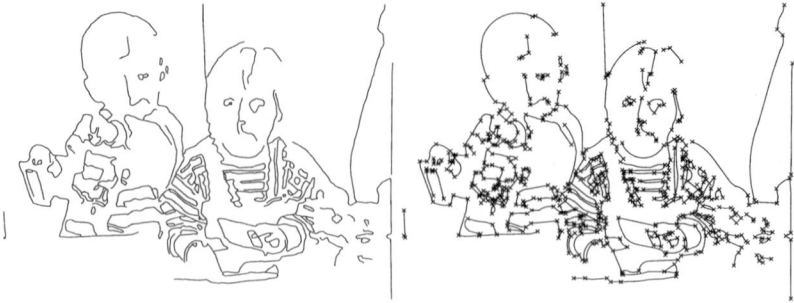

Figure 5.4 Image Segmentation 2: Lines and Corners

Alternatively, segmentation can be based on the detection of homogeneous regions. Contours of these regions are further inspected but the interface as a segmentation object remains the same.

Every segmented part has to be judged for its reliability; this measure will be used by the image analysis module (Sect. 5.7) in advanced recognition tasks.

Data abstraction of these objects yields a series of processing steps, which are shown in Figure 5.5. Proceeding from one level to the next means the introduction of a new class of data. This idea is further pursued in Part III.

5.6　Speech Segmentation

The segmentation of speech signals is correlated to a decomposition of the time ordered signal into linguistic units. Each unit represents an interval of the signal and can be for instance a single word or a syllable of a continuous spoken utterance. In general, those units computed by segmentation operators symbolize parts which are themselves homogeneous or heterogeneous among each other regarding some criterion. Different approaches for the segmentation of speech signals can be found in [Kun90, Nie90b, Noe91].

With the triumphal success of Hidden Markov Models (see Chapter 16) speech segmentation operations became of minor interest for speech recognition systems. It turned out that statistical methods give better recognition results

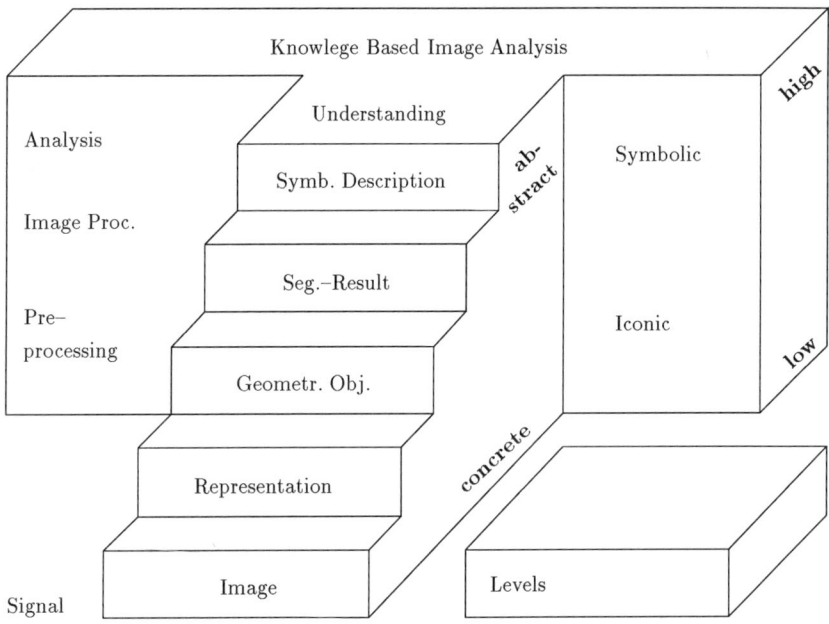

Figure 5.5 Levels of Abstraction with respect to data structures in image processing [Pau92b]

than structural analysis of the speech signal. The speech signal is divided into frames of equal length for which features are computed; we introduce common methods for this computation in Chapter 16. These features are input for a statistical analysis; we introduce basics of statistics for this purpose in Chapter 7 and apply them to speech processing in Sect. 16.8.

5.7 Pattern Understanding

Understanding a pattern within the present context requires knowledge stored explicitly in a knowledge base.

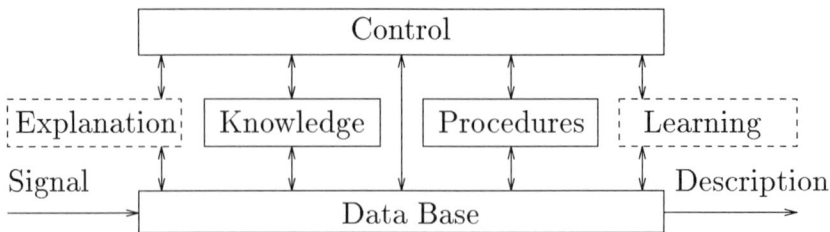

Figure 5.6 General structure of pattern analysis systems ([Nie90b]).

Image processing methods are applied to the data and are eventually transformed into a description as shown in Figure 5.6. This process is *controlled* by a separate module. The principle is generally observed through the *matching* of model data from the knowledge base with the segmentation data.

It is essential for the control module that the results of the segmentation are judged according to their quality and reliability. This problem dependent measure has to be provided by the segmentation methods. The search problem mentioned in Sect. 5.4 can then be solved by general search strategies in the control module, like the A^*–graph search or dynamic programming (see e.g. [Nie90b]).

Knowledge based pattern analysis as well as pattern understanding is related to problems of artificial intelligence (AI). In fact, speech understanding and vision were one of the first major ideas for machine intelligence. One of the important journal for speech and image analysis is called "Pattern Analysis and Machine Intelligence".

The following problems are directly connected to AI and refer to central ideas of AI (knowledge representation, searching, matching):

- representation scheme for the knowledge base

- matching of patterns with models

- search for best matching object

- dealing with uncertainty and false assumptions

- planning

In image analysis, the recovery of three–dimensional information from the visual data can be assisted by spatial or geometric reasoning. Speech analysis will use linguistic knowledge and dialogue strategies.

Object–oriented programming can assist to keep track of software dependencies in a large knowledge based system. C++ provides the extreme computational efficiency which is required for pattern understanding. Matching and optimization can be nicely implemented with object–oriented techniques; we will see an example in Sect. 16.7. Steps toward an object–oriented implementation of the knowledge base for image analysis are beyond the scope of this book; they are outlined in [Pau94].

It should however be noted that current research explores alternatives to "traditional" AI. Instead of an explicit model for speech or objects, statistical information is gathered and used for understanding. AI methods are left to dialogue strategies or planning, which is required in active vision tasks; active vision is introduced next.

5.8   Active Vision and Real Time Processing

Instead of, or in addition to, a symbolic description (which was the result of the system in Figure 5.5 and Figure 5.6), in active vision systems a series of commands for the active device is required. This will result in a top–down data flow all the way from control to low–level image processing (Figure 5.2).

Typical active methods change the focal length of a zoom lens; the aperture, or the focus (Sect. 1.6). Changes of the camera position are also possible if the lens is mounted on a robot. Examples can be found in [Den94].

Active vision usually requires a response of the system within fractions of a second; otherwise a feed back of the information can not be accomplished. It is crucial that the response delay is guaranteed not to exceed a maximum period. This is commonly called real time processing if the time period is reasonably short. Of course, this again relates to efficiency (Sect. 3.7). Typically, the images are captured at 25 frames per second (Sect. 1.7). A delay of less than 40 ms is therefore usually sufficient for real time processing. Since common algorithms require more computing time, other control algorithms with a shorter delay period have to be found.

In real time speech analysis, the maximum computation time is determined by by a human's senses while communicating with a machine. This can be used as an upper limit for the analysis of a complete utterance.

5.9   Top–Level Loop for Speech Analysis

In the following example we demonstrate the control structures introduced in Sect. 3.5 and 4.9. We describe a small program which waits until a speech signal is captured by a microphone and then tries to analyze the data until a spoken end command is heard. We assume that isolated words are spoken (in contrast to a continuously spoken language), and that each word is analyzed separately.

Following the idea of stepwise refinement (Sect. 3.2), we specify a top–level loop and leave the details to be filled in later. The details may be hidden in functions which are now simply called in the loop. For each function call, we mention the level of abstraction we are working on at the time.

```
main(int argc, char **argv)
{
    int wordNumber;         // words may be identified by numbers
    init_micro();           // start up recording
    wait_for_speech();      // record image frames until
                            // speech is observed
    do {
        get_frames();       // record until a pause is observed
        word = analyze();   // find word number from frames
        action(word);       // show some reaction on the input
    } while(wordNumber!=0); // 0 means "QUIT"
}
```
(32)

We left out any variables needed for the speech signal. In the initialization, the actual settings of the device and the noise level in the background are measured. Waiting for the word to start can be simply done by adding up all sampled values in the present frame. If this number is considerably higher

than a comparable computation for a frame in the initialization, a word is
supposed to start. This operation is typical in the preprocessing stage.

This example will be completed in the exercises of the following chapters.

Exercises

1. Explain differences and similarities of feature extraction and segmentation!

2. Think about formalisms for representing domain knowledge. Which techniques would you prefer?

3. Discuss the objectives of classification and analysis in detail!

4. Explain why the algorithms in chapter 19 are part of the preprocessing stage.

5. Create a modular program for the speech toplevel loop in Example 32. Use separate files for the function dummies which are called from the main program. Make sure that a header file defines all the required interfaces. Use a Makefile to build the program.

6   Arrays and Pointers

In the first chapter we explained that discrete speech signals can be represented by vectors. Images are usually stored as matrices or as higher dimensional arrays. Therefore vectors and matrices are very important data–structures in the field of pattern recognition and should be discussed in detail.

6.1   Vectors and Matrices

In general, arrays are indexed by integers beginning with 0. A one–dimensional array of size n therefore has the elements $f_0, f_1, \ldots, f_{n-1}$. Neither the compiler nor the runtime system check the range of the subscripts; nasty errors may occur with the use of improper values[1] (see also Exercise 2 on page 29).

Examples of the declaration of arrays are given in Example 33. A variable is declared as an array by placing the number of elements within square brackets following the variable name. With multidimensional arrays the size specification is repeated.

| Syntax: | *type ID [size]*;* |

For two dimensional arrays, the first size specifies the number of rows, the second specifies the number of columns. Access to single elements is done by supplying an index of range $0 \ldots n - 1$ as shown in Example 33.

---

[1]In section 10.8 we will learn how to avoid this "feature" in C++.

```
int    a[10];            /* integer array size 10    */
char  c[20];             /* character array size 20   */
float f[20][10];         /* float matrix size 20 * 10 */
int i = 9;               /* integer variable          */

unsigned char image[256][256]; /* a typical image     */
a[4] = 3;       c[9] = 'c';       f[4][2]    = 4.33;
a[0] = a[4];    a[0] += 4;        image[1][i] = 0;

a[++i] = 10; // syntactically correct, but wrong index! (i>9)  (33)
```

Example 33 also shows how eight bit gray level images are represented in C
and C++, i.e. pixels are unsigned char represented as byte. The size of the
image is fixed to 256^2 elements. A change of image size would most likely
cause many changes in the source code. It is better to use macros (Sect. 2.8)
or constants instead (Example 34).

```
#include <stdlib.h>
#define COLUMNS 256
#define LINES   256
static unsigned char image[LINES][COLUMNS];// global image
main(int argc, char ** argv)               // main program
{
    int s = atoi(argv[1]);                 // should check argc!
    for (int i = 0; i < LINES; ++i )       // loop over lines
      for (int j = 0; j < COLUMNS; ++j ) { // loop over columns
         image[i][j] = (i * s) ^ j;        // ^ introduced later
      }
    fwrite(image[0],COLUMNS,LINES,stdout); // ugly - raw write
    exit(0);                               // good exit code
}                                                          (34)
```

In Example 34, a change of the image size is done at one point of the file
only. The program creates a fancy synthetic image and writes it — the hard

way — to stdout.[2] It combines the indices i and j with the xor–operator ˆ
which will be introduced in section 8.3. The result for two different values of
s is shown in Figure 6.1.

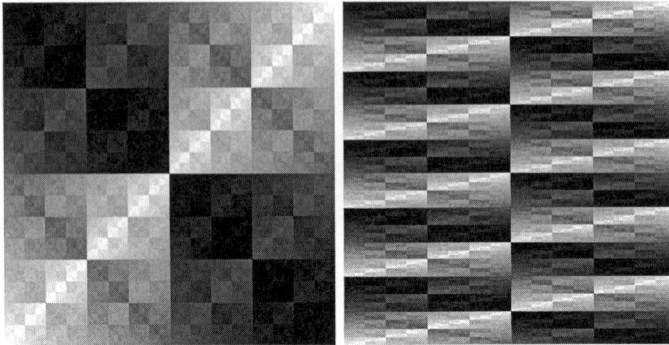

Figure 6.1   Result of Example 34 with argument 1 and 5

6.2   Pointers

People often are very suspicious of using pointers. Especially those whose
"native language" is Pascal. Nevertheless, the essence of C and C++ is in the
usage of pointers.

"First of all, don't panic".

Pointers in C and C++ are declared as variables pointing to data of a known
type, i.e. there are no pointers *per se* but pointers to integers, pointers to
floating point numbers, pointers to characters, etc.. The syntax was already
introduced in Sect. 2.4.[3] The * declares the variable immediately following as
a pointer to the type.

Syntax: *type* [*] *var1* [= *expr*] [, [*] *var2* [= *expr*]]* ;

---

[2]We will see better ways of storing images in chapter 11.

[3]There we did not specify, what ptr was.

Example 35 shows the definition of two pointer variables to integers (a and c); the variable b is a normal integer variable.

```
int * a, b, *c;   // Pointers to int a and c, normal int b
```

(35)

After the definition of a pointer variable, the value of the variable is undefined (as it is the case with normal values), i.e. the address in the value cell is arbitrary and — in general — not valid. Pointer values can be set by assigning one pointer to another of the same type. Pointers can be set to any location in memory where data of the expected type is present. In contrast to Pascal, for example, this location can be assigned by the address operator & on a normal variable and does not have to be allocated dynamically. The access of the data pointed to by the pointer is done using a *. Example 36 explains the various uses of pointers.

```
int b = 3;    char a = 'a';   // memory filled with values
int *bp;      char * ap;      // pointers (not initialized)
int *cp;                      // i.e., undefined value
bp = &b;                      // *bp == b
cp = bp;                      // *bp == *cp
ap = &a;                      // *ap == a
*ap = 'x';                    // a == 'x'
ap = NULL;                    // NULL-pointer
```

(36)

If a pointer is not initialized, it points *somewhere* — which is usually an illegal location. It is often required to have a pointer point *nowhere*; in Pascal this is done with the *nil*-pointer value. In C/C++ there is a macro in the file stdio.h named NULL; we then call the pointer a "NULL–pointer".

6.3   Vectors vs. Pointers

Vectors and Pointers are very similar in C/C++. A vector can be seen as a constant pointer to the first element of an array. Applications can be seen in Example 37.

```
char carray[64];
char * cptr;
cptr = carray;
cptr = &(carray[3]);
carray = cptr ;          // ILLEGAL
carray[3] = *cptr;
cptr[3] = 'a';           // [ offset ] is legal for pointers
```
(37)

Assignment to the whole vector with one operator is not possible (see the illegal line in the example), since an array is a *constant* pointer. However, a pointer can be set to an array. Assignment to single elements is obviously possible as well. Data pointed to by pointer can be accessed using [index] as in an array.

6.4   Vector Initialization

Global or static arrays can be initialized during the variable's definition. The values assigned are listed in curly brackets separated by commas. The size of the array can be implicitly determined by the number of initial values. If a size is specified, it may not be smaller than the size indicated by the number of elements in the initialization.

```
int iarray0[10] = {1,2,3,4,0,1,2,3,4,5}; // all values specified
int iarray1[]   = {1,2,3,4,5};           // int iarray[5]
int iarray2[10] = {1,2,3,4,5};           // remaining values 0
```
(38)

Static multidimensional arrays are initialized by nested lists of values as shown in Example 39. For two dimensional arrays, the inner list initializes the rows.

```
unsigned char bild[4][3]   =     /* image */
    { {  1, 0 ,  1},                 /* row 0 */
      { -1, 0 , -1},                 /* row 1 */
      { -1, 0 , -1},                 /* row 2 */
      {  1, 0 ,  1} };               /* row 3 */
```
(39)

6.5   Strings

In Example 33, the array c represents a string, i.e. strings are vectors (one–dimensional arrays) of characters. Their characterizing property is the trailing '\0' character. Initialization of a string (i.e. an array of characters) can be done using the lists described in section 6.4; it also can be simplified by supplying a string in double quotes (Example 40). In the first case, the 0 has to be added explicitly; in the later case, the 0 is added automatically, the array will thus be one element longer than the number of characters provided in the initialization.

```
char string0[10];                     // constant length 10
char string1[] = { 'a', 'b', 'c', '\0'}; // length 4
char string2[] = "abc";               // also length 4
```
(40)

Useful functions on strings can be found in the standard libraries. Comparison and manipulation of strings is facilitated by the following routines: strcmp compares two strings, strlen returns the length of the string (see also Example 42), and strcpy copies one string to another. These functions are declared in string.h and can be inserted into the program with #include <string.h>. Refer to the compiler or operating system manual for further information on these functions.

6.6   Pointers Operations and Allocation

Pointers can be manipulated by various operators; for example, they can be compared using the relational operators (> >= == != < <=). If an integer is added to a pointer, the address is incremented by the given number of elements; i.e. if 4 is added to a pointer pointing to an integer (int *), the result of the addition points to the fourth integer following the actual position of the pointer. The same holds for subtraction. This can be understood best if we look at the index operator [index]; the expression carray[3] is identical to *(carray+3).[4] Subtraction of two pointers (of the same type) yields the number of elements between the two positions.

Like in addition and subtraction of numbers, pointers can also be incremented and decremented. These operations are often combined with * to access the element pointed to as can be seen in Example 41. A pointer can be set to a legal address by assigning the address of a variable using the address operator. Alternatively, the pointer may be set to unnamed memory requested by new; this allocation can be discarded by the operator delete. A summary of the operations on pointers is given in Table 6.1. When arrays are created with new type[size] the corresponding delete operation has to use the syntax delete [].

```
cptr = &(carray[0]);
*cptr = 'a';
cptr++;
*cptr = 'b';
*++cptr = 'c';
cptr = new char[10];      // allocate 10 characters
delete [] cptr;           // discard allocation
cptr = new char;          // allocate 1 characters
delete cptr;              // discard allocation
```
                                                                    (41)

The function in Example 42 is a very common application for strings. It also shows the combination of assignment and relational comparison. The second string had better be long enough!

___

[4]Together with the commutativity of addition, this implies a[i] == i[a]. This is not a joke!

operator	operand 1	operator	operand 2	Explanation
*	ptr			Dereference
&	var			Address of
++	ptr			Increment
--	ptr			Decrement
	ptr	=	ptr	Assignment
	ptr	=	& var	Assignment
	ptr	=	new type [number]	Array allocation
	ptr	=	new type	Allocation
delete	ptr			Disposal
delete[]	ptr			Array disposal
	ptr	[number]		Array access
	ptr	+	int	Increment
	ptr	-	int	Decrement
	ptr	-	prt	Distance
	ptr	rel–op	prt	Compare addr.

Table 6.1 Operations on pointers. rel–op stands for any relational operator (Sect. 4.2).

```
void strcpy(char * to, char * from)
{
    while((*(to++) = *(from++)) != '\0')
        /* empty body */ ;
}
```
(42)

When a loop's body is empty (as in Example 42), this should be marked and commented clearly, so other readers will not suspect an error there.

6.7   Pointer and Array Arguments

The C programming language passes *all* function arguments by value. Changes
to the arguments in the function body are therefore local and have no global
effect.

Functions can change global data using pointer arguments. In Example 42
the pointers to and from are incremented; this does not, however, change the
value of the pointers provided in the call which are passed to the function by
value! The changes occur in the data pointed to by the arguments! This is
shown in Example 43.

```
void swapint(int * a, int *b) // swap the value of two integers
{
    int tmp = *a; *a = *b; *b = tmp;
}

void foo()
{   int i = 3, j = 4;
    swapint (&i,&j);                 // now i ==4, j == 3
}
```
(43)

Of course, global variables may be accessed inside a block or function. This is
generally not the best software practice, however. The return value of a function can be used in the calling sequence to promote the changes of a function.
Later we will see other argument parsing facilities for C++ (section 8.4).

When a multi–dimensional array is to be passed to a function, the size of
the argument has to be provided to the compiler; only the first size of the
argument may be left unspecified. An example is given in Example 44. There
is a trick for circumventing the problems with multidimensional arrays (see
e.g., [Pre88]) which is exploited in section 10.8.

```
void foo(unsigned char m[][3], unsigned char f[][256])
{
    f[3][4] *= m[1][1];
}
```
①① 44

6.8   Pointer to Pointer

Pointers are tied to a given type. Naturally, the data the pointer points to can again be a pointer. The declaration and application of a pointer to a pointer to an integer is shown in Example 45.

```
int i, * ip, ** ipp;
i = 3; ip = &i; ipp = &ip;
*ip = 4; ** ipp = 5;              /* i == *ip == **ipp == 5 */
```
45

Because of the dual nature of pointers and vectors, a twofold pointer can be seen as a two–dimensional array, i.e. it can be accessed using two indices. Although this looks similar as an array access (Example 33), it has a different meaning to the compiler. For static arrays, indices are evaluated using the type sizes contained in the array declaration; after an arithmetic expression, this will result in the address of the array element. Generally, addition and multiplication is required here.

For pointers to pointers, the indices are offsets to the pointer. The first index will be an offset to the pointer. This will yield an address to which the second offset is applied. No arithmetic other than addition is required here.

6.9   Main Function Arguments

In section 2.7 we used the main function with two arguments argc and argv; argc is already known as the number of arguments on the command line; we can now explain argv.

The argument argv is an array of strings, i.e. a pointer to a pointer to a character. It is passed to main as a pointer to the first string which contains the name of the program. The length of each string is known by the trailing 0 in the string. Example 46 shows a program that prints its own arguments.

```
#include <stdlib.h>
main(int argc, char ** argv)
{
    while ( argc-- > 0 )
      printf("%s\n", *(argv++));
    exit(0);
}
```
(46)

There exist several handy functions for parsing the arguments of a program. We use extensions of the functions defined in the following exercises.

Exercises

1. Declare, define, and initialize a static array of strings with its size determined by the number of initialization strings. Write a NULL string as the last string.

2. Write a routine cmp_arg with one string as an argument called opt. Compare opt to all the strings of exercise 1. If the string is a unique prefix of a string in the list, return its index in the array. If it is a prefix, but not a unique one, return -1; If it is not found in the list, return -2.

   Hint: use the function strncmp.

3. Write a routine `printargs` which prints all the strings of the list in exercise 1.

4. Write a routine `check_args(argc,argv)` which is called from `main`. Every command line argument starting with a '-' should be checked by the routine of exercise 2. Skip the '-' for that purpose. Use a switch on the return value of `cmp_arg`. In case of failure, use `printargs` and print an appropriate error message.

5. Write a simple function which generates a synthetic image containing a filled circle. Use a fixed size for the image. Provide filename, center, and radius from the command line. Write the image to a file using the raw write function in Example 34 — but hide the call in a separate function `write_image` and put the defines for the image sizes in a separate header file as shown in Example 47.

```
#include <stdlib.h>
#include "image.h"            /* defines for XS and YS */
void readimage(char*filename,unsigned char image[YS][XS])
{
    FILE * file = fopen(filename,"r");
    if (file == NULL) {
      fprintf(stderr,"Could not open file %s\n",filename);
      exit(1);
    }
    fread(image[0],YS,XS,file); // ugly - raw binary read
    fclose(file);
}
```

(47)

Your main program could look as in Example 48.

Make sure that your program works with arbitrary image sizes. Write a makefile and use `rcs`.

```
#include <stdlib.h>
#include "image.h"                    /* defines for XS and YS */
unsigned char image[YS][XS];
main(int argc, char ** argv)
{
    char * in, * out;
    // get args
    readimage(in,image);
    // etc.
}                                                                    (48)
```

6. Write a program that applies a filter (chapter 19) to an image. Proceed as in the previous exercise.

7. Extend exercise 5 in Chapter 5. Define a vector of signed short integers to contain the speech signal. Its length should be given as an argument to the main program. Put the *declaration* of this vector and its length into the header file and use it in all the functions which need it.

7 Statistics for Pattern Recognition

Applications of image processing have to deal with uncertainty and noise effects. These factors can be partially suppressed by normalization techniques or filters. For example, you can normalize the intensity of light, which is ordinarily different under varying illumination conditions. Probability theory and statistics provide a mathematical framework to handle these phenomena. As outlined in Sect. 1.4, pattern analysis deals with the *mathematical* part of perception. It is therefore natural to use all kinds of mathematical tools.

Other typical applications of statistics can be found in pattern classification (Sect. 5.1). Lots of examples can be found in [Nie83].

The subsequent sections explain the basics of probability theory and statistics that are required for the understanding of the algorithms and principles of Chapter 19. For more mathematical details, we refer to [Bre88].

7.1 Axioms

Many concepts of probability theory are inspired by numerical phenomena. For instance, you can measure the energy of a speech signal or the intensities for each pixel of a gray–level image. Such measurable quantities are called *random variables.*

The basic object in probability theory is the *probability space* $(\Omega, \mathcal{F}, p)$, where Ω represents the set of all possible outcomes of an experiment, $\mathcal{F}$ is the family of events, i.e. a set of subsets of Ω, and p is a probability function assigning to each event $A \in \mathcal{F}$ its probability $p(A) \in [0, 1]$.

The introduced probability space has to satisfy the axioms of probability theory:

Axioms of Probability Theory:

1. $\Omega \in \mathcal{F}$

2. if $A \in \mathcal{F}$, the $\bar{A} \in \mathcal{F}$

3. if for all elements of the sequence $(A_n)_{n \geq 0}$ we have $A_n \in \mathcal{F}$, then $\bigcup_{n \geq 0} A_n \in \mathcal{F}$.

4. $p(\Omega) = 1$

5. for any sequence $(A_n)_{n \geq 0}$ of pairwise disjoint events the following additivity condition is valid

$$p\left(\bigcup_{n \geq 0} A_n\right) = \sum_{n \geq 0} p(A_n).$$

Depending on the applications, the range of random variables can be discrete or continuous. These two cases are discussed separately in the following two sections.

7.2 Discrete Random Variables

The probability to observe a discrete random variable is written as $p(X)$; similarly, the probability that the value of X is in the interval $[A, B]$ is denoted by $p(A \leq X \leq B)$. Using the axioms of probability theory the following equation obviously holds:

$$p(X \leq A) = 1 - p(X > A).$$

In many practical situations it is necessary to *estimate* the probability $p(X)$ for each random variable X from the training samples. This is done using the relative frequency of the observed random variables. Let M be the set of observed random variables and $|M|$ the cardinality of the training set. For each random variable $X \in M$ we can compute

$$p(X) = \frac{|\{Y \in M \mid Y = X\}|}{|M|}.$$

This quotient is called the *relative frequency* of X.

The *cumulative distribution function* $P(x)$ for the random variable X is defined by

$$P(x) \quad = \quad p(X \leq x) = \sum_{X \leq x} p(X). \tag{7.1}$$

A cumulative distribution function is monotone and increasing and its maximum value equals 1.

One fundamental result of probability theory states that the probability of the difference between real probability of observing X and the relative frequency is greater or equal to an arbitrary small positive number converges to zero for an infinite sample set (see e.g. [Bre88]).

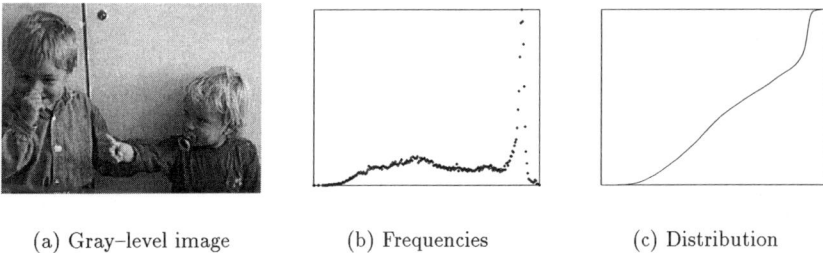

(a) Gray–level image   (b) Frequencies   (c) Distribution

Figure 7.1 Original gray–level image

Example:

In image processing applications random variables often are the gray–levels of image pixels. Figure 7.1 shows a gray–level image, its frequencies of gray–levels, and the associated distribution function. The relative frequency of each gray–level can be computed by dividing the value of the ordinate in the histogram by the number of image pixels, i.e. in our example 256^2. You can also see that the distribution has the value 1 for the gray–level 255.

7.3   Continuous Random Variables

Suppose we are working on analogous image data. In this case the random variable *gray–level* will have a real value, i.e. we have a set of random variables of infinite cardinality. From the axioms of probability theory we conclude that the probability of observing a specific gray–level equals 0. Of course, for each point in the image plane, we can measure a gray–level; nevertheless the probability of observing exactly this gray–level is 0. In analogy to the discrete case, we define the cumulative distribution function

$$F(x) \;=\; p(X \le x). \tag{7.2}$$

If there exists a nonnegative function f such that,

$$F(x) \;=\; \int_{-\infty}^{x} f(z)\,dz, \tag{7.3}$$

then we call $f(x)$ the *density function* of the continuous random variable X.

Example:

The most famous probability density is the *Gaussian density*.

$$f(x) \;=\; \frac{1}{\sigma\sqrt{2\pi}}\, e^{-\frac{1}{2}\frac{(x-\mu)^2}{\sigma^2}} \tag{7.4}$$

The parameters μ and σ^2 are called the *mean* and *variance* of the given distribution. A probabilistic interpretation of these two parameters will be given in the next section. The cumulative distribution of normal or Gaussian distributed random variable is

$$F(x) \;=\; \frac{1}{\sigma\sqrt{2\pi}} \int_{-\infty}^{x} e^{-\frac{1}{2}\frac{(x-\mu)^2}{\sigma^2}}\,dx \quad . \tag{7.5}$$

It is fairly easy to see that the value of the density function $f(x)$ can be greater than 1, if $\sigma < \sqrt{2\pi}$. So $f(x)$ should not be mixed up with the probability function p of the probability space (Sect. 7.1).

In the field of pattern recognition, Gaussian densities are used to model noise effects, for instance. We will use them in Chapter 18 for this purpose.

The support of mathematical functions and operations in the language definition of C++ is small compared to other languages, like e.g Fortran [Bra78]. In
Sect. 4.1 we saw arithmetic operators. For the computation of function values
with e.g. the formula in (7.5) we need the constant π, exponentiation, etc.
These values and functions can be found in a header file math.h and a mathematical library which as to be added by the linker (Sect. 4.7).[1] Example 49
shows an implementation of the Gauss function $f(x)$ (7.4):

```
#include <math.h>             // import constants and functions
double gauss(double x, double sigma, double mu)
{
   return ( 1 / (sigma *
             sqrt(              // sqrt: square root function
                2 * M_PI        // M_PI: from math.h
             )) *
             exp ((             // exp(..) exponentiation function
                - 0.5 *
                sqr(x - mu)     // sqr: square function
             ) / sqr(sigma)));
}
```
(49)

7.4   Mean and Variance

In general, the underlying statistics of gray–levels or other observable sensor
data is not known. Nevertheless, the statistical quantities can be estimated
from the random samples. The *mean* of given samples is defined in (7.6) and
the *variance* is given by (7.7).

$$\mu \;=\; \frac{1}{n}\sum_{i=1}^{n} f_i \qquad\qquad (7.6)$$

---

[1] Usually, a flag has to be passed to the linker like -lm to inform it that this library is
needed.

$$\sigma^2 \;=\; \frac{1}{n}\sum_{i=1}^{n}(f_i - \mu)^2 \tag{7.7}$$

Both values can be computed assuming that the gray–levels f_i are normally distributed and using maximum likelihood estimation of the parameters μ and σ^2. This is done by maximizing the likelihood function $L(\{f_1, f_2, \ldots, f_n\}, \mu, \sigma^2)$ of observing the set of gray–levels

$$L(\{f_1, f_2, \ldots, f_n\}, \mu, \sigma^2) = \left(\frac{1}{\sigma\sqrt{2\pi}}\right)^n e^{-\frac{1}{2\sigma^2}\sum_{i=1}^{n}(f_i - \mu)^2} \tag{7.8}$$

The computation of zero crossings of the partial derivatives with respect to μ and σ result in the above formulas.

Example:

The computation of mean and variance of the gray–levels of the video image shown in Figure 7.1 yields $\mu = 143.417$ and $\sigma^2 = 1959.78$.

7.5   Moments of a Distribution

The cumulative distribution or the density function characterize the distribution completely. The mean and variance introduced in the previous section can be computed using the above formulas. Even if the underlying distribution of the observed sample data is not Gaussian, we get a result for μ and σ. Therefore, we cannot conclude from these values the underlying distribution of the sample data. The mean and variance are coarse measures of the distribution. Therefore, we generalize these measures.

Let k be a natural number and $f(x)$ the density function of a distribution. If the function $g(z) = z^k f(z)$ is absolutely integrable, then we call

$$m_k(p) \;=\; \int z^k f(z)dz \tag{7.9}$$

the k–th absolute moment of the distribution p. Analogously, we call

$$\hat{m}_k(p) = \int (z - m_1(p))^k f(z)dz \tag{7.10}$$

the k–th central moment of the distribution p, if $g(z) = (z - m_1(p))^k f(z)$ is absolutely integrable.

The first absolute moment is called *expectation* and we commonly write $E[X]$ for the expectation of the random variable X. Above definitions are valid for continuous random variables. In the discrete case one has to substitute the integral sign with a discrete summation. The first absolute moment and the second central moment are the mean and variance in the discrete situation.

7.6 Random Vectors

The definition of random variables can be used for generalization purposes. We call a vector $\boldsymbol{X} = (X_1, X_2, \ldots, X_n)$ a *random vector* of dimension n, if the components $X_1, X_2, \ldots, X_n$ are real valued random variables. The multivariate cumulative distribution function of $\boldsymbol{X}$ is similar to the one–dimensional case defined by

$$F_{\boldsymbol{X}}(x_1, x_2, \ldots, x_n) = P(X_1 \leq x_1, X_2 \leq x_2, \ldots, X_n \leq x_n). \quad (7.11)$$

The nonnegative multivariate density function $f_{\boldsymbol{X}}(x_1, x_2, \ldots, x_n)$ can be computed from the following n–dimensional integral equation

$$F_{\boldsymbol{X}}(x_1, \ldots, x_n) = \int_{-\infty}^{x_1} \ldots \int_{-\infty}^{x_n} f_{\boldsymbol{X}}(y_1, \ldots, y_n) \, dy_1 \ldots dy_n. \quad (7.12)$$

The formulas for discrete random vectors follow immediately, if the integral signs are substituted by sums over all possible values of the discrete random variables.

Example:

A gray–level image can be viewed as a discrete random vector where the gray–levels represent the components of the vector.

Let $\boldsymbol{X} = (X_1, X_2, \ldots, X_n)$ be an n–dimensional random vector. The *mean vector* is now defined by the vector of means of each component, i.e.

$$E[\boldsymbol{X}] = \begin{pmatrix} E[X_1] \\ E[X_2] \\ \vdots \\ E[X_n] \end{pmatrix}. \quad (7.13)$$

The generalization of the variance is done by the *covariance* of two random variables X_i and X_j by

$$\sigma_{i,j} \;\; = \;\; E[(X_i - E[X_i])(X_j - E[X_j])]. \tag{7.14}$$

Obviously this results in the variance, if $i = j$. The *covariance matrix* is now given by

$$\Sigma \;\; = \;\; \begin{pmatrix} \sigma_{11} & \cdots & \sigma_{1n} \\ \vdots & & \vdots \\ \sigma_{n1} & \cdots & \sigma_{nn} \end{pmatrix}. \tag{7.15}$$

Example:

The generalization of the Gaussian density function to n dimensions is

$$f_X(x) = \frac{1}{\sqrt{2^n \pi^n |\det \Sigma|}} \; e^{-\dfrac{(x - \mu)^T \Sigma^{-1}(x - \mu)}{2}}, \tag{7.16}$$

where $x = (x_1, x_2, \ldots, x_n)^T$, μ is the n–dimensional mean vector, and Σ the symmetrical covariance matrix.

7.7   Statistical Features and Entropy

The defined statistical distribution characteristics constitute possible features of patterns. The speech signal, for example, is divided up into intervals of fixed size, usually a sampling rate of 10 kHz or a window of a duration of about 12.8 ms. In general, the interval size should be motivated by linguistics and has an averaged duration of 10–20 ms. Images are decomposed into blocks of fixed size, for example 16×16 pixels. Statistical measures like moments can be computed for each set of values. These are possible features for the given patterns and can be used for pattern classification (Sect. 5.1).

When we observe a random variable X_i, the information derivable from the outcome will depend on its probability. If the probability of observing the random variable is small, a large degree of information can be concluded, since the occurrence of this random variable is very rare. In contrast to that, random variables with a large probability of being observed have a very small degree of information. The amount of information is in coding and information theory defined as

$$I(X_i) \;\; = \;\; -\log p(X_i). \tag{7.17}$$

The important property of a randomized information source is the *entropy* which is defined as the average amount of information, i.e.

$$H(\boldsymbol{S}) \quad = \quad -\sum_{X_i \in S} p(X_i) \log p(X_i). \tag{7.18}$$

The entropy is the measure of the amount of information required in specifying which random variable has occurred on average.

7.8 Signal–to–Noise Ratio

By representing a real value f_i in the computer we have to use the discrete value f_i'. The error between the discrete and the real value is called *quantization noise* (compare Figure 1.9) and is given by

$$n_i \quad = \quad f_i - f_i'. \tag{7.19}$$

A measure for the accuracy of this quantization is the *signal–to–noise ratio* SNR defined by a quotient of means:

$$SNR \quad = \quad \frac{E[f_i^2]}{E[n_i^2]} \tag{7.20}$$

The assumptions that the quantization error is uniformly distributed, the quantizer is not saturated and the quantization is fine $(B > 6)$, leads to the following formula for the SNR:

$$SNR = 12 \cdot 2^{2B-6}, \tag{7.21}$$

where B is the number of bits used for quantization, i.e. we have 2^B different values for the digital range [Nie83]p. 29. The signal–to–noise ratio is used to measure the "quality" of a signal. It may happen, however, that a signal with high SNR looks worse than one with a lower ratio.

7.9   Histograms

Normally, the distribution of range values is an a priori unknown. One possible way to get information about the underlying statistics of the gray levels of an image is the computation of the relative frequency of possible values in the observed sample. Histograms render possible graphical representations of these frequencies. The discrete distribution of these quantities is shown in an empirical distribution by adding the relative frequencies successively from left to right. Figure 7.1 shows a gray–level image, the computed histogram of gray levels, and the associated discrete empirical distribution.

The transformation of histograms is quite easy. A frequently used technique in the preprocessing phase of image analysis systems is gray level scaling using histograms and the associated discrete distributions. In this connection, the discrete or continuous distribution is adapted to a special distribution – for example uniform distribution – with the help of a distortion function. The principle of this procedure is visualized in Figure 7.2.

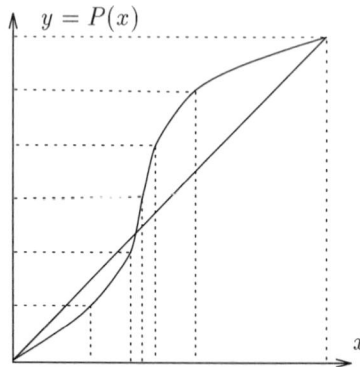

Figure 7.2 Linearization of the discrete distribution

For that, the y–axis is divided up into equidistant intervals and reflected to the x–axis. In Figure 7.3 the result of the described linearization is shown, including the gray–level image, the distribution, and the resulting histogram. The distribution is not exactly linear, but the differences in the gray–level frequencies are considerable compared to figurename 7.1.

Practically established transformations based on histograms are the linear or logarithmic representation of speech signals with eight bits, which are given with twelve bit. In image processing, the distortion of gray levels is used e.g. to raise the contrast of a picture.

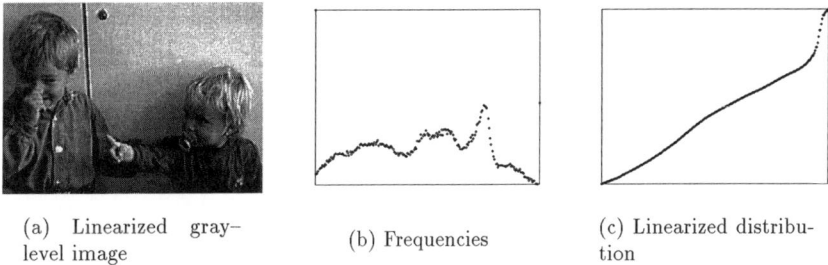

(a) Linearized gray–level image

(b) Frequencies

(c) Linearized distribution

Figure 7.3 Results of linearization

Exercises

1. Compute the probability that in a gray–level image of size $n \times m$ all pixels have the same gray–level. Assume that the discrete gray–levels are uniformly distributed on the integers $[0, g]$.

2. Usually, mathematical function libraries provide a random function which generates uniform distributed random numbers out of a fixed interval $[\min, \max]$.[2] Sketch an algorithm which permits the computation of uniform distributed numbers out of a parameterized interval $[l, u]$ using the available random generator.

3. Implement programs for the computation of histograms and discrete distribution of gray levels.

4. Explain why the distribution of Figure 7.3 is not a straight line.

5. Compute the SNR for music with CD quality (16 bit).

---

[2]Try `rand()` or `random()` on your machine.

6. Estimate the mean and variance of the gray–levels for each synthetic noisy image developed in Chapter 18.

7. Do a simple version of the projects in Chapter 19. Use a global array with fixed dimension (of course you should use macros for the size specifications as in Example 48!).

8 C++ as a better C

In this chapter we conclude the description of the conventional programming part of C++. We include the new features of C++, which amend some of the defects of C. Except for structures, most of the important features of C which are also valid for C++ will have been mentioned by the end of this chapter. We still miss conditional expressions and enumerations. These topics will be introduced through examples in Part II of the book. We also miss function pointers and other advanced applications of pointers.[1]

8.1 Type Declaration

New types can be introduced using already known declarations with the key word `typedef`.[2] Example 50 shows common declarations of the new types byte, string, and GrayValue.

```
typedef unsigned char byte;   // byte now identical to uns. char
typedef byte GrayValue;       // gray value identical to byte
typedef char * String;        // string types instead of char *
```
(50)

Type definitions may enhance the readability and portability of a program. Imagine, for example, a change of your image data format from eight to sixteen bits.

The operator `sizeof` returns the size (measured in byte) of its argument at *Compile-Time*. The argument can be a variable, an expression, or a type name. This operator again shows the difference between vectors and pointers. Applied to a pointer, the operator will give the number of bytes required

---

[1]These features can often be avoided in C++ by the use of virtual functions (Sect. 12.5).
[2]Although it sounds like "type definition" it is really a *declaration*!

for storing an address; applied to an array, it will give the size of the array. Example 51 shows how to enquire the number of elements in an array at compile time.

```
static char string[] = "abc";           // initialize static array
static char * cptr   = string;           // pointer
static int  arrayp[] = {1,2,3,4};        // initialize static array
int asize = sizeof(arrayp)/sizeof(int); // number of elements
int slen  = sizeof string;              // no () required
int plen  = sizeof cptr;                // different from slen
```
$\widehat{51}$

As can be seen, the `sizeof` operator may be used to write machine–independent programs which adjust their behavior according to the size of the same data type found on a different machine architecture (compare Table A.3).

8.2   Type Conversion for Pointers

As was already seen in section 4.1, types can be converted to others through the use of a type cast. Numerical values are then adjusted to the given type. A change of size and value is sometimes necessary (e.g. when converting from an unsigned character to a double value).

Pointers can also be converted using cast expressions. Normally, the size of the result is the same as before, i.e. a pointer requires the same number of bytes for storing the address no matter to which type it points. An example of type conversion for pointers is shown in Example 52. A special notation `void *` can be used for a generic pointer pointing to *any* type. Before the data pointed to can be accessed, however, the pointer has to be cast to the appropriate type.

```
char * cpt;            // some pointer definitions
int * iptr, i;         // not initialized
void * anyptr;         // can point anywhere
iptr = &i;             // pointer to an int
cpt = (char*) iptr;    // explicit conversion
anyptr = &i;           // now points to an int
* (int *) anyptr = 3;  // cast required
```
(52)

Note that the result of a pointer cast may in some cases give illegal values of the address or may even change the value of the pointer. For example, on most machines you should not try to cast a character pointer to an integer pointer, if the character pointer has an odd address.[3]

8.3 Bit– and Shift–Operations

Often operations are defined on integer values so that they can be used to analyze data bit by bit. They are used this way mainly in operating system interfaces or in highly efficient parts of a program.

Bit– and shift–operations for C and C++ are listed in Table 8.1. A zero value is inserted on left shift operations (LSH). A right shift (RSH) of an unsigned value will insert a zero in the highest bit. A right shift of a signed integer will do an arithmetic shift corresponding to a division by two; i.e. the highest bit is left unchanged and the second highest is filled with the value of the highest bit.[4] The operators & and | combine their operands bitwise. In contrast, the boolean operators && and || combine the values of their operands logically.

Binary bit and shift operations can be combined with an assignment as shown in Example 53.[5]

---

[3]Try for example:
`float f=1, * fp=&f; char * cp=1 + (char *) fp; fp=(float*) cp; *fp=3;`
Do not forget to remove the **core** file!

[4]This behavior is machine dependent; you should not rely on it.

[5]See also Table 4.1.

Operator	Description	Example
&	AND	a & 0xff
|	OR	a | 0x13ff
^	XOR	a ^ b
~	NOT	~0
<<	LSH	a << 3
>>	RSH	a >> 2

Table 8.1 Bit operations on integral values

```
int b = -2;              // not spectacular
int a = b | 0x33;        // bitwise OR connection
int c = a << 4;          // see the operator precedence
b ^= (a & 0xffff);       // parentheses look better
b = a || c;              // logical connection
```
⑤③

8.4   Type Specifiers and Variable Declaration

Variables can be *specified* with additional keywords in the declarations. C++ offers several choices: const declares the variable to have a constant value, & makes it a reference, register is used for compiler optimization, extern, auto, and static control scope and life time.

When a variable is declared extern, the statement is a declaration and not a definition. These modifications are valid for function arguments as well.

Reference arguments in function declarations provide a twofold benefit. First, changes to a non–local variable can be done through the use of reference arguments. This introduces arguments with the "call by reference" semantics as found, for example, in Pascal or Fortran. An example is shown in Example 54 (compare to Example 43).

Secondly, it is often advantageous not to pass large objects to a function. Arguments passed by value require a copy operation on the data. Argument references are not copied when they are passed as arguments; only a reference to the object is passed to the function. To make this intention explicit, a combination of reference and const should be used as shown in Example 55.

```
void swapint(int &a, int &b)
{                        // swap the value of two integers
    int tmp = a; a = b; b = tmp;
}

void foo()
{   int i = 3, j = 4;
    swapint (i,j);       // now i ==4, j == 3
}
```
(54)

```
static int globalint = 0; // local in this module
static void foo(int a,    // pass by value
        int & b,          // pass by reference
        const int & c,    // pass by constant reference
        int * d,          // pass as a pointer
        const int * e)    // pass as pointer to constant
{
    auto      int i = 0;  // same as int i = 0;
    register int k = 10;  // hint to the compiler
    static    int j = 1;
    const     int l = 0;
    a = i;                // local effect
    b = i;                // will change the referenced arg
    c = i;                // error
    *d = 1;               // global effect
    e = d;                // ok, only data pointed to is const
    *e = *d;              // error
}
```
(55)

We can now specify a more complex (but still incomplete, see [Str91a]) syntax for a variable declaration; for simplicity we leave out initialization and multiple variables in one declaration statement.[6]

Syntax:

[<u>extern</u> |<u>static</u> |<u>register</u> |<u>auto</u>] [<u>const</u>] *type* [<u>*</u>*|&] *var1* [[<u>*size*</u>]]*

Various combinations of * and [] can result in cryptic sequences of characters. Through the use of **typedef**'s it is often possible to reduce the complexity of such expressions. A declaration and an explanation[7] is shown in Example 56.

```
int * const f[10];

c++decl> explain int * const f[10]
declare f as array 10 of const pointer to int
```
(56)

8.5   Type–Safe Linkage

When using different modules, inevitably names for functions and variables have to be shared between different files. In C only the name is exported to the linker. For example, if a function **foo** is defined in one module and used as an integer **foo** in another module, this will not result in a linkage error. The runtime system will however show the disastrous effects.

C++ introduces type-safe linkage and treats the integer **foo** different from the function **foo()**. The technique used generates function names that include an encoding of both the function's type and its respective argument types into the external name. It does this through the use of a unique naming scheme (called "name mangling"). Occasionally, the linker will report such unresolved symbols. A program called **demangle** can be used to decode these cryptic messages into more readable ones.

---

[6]We still miss the possibility to express pointers to functions etc.

[7]The program **cdecl** is in the public domain (see Sect. C.1). It explains in clear English a given variable definition or declaration or cast expression for C or C++.

A special notation **extern** "C" can be used to circumvent the coding of arguments into the external name. This is useful when modules compiled in the C language have to be linked with C++–modules. Example 57 shows a C and a C++ program which can be linked together into one program.

```
/* ANSI C Program */
int verbose;
int foo(int i)
{
    return i;
}
```

```
extern "C" int verbose;
extern "C" int foo(int);
main(int argc, char **argv)
{   if (verbose)
        printf("%d\n", foo(argc));
}
```
(57)

8.6   Overloaded Function Names

Several different functions may share a common name as long as the function can be uniquely identified by its arguments. Of course, this makes only sense for groups of functions which essentially do the same as those in Example 58. Name mangling ensures that such functions can be distinguished by the linker.

```
double sqr(double a) { return a*a; }  // sqr for double and float
int    sqr(int a)    { return a*a; }  // sqr for integers
```
(58)

Functions which can not be distinguished by the compiler are shown in Example 59.

```
typedef unsigned char byte;
double sqr(unsigned char) { return a*a; }
int    sqr(byte a)        { return a*a; } // error
```
(59)

8.7 Return Value and Arguments

A function can have a variable number of arguments in the call syntax, such as the function `printf`. The implementation of such functions in C is possible using macros from an include file `varargs.h`. This is however error prone, since the compiler can not check whether a sufficient number of arguments is provided when the function is called. A safe and easy solution in C++ is to provide default values for the arguments in the *declaration* of the function. These values can then be left out when the function is called. Only the trailing arguments can have initial default values. Another possibility is the use of "..." which declares the function with an unspecified number and type of arguments.[8] This should be avoided in general; but it is necessary for both C and the Unix interface of the language.

```
void foo0(int i, int j = 3) {}            // definition
void foo1(int i, char c=' ', float f = 0.0);   // declaration
int  foo2(int i ... );                    // declaration

void foo1(int i, char c, float f) {}      // definition

main()
{
    foo0 (1);               // call foo0(1,3)
    foo0 (1,2);
    foo2 (1,2,3,4,5);   // foo2 will have to take care of the args
}
```
(60)

The specifiers described in Sect. 8.4 are valid when declaring the return value of a function as well. Returning a reference is rather interesting because the return value of the function can be assigned to a variable (Example 61).

---

[8]The function then has to use **varargs** to recover the argument list.

```
int & elem(int i)
{
    static int f[10];   /* must be static !*/
    return f[i];
}
foo(int i)
{
    elem(i) = 3;
}
```
(61)

It is an error to return a reference to a function's local variable — which is not static — upon its return, since the memory location is no longer valid after the return from the function that was called.

8.8   Macros and Inline Functions

Macros (see Sect. 2.8) are often a source of nasty errors, especially if they have side effects as shown in Example 62.

```
#include<stdio.h>
#define sqr(a) a*a
main()
{
    int    i = 3;
    float  g = 3.0;
    int    j = sqr(++i);      // surprise
    float  f = sqr(g+2);      // surprise
    printf("%d %f\n", j, f);  // prints 20 11.0
}
```
(62)

Although it looks like a function call, sqr in Example 62 is just a textual substitution and has no function semantics. C++ introduces inline functions, which in many cases replace the use of macros with a safer tool.

Inline functions provide the runtime efficiency of macros and the flexibility of functional semantics including local variables and scoping rules. Example 63 shows the new version of Example 62 which now works as expected. However, we need two function definitions in order to provide the square of integral numbers and of floating point numbers.

```
#include<stdlib.h>
inline int    sqr(int a)    { return a*a; }  // sqr 1
inline double sqr(double a) { return a*a; }  // sqr 2
main(int argc, char ** argv)
{
    int   j = sqr(atoi(*++argv));        // call sqr 1
    float f = sqr(atof(*++argv)+2);      // call sqr 2
    printf("%d %f\n", j, f);             // works as expected
}                                                            (63)
```

The function `atof` in Example 63 works like `atoi` but returns a floating point value. Inline functions are "expanded" like macros but provide functional semantics. They should be used in C++ instead of macros wherever possible.

8.9 Function Pointers

In Chapter 6 we introduced pointers to data. Pointers may as well be set to functions. The syntax of the declaration is basically as follows:

Syntax: [extern |static] *return_type* (* *name*) (*arguments*)

This means that a function pointer variable is declared which can be set to a function of a given type; this declaration includes the return type and the argument declaration of the function. It is possible to circumvent this kind of type checking, but in general this can introduce problems during run time of a program.

Functions can be called *indirectly* via pointers as shown in Example 64. This technique is very powerful and used in large C programs. In C++, other mech-

anisms exist which are safer in respect to type checking and simpler in terms
of programming. We will hear more about that in Part II.

```
static int foo1(int i) { return i; }
static int foo2(int i) { return i*i; }

static int (*fptr) (int)     // declare fptr as ptr to function
          = foo1;            // and initialize to foo1

main()
{
    printf("%d\n", fptr(2)); // indirect function call to foo1
    fptr = foo2;
    printf("%d\n", fptr(2)); // indirect function call to foo2
}
```
(64)

Since C++ provides better features than function pointers, we will not go into
details here. This language feature is however required if functions from the
system libraries are to be used, for example a quick–sort function as declared
in Example 65 and used in Example 66.

```
extern "C" void
qsrt(                      // extern C quick sort function
     void *base,           // pointer to start of data
     int nel,              // number of elements
     int size,             // size of an element
     int (*compar)(const void *, const void *) // compare function
);
```
(65)

A complicated cast of the function pointer compare is required to bypass C++
argument type checking. Such casts can occasionally be made more readable
by a typedef for a function pointer.

```
static int cmp(const int* i1,const int* i2) {return (*i1)-(*i2);}
main()
{
    int * ia = new int[20];
    // do something with ia
    qsrt(ia,20,sizeof(int), (int(*)(const void*,const void*))cmp);
}
```
(66)

Exercises

1. *The Functions* sscanf *and* fgets

   The function sscanf extracts values from a string and is part of most C
   libraries. This function can be used when atof and atoi is not sufficient.

   In combination with the function fgets which reads a string into a buffer,
   simple formatted input can be parsed. The formatting parameters are
   essentially the same as for printf (Table 2.1). However, the arguments
   have to be provided as pointers to be filled with values. An example is
   shown in Example 67.

   ```
   int i; char c; float f;
   char buffer[256];
   fgets(buffer,sizeof(buffer),stdin);
   sscanf(buffer,"I = %d, F = %7.2f, c = %c",&i,&f,&c);
   ```
   (67)

   The functions fscanf and scanf read directly from a stream and are not
   as handy as sscanf and fgets. C++ provides other facilities for input from
   streams ([Str91a]pp. 325, cmp. Sect. 14.5).

   Declare the functions fgets, fscanf, and sscanf with their argument
   lists. Check your result against the declarations in the file <stdio.h>.

2. *Repeat Macro*

One syntactic macro — in contrast to Example 68 — will make the code more readable,[9] since the multiple use of the key word `while` is avoided:

Write a macro `repeat` and `until ( expression )` which will work as expected (refer to the Pascal manual). Use proper parentheses for the expression!

3. *Debug Macro*

Even if your system has a nice debugger, messages for debugging a program are often very handy. On the other hand, it is a nuisance to remove them for the final run. Often, some lines are removed which should be kept, etc.

Define a simple macro called `DEBUGMSG`.

It should have one (!) argument which is used for the function `printf`. Since `printf` directs its output to `stdout` — which is a buffered file — messages are delayed until the buffer is full. Use the function `fflush` to avoid this behavior.

Hints:

- Create two files:

    - `debugmsg.h` containing the macros
    - `debugmsg.C` containing the functions

    Write a test program, use a makefile and `rcs`.

- The resulting lines in the program should look as in Example 3.

- Check the file `<assert.h>` for further ideas. Try `man assert` as well.

```
#include "debugmsg.h"
main (int argc, char** argv)
{
    DEBUGMSG(("starting main %s\n", *argv));
    // do something
    DEBUGMSG(("End of main\n"));
}
```
(68)

---

[9]This is at least the opinion of the authors of this book.

Then redefine the macro in a way that

- No output is printed
- No code is generated for this line

4. Extend exercise 7 in 6. Now define the vector for the speech signal locally in the main function. Pass the vector and its length as arguments to all the functions which need it.

   If your computer has an audio input device, put all the device dependent code into a separate module and run the program. Try to recognize three different spoken words which are spoken isolatedly:

   - "Start"
   - "Stop"
   - "Quit"

   Use simple features, like the duration of the speech signal, or try the features learned in Chapter 7.

Part II
Object–Oriented Pattern Analysis

Edge strength computed on the image on page 3.

Part II of the book introduces C++ as an object–oriented language. We describe class hierarchies for general object–oriented programming (nihcl) and for object–oriented image processing and analysis (part of ἵππος).

9 Object–Oriented Programming

In this chapter we introduce the object–oriented programming paradigm and other related subjects for object–oriented software construction. The term "object–oriented programming" has recently become very popular. Many applications of object–oriented programming and software design principles exist and there are many journals and scientific publications which are specialized on the philosophy and the possibilities of object–oriented systems. The following sections can only summarize the fundamental concepts of object–oriented programming languages. The interested reader may find more information in the references. A summary can be found e.g. in [Bus92]. We give an overview in Sect. 9.2 and elaborate the ideas further in the remainder of the chapter.

9.1 Object–Oriented Software Techniques

The object–oriented programming style suggests the decomposition of a problem domain into a hierarchy of classes and a set of communicating objects, which are themselves instances of classes. The object oriented programmer then specifies *what* is done with the objects. The procedural way of programming uses aspects of *how* something gets done. The advantage of object–oriented software design is that a one–to–one correspondence between objects of the real world and the objects in the program can be made. Even the analysis of the problem domain has to be involved in this mapping. Analysis and program design are no longer separated in the software development process (cmp. Chapter 3); object–oriented analysis and design share the same terminology and tools.

The first phase of object–oriented software development is to define the requirements (RD). In the object–oriented analysis (OOA) stage of a problem, concepts of the problem domain and their correspondences are identified and specified. Hierarchical relations between the concepts are used; information which can be shared by several special concepts will be included in a general concept and passed to the special cases through *inheritance*. In the object–oriented design (OOD) phase, the conceptual class hierarchy is overlayed with links which are meaningful for the implementation only. This provides a transition from the problem domain to the *solution* domain. After analysis and design, the object–oriented coding can take place (object–oriented programming, OOP). Conventional tools as well as the corresponding object–oriented terms are shown in Figure 9.1; structured design (SD, [DeM79, PJ80]) and structured programming (SP) are now integrated into the new object–oriented techniques. Whereas conventional software engineering is mostly sequential with some optional loops (Figure 3.1), object–oriented software development has a main stream from RD to OOP, with possibly opposite direction as well.

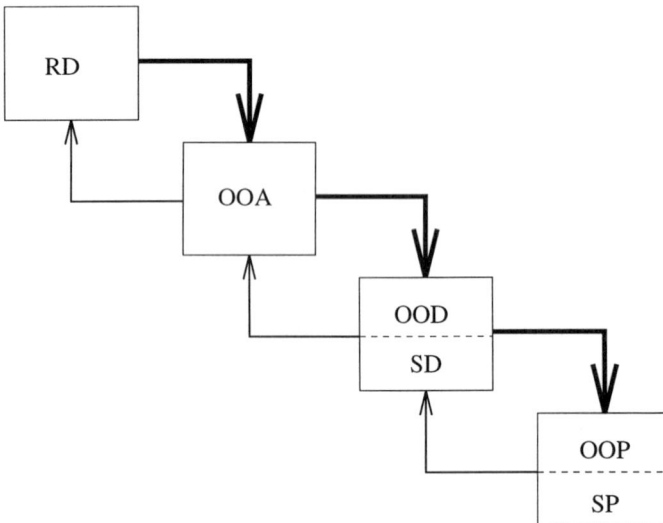

Figure 9.1 Object–oriented software engineering techniques (explained in the text).

Several graphical representations and mechanisms have been proposed for OOA and OOD. The books of Booch [Boo91], Coad & Yourdon [Coa90], Rumbaugh et al. [Rum91], and Shlaer & Mellor [Shl88] are commonly used in this stage of software development.

9.2   Basic Concepts

Due to [Weg87], the characteristical features of the object–oriented programming paradigm are:

- objects,
- classes,
- inheritance,
- data abstraction,
- polymorphism,
- message passing,
- methods,
- types, and
- durability.

Objects can be for example integers, reals, gray–level images, lines, addresses, or any other concept conceivable in the problem domain. Objects themselves are *instances* of classes. Classes consist, in general, of member variables and methods which can be used for manipulating the member variables. Classes describe the layout of objects.

For example, a class "gray–level image" should have member variables like a matrix including intensity–values and the focal length of the used camera (see Chapter 11). Necessary methods are, for instance, selectors for reading a gray–value at a certain image point and a method which returns the focal length of the camera. This example shows that the assumed class for gray–level images includes a matrix as a member variable. This matrix can also be instance of a class. The image class for gray–level images is derived from a more abstract class, where all images like the range images or others can be specified. The provided technique for the implementation of such dependencies is inheritance. Data shared by all variants of images — e.g. a recording time stamp — can be defined in the common base class.

Another basic feature of object–oriented paradigm is the concept of polymorphism. In combination with inheritance, objects may exhibit "polymorphic" behavior and react on messages differently depending on the class the object actually belongs to. For example, matrix elements of a general matrix class can be integers, reals, gray–levels, or of some other type. The addition of two matrices is defined by a component wise addition; this is the case for all data types of the matrix entries. Thus, the code should be written independent on the types of the matrix entries. If a programming language supports parameterized member variables, a general matrix class can be implemented, where the type of the matrix entry is not specified.

Operator overloading, where functions with the same function name are distinguished by their arguments, is also a common technique in object–oriented systems.

In the following sections we will elaborate the above features a little further. One representative object–oriented programming language, which satisfies them, is C++. In the following chapters we will introduce the characteristics of an object–oriented programming language by using C++.

9.3   Data Abstraction and Modules

One of the aims of object–oriented software design is to provide an abstract interface for programmers using the technique of *information hiding*. The user of a class only needs to know the methods of a class and its semantics. The internal data representation and the implementation details of several methods should in general not be in the scope of users. The method of information hiding renders a high degree of modularity and supports the teamwork required in large programming projects.

Data abstraction provides the tools for modular programming. For example, you want to add two matrices in a part of a function. Since the matrix class provides a method for the addition of two matrices, we will not have to reimplement the addition using the components of the matrix. Furthermore, the code becomes more readable and thus reusable for other programmers (presupposing that the code is well documented). Changes in a special operation, like e.g. addition of matrices, can be done locally in the method's definition. The code which uses this function has only to be recompiled.

Computer scientists invented the concept of *abstract data types* (ADT). In this concept, data and the operations which alter the data are strongly connected. The data representation is no longer relevant. All access to the information is done using the operations provided in the data type. This is what we mean by information hiding. The definition of abstract data types is a more theoretical concept that combines data representation with formal aspects of implementation and representation [Gut78, Gog78]. Some programming languages have implemented this concept; one typical example is Modula 2 [Wir83]. Abstract data types are defined in some programming structures together along with the appropriate functions which define the interface for the given data type. Variables of this type can now be defined. The programmer can operate on these variables using the methods which were associated with the abstract data type.

Using the graphical elements of [Coa90], an abstract data type can be depicted as in Figure 9.2. If one data type A uses or references another type B, this can be visualized by a line connecting the two corresponding boxes, marked with a triangle pointing to A. This link is often used for the "part–of" relationship. Type A has to apply the operations for B in order to access data of B.

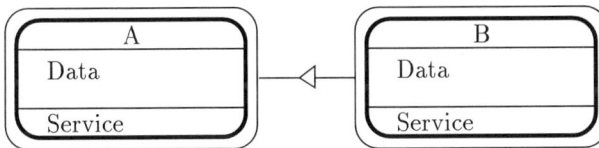

Figure 9.2   Two related abstract data types (ADT)

9.4   Inheritance

Classes as well as ADTs may be understood as descriptions of special terms; objects result out of classes by aligning special values to their descriptions. Classes can arise by inheritance from one or more base classes. This process is generally called the derivation of a new class. In the terminology of object–oriented programming the base class is often called *superclass* and a derived class *subclass*. We call this inheritance graph a hierarchy no matter whether it is actually a directed acyclic graph or really a tree.

The use of class hierarchies and inheritance forces programmers to think about an ordered structure of the underlying problem domain. The resulting source code has in general less lines, is more structured, and has a higher degree of reusability.

One class can be derived from another one – the *superclass*. This derivation inherits both the class' methods and the class members. Furthermore, the derived class should have also the same rights for the access of inherited members and methods (see Chapter 12), i.e. inheritance grants more insight to a class than the usage relation in Figure 9.2.

Inheritance can appear in two different ways: on the one hand we have *simple* on the other hand *multiple inheritance*. If a class is derived from one super class, we call the inheritance simple. If a class has more than one base class, multiple inheritance is being used.

Many authors suggest the use of simple inheritance because there exists no possibility for conflict. If multiple inheritance is used, it can be possible to construct cycles in the inheritance graph. Those cycles support the appearance of inconsistency. Consequently, algorithms have to be implemented which supervise the consistency in the inheritance graph. The development of such algorithms is a nontrivial problem.

A provisional and simplified characterization of object–oriented programming can be itemized as follows:

- classes (represent abstract units),

- inheritance of classes (abstract generic terms), and

- objects (concrete terms associated with values).

Using the graphical elements of [Coa90], inheritance of two classes A and B from C can be depicted as in Figure 9.3. The line between the boxes now contains a semi–circle with the round edge towards the base class.

9.5   Abstract Classes

The examples explained so far were concrete classes including methods which are explicitly suitable for implementation purposes. Assume you have to implement a class for lines. Obviously there are different possibilities to represent lines. For instance, you can use chain codes, polygons, arcs, or a set of affine

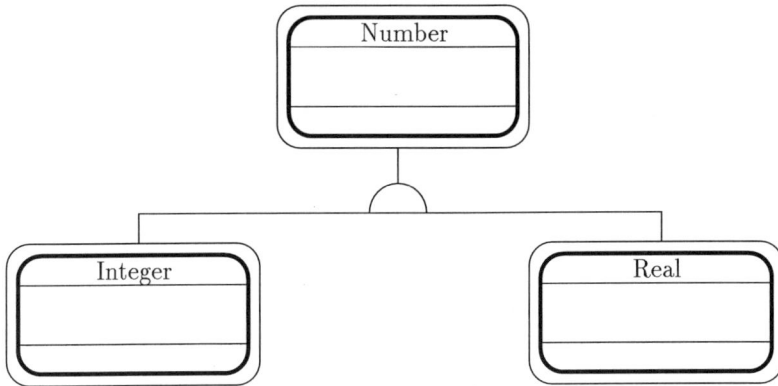

Figure 9.3 Inheritance

functions. Furthermore, you have to distinguish between lines of different dimensions. Independent of the internal representation a class for lines should include methods for the determination of line–length or for traversing the line points. It can not be the aim of an object–oriented programming system to implement all different classes for lines without the use of the more abstract concept of lines. Abstract classes provide the declaration of a class where no concrete members have to be specified and the methods can be declared in an abstract manner. In these abstract classes no implementation of the methods has to be made. The concrete definition of the methods then must be developed in derived classes, where the explicit line representation is known. The advantage of abstract classes is obviously the development of modular and well structured software, where classes which depend on each other in an abstract way are reflected within the network of classes. Abstract classes may specify concrete members and methods which are shared by all derived classes — even without redeclaration.

The class **Number** in Figure 9.3 had better be an abstract class, since an object is not simply a "number" but either a real number or an integer or what ever class of concrete numbers are used in the program. Using the graphical elements of [Coa90], an abstract class looks as in Figure 9.4.

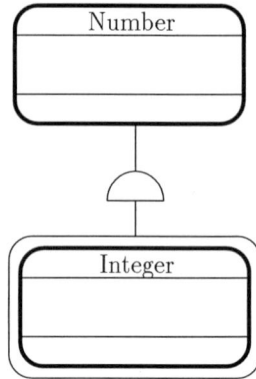

Figure 9.4 Abstract class and concrete derived classes

9.6   Object–Oriented Classification

The term "classification" was introduced with pattern analysis in Sect. 5.1. This term is also used in the description of object–oriented systems. Classes can be defined as representatives of a class of objects. The universe of objects is divided into classes by a partition. Objects of similar purpose are grouped into equivalence classes. Classes in this sense correspond to the term "class" in set theory.

> A class is a set of objects that share a common structure and a common behavior.

This approach allows for the distinction of types and classes. Objects belonging to one class may still have separate types. However, this is relevant only in "real" object–oriented programming languages. In C++ we can handle classes as types.

Classification is thus a fundamental problem of OOA. Objects have to be grouped according to their behavioral and structural similarity. However, it is context–dependent, which kind of behavior is regarded as similar. Class boundaries tend to be fuzzy rather than clear.

9.7 Polymorphism

Another basic concept of object–oriented programming languages is the use of polymorphism.

> A concept in type theory, according to which a name (such as a variable declaration) may denote objects of many different classes that are related by some common superclass; thus, any object denoted by this name is able to respond to some common set of operations in different ways, [Boo91]p. 517.

Sometimes algorithms can be formulated in an abstract manner independent of the data types it operates on. Mathematicians are well versed in those problems. For example, the determination of the maximum element of a set or a sort algorithm on a set of elements depends only on the ordering of the elements' domain. So, routines are needed which can be applied to many different data types, for instance numbers, letters, or vectors. These functions are called *polymorphic* and they serve for the sparing of code. Another consequence of polymorphism is a compact and a more easily surveyed source code, which can easily be reused by others.

Polymorphism together with dynamic binding and inheritance is a key concept in object–oriented programming.

Often operator overloading is called weak polymorphism. Examples for overloaded functions names are addition and multiplication for integers, reals, and complex numbers.

9.8 Other Object–Oriented Concepts

If one class has more than one base class, we will call this *multiple inheritance* (Sect. 12.8). The ancestor Smalltalk did not allow multiple base classes. Several modern object–oriented programming languages do, however, implement this concept. It is by far more complex to maintain a class hierarchy with multiple inheritance, than with single inheritance. One typical use of multiple inheritance is the introduction of a new *aspect* of a class. Consider for example the classes `animal`, `rabbit`, `horse`, `vehicle`, and `truck`. In addition to the natural inheritance from general to special concepts, one may introduce a class `transportation`. Now `horse` and the `truck` are additionally derived from `transportation`.

In general, multiple inheritance may be difficult to implement, but as soon as someone else has written the system, application programming is fairly easy. The concept of multiple inheritance has many applications, e.g. in the graphics world. For instance, a window system may have graphics windows, text windows, and scrollable window classes. An application programmer may want to create a new class with properties from all three. Without multiple inheritance, this is very messy.

One class may contain members of another class. We call the classes of the member objects *clients*. Instead of inheriting classes we may also in some cases use a client and define all the methods of the client in the new class. These methods will just pass the arguments to the corresponding methods of the clients. This is called *delegation*. In many cases multiple inheritance can be avoided using delegation.

Often, a system contains several classes which are identical except for the type or class of some member variables. *Parametric types* allow to create classes from a description including parameters. A general scheme is expanded to the actual classes. In C++, this can be done with templates (Sect. 11.2).

9.9   Class Libraries

Object–oriented programming has been used in various libraries. For example, object–oriented ideas are used in the implementation of the X11 graphics system, even if no object–oriented language is used. A real object–oriented implementation of X11 is available in the public domain, the InterViews system (see Sect. C.3).

The Smalltalk system was distributed with an extensive library for graphics and all common programming applications. It included sets, collections, dictionaries, all sorts of mathematical applications etc. It also contained a windowing environment.

In contrast, C++ is a programming language without any advanced programming libraries. The only classes contained in the standard distribution are those for input and output with streams. This is a great disadvantage for those who want to start with object–oriented programming. Every little concept has to be individually programmed. There are however class libraries in the public domain which add some of the power of Smalltalk to C++. We will see more about this in Chapter 14.

Exercises

1. Develop a class hierarchy for lines. Which methods should be declared in the abstract class? Is it useful to use multiple inheritance? Where can concepts like polymorphism and operator overloading be used in this example?

2. Define an parametric matrix class. Which members do we need? Which methods should be provided by the class?

3. Check the advertisements in your favorite computer journal for occurrences of the term "object–oriented". Try to find out whether this term is correctly applied there.

10 Classes in C++

C++ is not an object–oriented language. It *allows* for object–oriented program-ming. The features of object–oriented programming introduced in chapter 9 can be mapped to features of the C++–language. In this chapter we intro-duce the design of classes in C++ and show the use of abstract data types for realizing encapsulation.

10.1 Structures

Like most modern programming languages, C++ has a mechanism for gluing already known data types together into a new data type. In C++ this is called a `struct` and usually has a type name.[1] The syntax is basically as follows:

Syntax:	`struct` [*sname*] { *declaration** } [*vdef*] ;

This introduces a new type name (*sname*). The semicolon at the end is very important and is a common source of errors when it is forgotten. Declarations of variables inside the braces declare storage locations which are the *members* of the data structure; the names are called *structure tags*. Variables may be immediately defined with a type declaration (*vdef*); more commonly, they are defined separately using the structure name (*sname*). Example 69 shows the new data type `PointXY` for point coordinates. The variable `p0` is defined using this new data type. Access to the members of a structure is possible via a variable followed by a dot and the member tag.

---

[1]Occasionally the name is left out; see Example 121 for an example.

```
struct PointXY {      // declare new data type
   int x,y;           // members are x and y
};                    // do not forget the ;

PointXY p0;           // define a variable
p0.x = 1;             // access the member x
p0.y = 1;             // access the member y
```
⟨69⟩

As with standard data types, pointers may be set to user defined data types. Members can be accessed by the use of pointers to structures. The combination of pointer access and member ((*ptr).member) can be abbreviated by a new operator -> (Example 70). Like arrays, the structures can be initialized by lists in curly brackets. In contrast to C, the structure name can be used as a type without a typedef.

```
PointXY p = { 1, 2 };    // initialize a variable
PointXY *pp = &p;        // define a pointer variable
p.x = 1;                 // access via variable
(*pp).y = 1;             // access via pointer
pp->x = 2;               // short hand for (*pp).x = 2;
```
⟨70⟩

10.2   Methods and ADT's

Example 69 showed the data structure PointXY consisting of two data entries. This basically looks like Pascal. No restrictions on the access, modification, and use of the structure members were specified. Good programming practice requires the definition of functions which use the new data type (Example 71). All these functions have been prefixed with the data type name to avoid name conflicts. Misuse or failure to use the new functions can, however, not be controlled by the compiler. The use of these functions can be recommended but not enforced. Information hiding — as required in ADT's (section 9.3) – is thus only partially possible.

```
void PointXY_setXY(PointXY& p, int x, int y) { p.x = x ; p.y = y; }
int  PointXY_getX(PointXY& p)                { return p.x; }
int  PointXY_getY(PointXY& p)                { return p.y; }
```
⑺₁

Now, in addition to data members, functions can be declared *inside* the structure. These functions are used only in conjunction with the data of the structure type. Example 72 shows a structure for rational numbers consisting of a numerator and a denominator. This already looks more like an ADT, since operations on the data type are declared with tight adherence to the data specification. These functions are called "methods" (see chapter 9).

```
struct rational {          // structure declaration
   int d,q;                // two data members
   void cancel();          // member function declaration
   rational set(int,int);  // member function declaration
   float asFloat()         // member function definition
     {return d/float(q); }
};

rational r, *rp = &r;      // variable definition
```
⑺₂

Functions *defined* within the body — the method `asFloat` in Example 72 — are automatically inlined (section 8.8). The `inline` key word can be used for better readability.

Methods can be accessed like data members using a variable and a tag — the method name — separated by a "." or a "->" in the case of a pointer. In addition, a parameter list can be given. As can be seen from Example 73, structures can be assigned as a whole; they can also be returned from functions.

```
r.set(3,3);
float f = rp->asFloat();
rational r1 = r, r2 = *rp;
```

⑦③

Definition of methods outside the structure use the structure name followed by
:: [2] and the method name (Example 74). Inside the methods, other methods
and data members are known without the explicit mention of the class name.
They can be accessed explicitly by the **this** pointer, which points to the actual
object for which the method is invoked.[3] In some cases, the **this** pointer is
required to access the actual object as a whole (**return** statement in the
second implementation of the method **set** in Example 74).

```
#ifndef USE_THIS
rational rational::set(int x, int y)
{
    d = x; q = y;   // will give a warning
}                   // non void function without return value
#else /* alternatively */
rational rational::set(int x, int y)
{
    this->d = x;    // just to give an example
    (*this).q = y;  // just to be different
    return *this;   // this is returned
}
#endif
```

⑦④

Note also the preprocessor statement for conditional compilation depending
on the existence of a defined (in terms of the preprocessor) macro in Example 74. This kind of definition is often passed to the preprocessor from the
compiler command line e.g. with CC -DUSE_THIS -c prog.C.

---

[2]The scope resolution operator — like all other two character operators — may not be
separated by a blank character.
[3]The compiler implicitly prefixes all the access expressions to class members by a **this->**
pointer.

10.3   Class Declarations

Structures as introduced in the previous sections partially satisfy the requirements of ADT's. The primary feature that is missing is "Information Hiding".
This is possible with the `class` declaration in C++. Variables of a class type
are called *objects*.

Classes are structures with access regulations. Data members and methods
can be excluded from external usage; they are then applicable only inside
other methods. Three key words are used for access regulations: The label
`public:` introduces unrestricted parts of the class. The label `private:` re-
stricts the following entries for internal class use. The label `protected:` will
be introduced in section 12.2. Example 75 shows a class declaration of a so
called `assoc_int`.[4] A key (e.g. a name) is associated with an integer (e.g.
a telephone number). The data members are accessible only by the public
methods. These labels can be repeated and occur in any order.

```
class assoc_int {     // association between integer and string
private:               // can be omitted: classes start private
    int value;
    char * key;
public:                // the following defines the interface
    const char * Key() { return key; }   // read access to data
    void Key(char * k) { key = k; }      // set key
    int Value() { return value; }        // read access to data
    void set(int v, char * k);           // set value
};                                                                (75)
```

Structures in C++ are exactly the same as classes except for one small difference; the initial access mode for structures is public; the initial mode for
classes is private. Several uses, both legal and illegal, of the class `assoc_int`
are shown in Example 76. Making the return value of `Key` a `const char *`
protects the association string from manipulation after a call to the method.

---

[4]We will later see applications of this class.

```
assoc_int ai1, ai2;        // object definition
ai1.set(857895,"Paulus");  // legal use of method
ai2.set(857826,"Hornegger"); // legal use of method
ai1.value = 33;            // error, value is private
char * n1 = ai2.key;       // error, key is private
char * n2 = ai2.Key();     // warning, constant assigned
                           // to char *
```
(76)

10.4 Object Construction

It would be tedious and error prone if every class or structure had a method for initialization (as in Example 75 the method set) which had to be called explicitly for every object.

C++ introduces special methods for classes called *constructors*. These — usually overloaded — functions share the class name as their method name. They are used upon definition of an object and can initialize internal and external data automatically. Syntax and usage is best seen through an example. Example 77 shows a modification of the class introduced in Example 75. The method set is now left out.

```
class assoc_int {
   int value; char * key;  // private
public:                    // the following defines the interface
   assoc_int();            // default constructor
   assoc_int(int,char*);   // alternative constructor
   const char * Key();
   int Value();
};
```
(77)

Example 78 is a modified version of Example 76. Instead of explicitly initializing the objects we use constructors. The example also shows the use of the new operator on classes. The so called "default constructor" is used when no argument list is provided. As for overloaded functions, the choice of the appropriate constructor depends on the argument list. Example 79 shows the definition of the default constructor for this class.

```
assoc_int ai1;          // definition and call
                        // of default constructor
assoc_int ai2(10,"a");  // definition and call
                        // of second constructor
assoc_int * aip1 = new assoc_int;        // use default constructor
assoc_int * aip2 = new assoc_int(11,"b");// use second constructor
```
(78)

```
assoc_int::assoc_int()
{
    value = -1;
    key = NULL;
}
```
(79)

Arrays of objects can be defined similar to arrays of simple types (section 6.1). A default constructor is called for every object in the array. If no default constructor is defined for the class, the compiler should emit an error message (Example 80).

```
assoc_int aia[10];       // definition and call of
                         // default constructor
assoc_int * aip3 = new assoc_int[11];  // use default constructor
                                       // 11 times
```
(80)

It is often useful to initialize one object with the contents of another object of the same type. The "Reference Constructor" is used for this purpose. Declaration and use is shown in Example 81 which extends Example 69.[5] This constructor is used when an object is returned from a function or passed to it as an argument. Note, that it is *not* called, if the argument is passed as a reference!

```
class PointXY {          // declare new data type
    int xa,ya;           // members are xa and ya
public:
    PointXY();               // default constructor
    PointXY(const PointXY &);  // reference constructor,
                             // always const arg.
    PointXY(int, int);       // third constructor
    int x();                 // access to member xa
    int y();                 // access to member ya
};                                                            (81)
```

Example 82 shows the definition of the constructor methods declared in Example 81.

```
PointXY::PointXY() { xa = 0; ya = 1; }
PointXY::PointXY(const PointXY & r) { xa = r.xa; ya = r.ya; }
PointXY::PointXY(int i, int j) { xa = i; ya = j; }            (82)
```

Constructors never have a return type. However, they can be terminated by a return statement like any other void function.

10.5   Destruction of Objects

Similar to object construction, the destruction code of an object is generated automatically by the compiler if it is not declared explicitly. The "destructor"

---

[5]If there is no declaration of a reference constructor, the compiler will automatically create one which copies all components recursively.

is a special method; its name is the class name prefixed with a tilde (resembling the unary not operator, Table 8.1). A string class with destructor is shown in Example 83.

```
class string {        // declare new data type
   char * st;
public:
   string(char *); // constructor
   ~string();        // destructor
};
```
(83)

Typically, destructors release the memory which was allocated in the constructor (Example 84). Other examples can be found in the following sections.

```
#include <string.h>
string::string(const char * s)
 { st = new char [1+strlen(s)]; strcpy(st,s); }
string::~string() { delete [] st; }
```
(84)

The destructor is called on an object when this object goes out of scope (and is not static, of course). Objects created by new can be destroyed by delete. This will call the destructor as well (Example 85). For arrays, the destructor is called for every element. There is only *one* destructor per class which always has no arguments and no return type. As with constructors, a return from the destructor with a return statement is possible. Objects are also deleted, when the function exit is called from any point in the program. This feature can be useful for example for files which have to do some cleanup on permanent storage: like removing temporary files or locks on devices as the program terminates.

```
void foo(char * sa)
{
    string s(sa);                     // allocate string
    string *sp = new string("ab");    // constructor call
    delete sp;                        // delete using destructor
    return;                           // quit function
}                                     // s will be destroyed
```
(85)

10.6 Overloaded Operators

Several operators were introduced for simple types (Sect. 4.1). They all have their fixed association rules. Some of them can be redefined for classes. The syntax of operator declarations is as follows:

| Syntax: | *return–type* operator *op* (*argument-list*) |

where user definable operators are, for example; +,*,-,=, or ==.[6]

Redefinition of an operator is called "operator overloading".[7] When used with care, this can facilitate programming and make programs easier to read. When misused, the results may be disastrous.[8] Operator overloading is possible only for classes.

Example 86 shows the definition of the overloaded assignment operator for the class rational (Example 81) (the declaration in the class is obvious). By passing the actual object as a return value, sequences of assignments are possible.

---

[6]For a complete list refer to the manual [Str91a].

[7]We will not treat this topic in detail. We give some clarifying examples and leave the rest to the reference.

[8]Imagine a program with + defined as multiplication on some numeric class ...

```
rational& rational::operator= (const rational& r)
{d = r.d; q = r.q; return *this}

rational r, q, s;
r = s;
s = q = r;
```
(86)

Other overloaded operators will be explained and applied in later sections.

10.7   Advanced Methods and Constructors

If a class contains data members of class type as shown in Example 87, the question arises how to provide constructors for these objects.

```
class A {
    int a;
public:
    A(int i) { a = i; }
};
class B {
    int b;
    A    a1, a2;
public:
    B(int, int, int);
};
```
(87)

The solution is shown in Example 88. After a colon, a list of constructor calls for member objects can be given before the definition of a constructor function body. The member objects are constructed before the body of the constructor function for B is executed.

```
B::B(int i, int j, int k)
     :                // start member constructors
    a1(j),            // constructor for first object
    a2(k)             // constructor for second object
{
    b = i;
}
```
(88)

We now introduce a simple vector class which will reveal several new features for classes and methods. We first restrict our class to a vector of **byte** elements (Example 89).

```
class bytevector {
    byte * row;                  // the actual data
    unsigned int size;           // number of elements
public:
    bytevector(int);                 // constructor
    byte   operator [] (int i) const; // access also for const
                                     // objects
    byte & operator [] (int i);       // access as usual
};
```
(89)

In Example 89, note the following things:

1. the overloaded operator []: this operator has one argument of type **int**. We can now access **bytevector** objects like arrays with an index in square brackets.

2. the **const** method (resp. a **const** operator): methods can be declared as **const**. This indicates to the compiler that the method will not change any data internal to the object. In particular, these methods are used when the object is itself a **const** object.

   Since the compiler can decide a constant from a variable object, the two declarations of the operator are legal.

3. reference as return value: to allow for an indexed expression of a `bytevector` on the left side of an expression, we use a reference to the element as return value.

Example 90 shows the implementation of the vector access methods. The meaning of the `const` operators and the reference return value will be exemplified in the following.

```
static void checkit(int i, int s)          // local helper function
{
    if (i >= s) {
    fprintf(stderr,"Index %d out of range (max is %d)\n",i,s);
    exit(1);
    }
}
byte bytevector::operator [] (int i) const // access also for
                                           // const objects
{ checkit(i,size); return row[i]; }        // return byte
byte & bytevector::operator [] (int i)     // read/write access
{ checkit(i,size); return row[i]; }        // return reference (90)
```

10.8   Vector Class

We now extend Example 89 to a complete simple and efficient vector class. We define constructors and introduce a new `operator byte*` which greatly increases the efficiency of this class (Example 91). This operator method is invoked when an object (not a pointer)[9] is cast to a `byte *`.

---

[9]It is a very common error, to cast the pointer instead of the object itself. The compiler will think this is intentional and will not give a warning!

```
class bytevector {
    byte * row;                 // the actual data
    unsigned int size;          // number of elements
public:
    ~bytevector();                      // destructor
    bytevector(int);                    // constructor
    byte    operator [] (int i) const;  // access also for
                                        // const objects
    byte & operator [] (int i);         // access as usual
    operator byte * () { return row; }
    int Size() const { return size; }
};
```
(91)

The implementation of the constructor and destructor methods is shown in Example 92. The file assert.h contains handy macro definitions for assertions. If the assertion fails, the program terminates with an error message at that point in the program.[10]

```
#include <assert.h>
bytevector::bytevector(int i) // constructor
{
    assert(i>0);
    size = i;
    row = new byte[i];
}
bytevector::~bytevector()     // destructor
{
    delete [] row;
}
```
(92)

The use of this class and its methods can be seen in Example 93.

---

[10]The macros can be defined to an empty statement when the program is compiled with -DNDEBUG; see your local compiler manual. Compare also exercise 3 on page 107.

```
void foo1(bytevector & bv)
{
    for(int i = bv.Size() - 1; i >= 0; --i ) bv[i] = 0;
}
void foo2(byte * bp, int s)
{
    for(int i = s - 1; i >= 0; --i ) bp[i] = 0;
}
main(int argc, char ** argv)
{
    bytevector bv(10);
    byte * bp = (byte *) bv; // call operator byte *
    foo1(bv);
    foo2(bv,bv.Size());       // convert to byte * using operator
    exit(0);
}
```
$$\text{\textcircled{93}}$$

The function foo1 in Example 93 uses the index operator [] and allows assignment to vector elements, since this operator returns a reference to the indexed byte. In contrast, the function foo3 in Example 94 has a constant argument. The index operator on this object uses the method for constant objects which returns a byte instead of a reference. Assignment and modification of the object is thereby disabled. Read access is, however, possible. The method Size() can be used, since it is also declared as a constant method. The vector access in foo2 is unprotected; when the function is called in the main program, the compiler already knows the argument type of the function which is a byte*; the actual argument is the object bv which will be converted to a byte* using its cast operator.

```
void foo3(const bytevector & bv)
{
    int s = 0;
    for(int i = bv.Size() - 1; i >= 0; --i ) s += bv[i];
}
```
$$\text{\textcircled{94}}$$

An explicit cast to a `byte` * as in the main function body of Example 93 will also invoke the cast operator.

10.9   Class Design

We conclude this chapter with several useful hints for class design in C++. Some of them are not obvious from the language definition but are required because of compiler limitations. The goals for class design in image analysis applications have to be

- efficiency (due to the time limitations) *and*

- clean design (due to general software rules and the difficulty of the problem in particular).

Classes or data structures should be declared for every unit in the description of the problem for which you have a clear conception in mind. Internals should be hidden to provide a clear interface in a modular programming style. It is good practice to put all data members in the private section of a class and to provide read only access methods for those values which should only be changed in a controlled way. Often the same message (i.e. function name) is used for read and write access with two overloaded functions as in Example 75.

If you split the program source for the methods of one class to several files, this can in some cases extend the time for the program to be linked. On the other hand, it can also reduce the program size. Keep in the middle between high granularity (i.e., many small files) and a monolith (i.e., one huge program source file). Generally, definitions (except for inline functions) should be separated from declarations. Class, variable, and function declarations should be put into a header file (.h); definitions should be put into several modules (.C) which are independent in the sense that they do not contain functions that mutually call each other.

Inline constructors for objects should in general be avoided for non trivial construction tasks. Some compilers will generate a lot of code for each construction and the overhead of a function call will be small in comparison to the overall time for object construction.[11] The same holds for destructors.

---

[11]Look at Example 87; what will the compiler have to generate in the case of an inline constructor?

Exercises

1. Define a structure with 3 members: an argument string , an explanation string, and the number of arguments required. The goal is to extend the exercise 1 on page 80 to handle command lines like

   ```
   prog -arg1 3 -arg2 3 4 -arg3 file file.
   ```

   Define a table consisting of elements of the structure. Two entries of the table could be:

   ```
   "arg1", "integer value", 1
   ```

   ```
   "arg2", "integer value, integer value", 2
   ```

   Extend the functions in the exercises on 80 accordingly.

2. Implement a `String` class with useful methods for substrings, modification, indexing etc. Extend Example 83 accordingly.

   Include overloaded operators (`operator+`) for assignment and concatenation. Which other operators can you think of?

3. Implement a class for points as a modification of Example 81.

   Include overloaded operators for assignment and vector addition. Which other operators can you think of?

11 Intensity Images

Intensity based images are the most common input data structure for image processing and analysis. In practice, matrices are used for the representation of these discrete gray–level images. Each element of the two–dimensional matrix describes the gray–level of the digital image at its associated location. These "picture elements" are called *pixels*.

In this chapter we define a simple class for images and show several of their applications. Motivated by the given examples we introduce the concept of templates for classes in C++ and demonstrate its advantages with respect to software engineering projects.

11.1 Array Class

In chapter 6 we introduced the representation of images using two–dimensional arrays. It was explained in detail how those arrays are declared and used in C and C++ programs. The declaration of a matrix as an argument to a function requires that the fixed size of the arrays is known at compilation time. In general, it is expected that image processing modules are suitable for images of arbitrary size. A compilation for each image size is – obviously – unreasonable. Other ways of dealing with images thus have to be found.

As was shown when the definition and implementation of the class `bytevector` was presented (Example 89), the use of the C++ `new` operator allows the dynamic allocation of storage for arbitrary arrays during the execution of programs. For that same purpose we now define a class `byteArray2d`. The class declaration for the abstract data type `byteArray2d` is designed to provide a constructor, whose arguments are the size of the two–dimensional array. The size of an array is thereby no longer required to be known during compilation. Parts of the header–file of the required class `byteArray2d` is shown in Example 95.

```
class byteArray2d {
  int xsize;                        // number of rows
  int ysize;                        // number of columns
  byte** matrix;                    // array
public:
  ~byteArray2d();                   // destructor
  byteArray2d();                    // default constructor
  byteArray2d(int, int);            // constructor
  const byte* operator[] (int) const; // access to vector with
                                    // index check
};
```
⑨⑤

The implementation of the constructor `byteArray2d::byteArray2d(int, int)` is shown in Example 96. Notice that a vector is first allocated to hold the complete array in consecutive memory locations. Then, a pointer array is allocated and initialized to the starting positions of each row in the array.

```
byteArray2d::byteArray2d(int x, int y){
  xsize= x;
  ysize= y;
  byte * array = new byte[x*y];    // vector of size x*y
  matrix = new byte*[y];           // generate byte matrix
  for (int i = 0; i < y; ++i)      // all rows
    matrix[i] = & (array[i*x]);    // fill in vector pointers
}
```
⑨⑥

The internal representation of a matrix is shown in Figure 11.1. We allocate the storage for this array dynamically by defining a one–dimensional array of length xy. Then, the pointers to each row of the matrix are assigned to the matrix components.

This technique allows for index checking of the first index in an array access operation (Example 97). If instead of a `byte**`, a vector of byte–vectors (see Example 89) is used, the indices are checked for both dimensions. This idea, however, requires changes in the class `bytevector`. In order to allocate a variable length vector of bytevectors, the `new` operator has to be used. Thus,

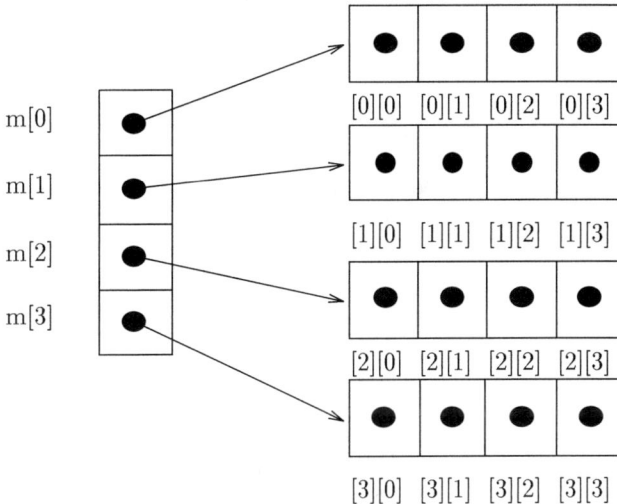

Figure 11.1 Internal representation of a two–dimensional array.

the byte vector class has to provide a default constructor. In addition, after creation with the default constructor, the actual length has to be set and the internal pointer has to be allocated. These extensions are left as an exercise (Exercise 1).

```
const byte * byteArray2d::operator[] (int i) const
{
  if (i > ysize)
    { printf("out of bounds\n"); } // need smarter routine!
  return matrix[i];
}
```
(97)

The destructor of this class just has to release the memory allocated in the constructor (Example 96). The memory allocated in **array** is accessible as **matrix[0]**. This is shown in Example 98.

```
byteArray2d::~byteArray2d()
{
 delete [] matrix[0];
 delete [] matrix;
}
```
98

11.2   Templates in C++

We now have a matrix class for components of the type **byte**. This class is sufficient for the representation of gray–levels in intensity images. But range images (Sect. 11.3), for example, expect that each component of the matrix is a real number and represents the distance of a point in the scene relative to a specified reference plane. What happens, if we need a class of real matrices? We have to implement the class **realArray2d**. The only difference between **byteArray2d** and **realArray2d** is that we have to substitute the data type **byte** with **real**. It would be annoying, if we had to program the matrix classes for different types of elements over and over again. Thus, it would be advantageous to have the possibility of "parameterized types" (Sect. 9.8). Operations like multiplication or addition are reduced to multiplications and additions of the components which are parameterized. The arithmetic of matrices would not depend upon the special types of the entries. Fortunately, C++ offers a feature to realize these parameterized classes automatically. This concept is called a *template.*

Different array types are, for instance, integer, byte, and float arrays. More complicated structures like arrays of vectors or matrices are also needed (see for example Chapter 13).

The syntax for declaring a class template is

Syntax: ▌ template **<** class *T* **>** *class–declaration*

A declared template specifies that an argument of type **T** will be used in the declaration of the parameterized class immediately following the template prefix. Formally expressed, type **T** is used within the declaration in exactly the same way as other types are. It does *not* have to be a class; it may as well be a simple type like an `int`. The concrete type of the parameter T is specified when a variable is declared. The name of the template class followed by the special type in brackets < > can be used exactly like the conventional classes.

The following Example 99 shows the implementation and the use of a template class for matrices. It directly extends Example 95.

```
template<class T> class Matrix {
  unsigned int xsize;              // number of rows
  unsigned int ysize;              // number of columns
  T ** matrix;                     // parameterized array
public:
  ~Matrix();                       // destructor
  Matrix();                        // default constructor
  Matrix(int, int);                // constructor
  T* operator[] (int);             // access to vector
  operator T**(){ return matrix; } // efficient access
  int SizeX()const{return xsize;}  // access
};
```
(99)

The template class for matrices is used in a C++ program as shown now in Example 100. For an actual variable, a type has to be specified in < >.

```
Matrix<int> m1(256,256);
Matrix<float> m2(512,256);
int c1= m1[2][100];
float c2= m2[5][120];
```
(100)

The compiler and linker have to take care that code for every parameter type is generated. This should be transparent to the user. The implementation of methods uses the class template as shown in Example 101. The allocation is done exactly as in Example 96.

```
template <class T> Matrix<T>::Matrix(int x, int y)
{
   xsize= x; ysize= y;
   T * array = new T[x*y];        // vector of size x*y
   matrix = new T*[y];            // generate byte matrix
   for (int i = 0; i < y; ++i)
      matrix[i] = & (array[i*x]); // fill in vector pointers
}
template <class T> T* Matrix<T>::operator[] (int i)
{
   return matrix[i];
}
```

(101)

11.3   Images

We now introduce image classes as the primary data structure for image processing and analysis. It quickly turns out that intensity images are not simply byte matrices. In real applications, we need further information about the image generation process. For example, it is necessary for recognition and classification purposes to know the camera geometry, i.e. the focal length or other parameters. Matrices are used as an internal representation of the image signal. Most common imaging devices use gray–level images with 256 gray levels which can be stored in one byte (see Figure 11.3 or Figure 11.2 for an example). The components of the image's byte–matrix represent an intensity value. Color–images generally need three matrices for the representation of their image information — each color channel corresponding to a one byte matrix (Sect. 11.6).

Another type of signal used for three–dimensional image processing are *range–images*. Each component of the image matrix no longer represents an intensity value; instead, the *distance* of the scene points with respect to a given reference plane are stored within the matrix. The matrix elements in an image can be any one of the types byte, int, float, or double. It depends only upon the discrete step–sizes chosen for the depth values. Additional information in the class range–image could include the position of the reference plane or the

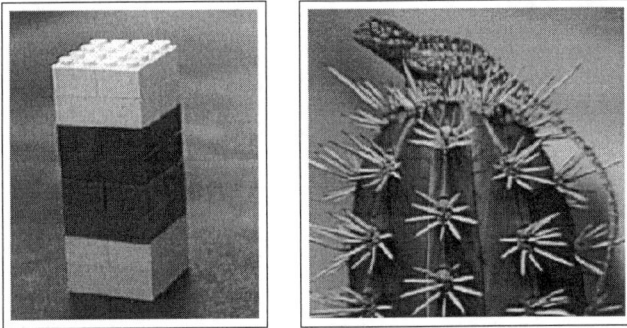

Figure 11.2 Example images: on the left a color image (printed as gray–level image), on the right a gray–level image

scaling of the depth values. Figure 11.3 shows an example of a range–image. The depth values of the industrial part are encoded as gray–levels. The higher the gray–level, the lower is the distance of the scene point with respect to the optical sensor.

Figure 11.3 An example for a gray–level image (left) and the corresponding range–image (right)[1]

The declaration in Example 102 introduces the abstract data type GLImage for gray–level images, wherein the defined template class for matrices is used,

---

[1](Ref. to Figure 11.3) Images by the Institute for Physics, University of Erlangen–Nürnberg

i.e. the class **Matrix** is a client of the abstract data type **image**. Additionally, we have members which represent the focal length and the aperture of the camera lens as well as a scaling factor which describes pixel characteristics.[2] Later, we will enhance this class definition (Example 138).

```
class GLImage {
    float focus;           // focal length
    float aperture;        // lens aperture
    float scaling;         // pixel side relation
    char * description;    // textual information
    Matrix<byte> image;    // the pixels
public:
    GLImage(int,int);               // constructor
    int isEqual(const GLImage&); // test equality
    // etc.
    byte * operator [] (int i) { return image[i]; } // delegation
    int SizeX() { return image.SizeX(); }
};                                                              (102)
```

Pixel access is simply delegated to the image array with an inline operator. The method **isEqual** tests whether two images are equal.[3]

11.4   External Data Formats

Images require a large amount of external storage due to the large number of pixels. The image in Figure 11.2 has a dimension of 511×491 which requires 250901 bytes on disk. The simplest form of storage is the so called raw format (cmp. Example 34). For odd image sizes (as in Figure 11.2), raw format may be insufficient; the image can only be read, when the dimensions are known. How should the computer decide whether the image is 511×491 or 491×511?

---

[2]Pixels may be either quadratic (the rare case), or rectangular depending on the layout of the CCD. The relation of the sides is stored in the scaling factor.

[3]This is the test for equality — a complicated topic which will be discussed in Sect. 11.8. It is different from the test for identity (**isSame**).

Normally, various information about sizes, contents, resolution etc. is stored in the image files (e.g. in the common TIFF **T**ag **I**mage **F**ile **F**ormat, see [Poy92]).

If the image elements are of a more complex data type than bytes, the external storage has to be conformant with machine dependent internal formats. Machine independent storage is essential for the exchange of images between different computer architectures. Byte order of integral data types and floating point format are the major problems one has to deal with. Several standards exist for data representation, either by a standard committee (ISO/ANSI/DIN) or as a "de–facto" standard imposed by the leading market position of some company (see also IIF e.g. in [Cla92]).

Images often contain a lot of redundancy. For that reason, image compression algorithms and strategies are of major importance. The JPEG (Joint Photographic Expert Group, [Wal90]) image compression standard and the MPEG (Motion Pictures Expert Group, [Gal91]) are the commonly used for image transmission. Since the data compression using these algorithms discard information, these techniques are generally not useful for image analysis. The program `compress` which is distributed with most Unix systems is designed for text compression. It is also applicable to images without loss of information, but of course with lower compression rates than JPEG or MPEG.

An image format suitable for object–oriented programming will be introduced in Chapter 14 and Chapter 15.

11.5 Binary Images

When every pixel in an image may be either black or white, and no values in between (gray) are allowed, then we are then talking about *binary images*. This class of images is particularly useful in many areas. The speed of computation may be higher when only few cases for pixel values have to be considered.

Using the histogram of a gray–level image (Sect. 7.9, Chapter 20), a threshold for binarization can be computed (Sect. 20.1) and through which a gray–level image may be transformed into a binary image. A gray–level image binary images are shown in Figure 11.4. The thresholds are determined automatically by the algorithms described in Sect. 20.1 and 20.2.

Logically, binary images and gray–level images are different image classes, since different operations are applicable to them. However, internally they may both use a byte matrix, since only few computers allow efficient direct bit access. Most often, the smallest addressable unit is a byte anyhow.

Figure 11.4 Gray–level image and two binary image with different thresholds

11.6 Color Images

This section briefly describes a class for color–images . First we consider which internal structure, which members, and which methods are useful. Finally, we draw some conclusions concerning the conversion to and the relationships to other data types or classes.

Usually colors are represented through the combination of the colors red, green, and blue (RGB). An example is shown in Figure 11.5. For each basic color we need a matrix. The declaration of a class `ColorImage` is shown in Example 103.[4]

---

[4]Would you prefer a matrix of a structure containing three bytes for each pixel? Discuss advantages and disadvantages!

Figure 11.5 Three color channels (red,green,blue) for image Figure 11.2

```
class ColorImage {
  Matrix<byte> red;        // color channel red
  Matrix<byte> green;      // color channel green
  Matrix<byte> blue;       // color channel blue
public:
  // ...
};
```
(103)

The class for color images should include conversion to *color spaces* of other kinds, for example YUV, XYZ, or HSL (see e.g. in [Sti82]). These conversions are mappings from one three–dimensional vector to another. The transformations of RGB to YUV or XYZ are linear transformations. The conversion to HSL (hue, saturation, luminosity) is much more complicated and non–linear. Two examples are given in (11.1) and (11.2).

$$\begin{pmatrix} Y \\ U \\ V \end{pmatrix} = \begin{pmatrix} 0.299 & 0.587 & 0.114 \\ -0.299 & -0.587 & 1-0.114 \\ 1-0.299 & -0.587 & -0.114 \end{pmatrix} \begin{pmatrix} R \\ G \\ B \end{pmatrix} \qquad (11.1)$$

$$\begin{pmatrix} X \\ Y \\ Z \end{pmatrix} = \begin{pmatrix} 0.607 & 0.174 & 0.200 \\ 0.299 & 0.587 & 0.114 \\ 0.000 & 0.066 & 1.111 \end{pmatrix} \begin{pmatrix} Y \\ U \\ V \end{pmatrix} \qquad (11.2)$$

Also, a conversion to gray–level images seems to be useful as shown in (11.3).[5] This is in fact the Y channel of (11.2).

$$f_{ij} = 0.299 \; r_{ij} + 0.587 \; g_{ij} + 0.114 \; b_{ij} \qquad (11.3)$$

Color images can also be created from gray level images by "pseudo coloring". A color vector has to be generated for every gray–level. This can easily be accomplished with the histogram mappings in Chapter 20.

11.7 Sub Images

Logically, image elements are accessed by the indices of the image array. In practice however, pointers are often used which are set once and then incremented to gain speed. Therefore, it is essential for reliable programs to know something about the memory layout of images.

It is convenient, if an algorithm can be applied to a sub–image, i.e. only a rectangular section of the image, without knowing about the size and offset to the enclosing image, will be processed. If we assume continuous allocation of pixels in the large image, the rows of the sub–image have to be split in memory as indicated in Figure 11.6.

The implementation of sub–images is straightforward when using the technique introduced in Example 96 (compare [Pau92b]). Images have to use reference counters in order to release memory correctly in the destructors.

Sub–images provide a source of great performance gain in real time image analysis. For sub–images to work properly, it is essential that all image operations make the assumption that image rows are allocated consecutively. Only there it is possible to use pointer access. When skipping from one row to the next, the pointer has to be initialized again using the sub–image information. This is shown in Example 104 for the computation of the mean of an image or a sub–image.

---

[5]The image in Figure 11.2 was created from the color image in Figure 11.5 using this formula.

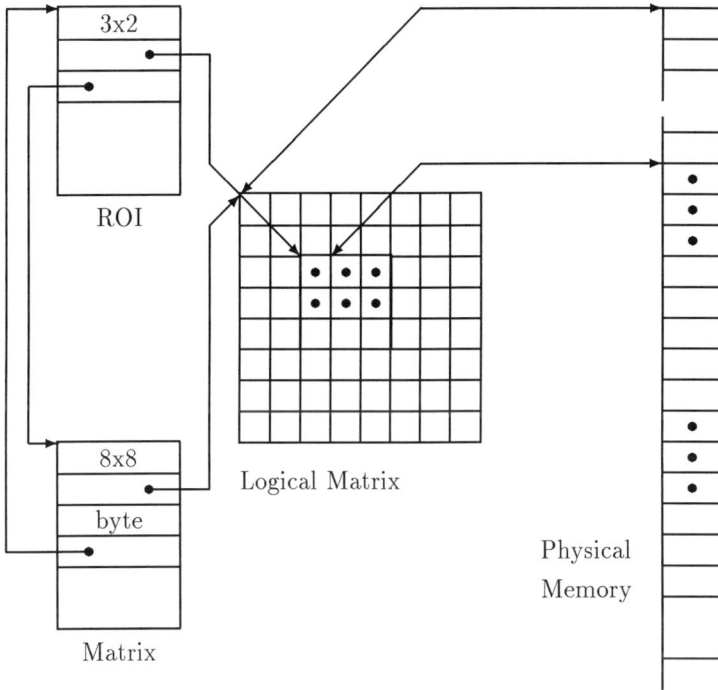

Figure 11.6 Logical and physical matrix mapped to a conventional linear storage. There exists no connected allocated storage for sub images (from [Pau92b]).

```
double mean(byte** image, int xs, int ys)
{                        // computes mean gray-value
   double res = 0;
   for (int i = ys-1; i >= 0; --i) {
   byte * ptr = image[i];          // use [ ]
     for (int j = xs-1; j >= 0; --j)
       res += *(ptr++);            // may use pointer
    }
   return res / (xs * ys);
}
```

104

11.8   Image Transformation and Registration

Image processing systems have some typical operators to perform image to image transformations (Sect. 5.2). For example, it is often advantageous to use filter operations. For data reduction some applications suggest the binarization of images, the reduction of size, or the extraction of regions of interest. All operations on images which assign one image I to an image J will be called *transformations*. Whether the implementation of those transformations should be done in the class definition as a method or as a separate function is mostly up to the programmer. A general guideline is to keep the class interface at a reasonable size. We suggest to include all access functions as methods and to leave out all those algorithms which can have more than one implementations; e.g. it is better to have a *function* smooth with accompanying documentation for the actual algorithm, than to have it as a method — some users will not be satisfied with the results and will have to define their own smoothing function anyhow.

Several images of one object are often recorded under different viewing conditions, e.g. different illumination. Even if the images are taken with the same camera and scene, the two images may differ slightly due to sensor noise. Therefore the decision whether two images are equal or not is a nontrivial problem. The pixel wise comparison would fail. Thus, we need a similarity measure for images. For that purpose the correlation of sub-images can be used. Sub-images may be chosen at random positions for that purpose ([Nie90a]p. 45 or [Pra78]p. 562–566).

The distance between the $N \times M$ image $\boldsymbol{f}$ and and the $K \times L$ image $\boldsymbol{s}$ for sequential registration can be computed using the distance

$$d(r,i,j) \quad = \quad \sum_{\varrho=1}^{r} |f_{i+k(\varrho),j+l(\varrho)} - s_{k(\varrho),l(\varrho)}|^p \quad , \qquad (11.4)$$

where $r \leq KL$ and $\{(k(\varrho), l(\varrho)) \mid 1 \leq \varrho \leq r\}$ represents the set of random position pairs. If the distance measure exceeds a special threshold value for all window points, then the similarity test fails.

This technique may be used to implement the equality operator on images which is fast and tolerant to little changes (cmp. Example 102). Imagine a set of images and add a *new* image to the set. Due to the nature of a set, no two images may be contained which are equal. If the equality of pictures is implemented on a pixel basis, the new image will have to test each pixel against the corresponding pixels in *all* other images. This may require an non-feasible number of comparisons even for relatively small sets of images.

11.9 Neighborhood

Rectangular or quadratic tessellation of digital images induces the problem neighborhood. A pixel (i, j) is usually considered closer to $(i + 1, j)$ than to $(i + 1, j + 1)$. Two alternatives can be chosen for those pixels which are assumed to be directly adjacent to (i, j):

- *4–connectivity*, for which the four pixels { $(i + 1, j)$, $(i - 1, j)$, $(i, j + 1)$, $(i, j - 1)$ } are used, and
- *8–connectivity*, for which eight pixels are used, namely the 4–connected pixels and { $(i - 1, j - 1)$, $(i + 1, j - 1)$, $(i - 1, j + 1)$, $(i + 1, j + 1)$ }.

Both versions have advantages and drawbacks, when sets of similar pixels are searched in segmentation, which should result in a connected region (cmp. Exercise 6). The neighborhood definitions are visualized in Figure 11.7.

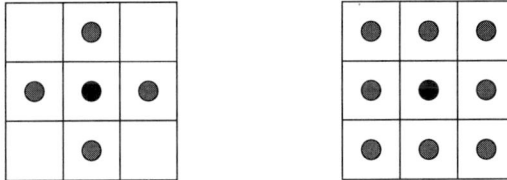

Figure 11.7 Neighborhood of a pixel: 4–connectivity (left) and 8–connectivity (right)

Exercises

1. Implement a matrix class using a vector of byte vectors (Example 89). Extend the class `bytevector` as indicated in Sect. 11.1.

2. Write a program to convert to and from your favorite image format.

3. Implement the concept of sub–images [Pau92b] for the image classes introduced in this chapter.

4. Make the projects in chapter 18 work on images of arbitrary size.

5. Implement an equality operator in gray level images using ideas of Sect. 11.8.

6. Explain different neighborhoods on a chess board.

7. Write a program to create a color image object from a gray level image with pseudo colors using gray level mappings as in Figure 20.5.

8. Compute reverse transformations for (11.1) and (11.2). Apply the transformation back and forth several times. What kind of an error will you get?

12 Inheritance in C++–Classes

As already explained in Chapter 9, object–oriented programming is mainly characterized by the features encapsulation, dynamic binding, and inheritance. The introduced classes in Chapter 11 show implementations of ADT's (section 9.3). They serve for the realization of encapsulation. In this chapter we give a detailed description of the fundamental and powerful principles of inheritance and their implementation in C++. We introduce the concepts for both simple inheritance and – its more complicated form – multiple inheritance. With the use of inheritance, the real world dependency structure of objects can be mapped into a C++ class hierarchy in a "natural manner".

Often, classes have similar methods which operate on completely different data. For the projection of those dependencies into the class hierarchy abstract classes are necessary. The methods cannot be concretely implemented in those abstract classes. C++ provides virtual functions for that purpose. Those virtual member functions hide the differences among the methods of the derived classes. Dynamic binding is used to get the correct functions needed by the client programs.

In what follows, each thoroughly introduced object–oriented mechanism is actually used in practical everyday applications of image processing.

12.1 Motivation and Syntax

The task of implementing a new function can be simplified by using inheritance. In general, a new class is derived from an existing class. If the new class will have additional members, some additional functions, or possibly a redefinition of an already implemented function; programmers have only to describe the differences of their new classes to the classes upon which they are based. By using inheritance a complete reimplementation can be avoided. Inheritance, therefore, provides a high degree of reusable code and concepts. For example, rectangles are a special kind of geometric shape. Consequently, the class **Rectangle** is derived from the more general class **Shape**. Other related concepts are circles and triangles which can also be derived of the general class. Squares are a special case of rectangles and should therefore be derived from the class for rectangles.

The derivation of a class from one base class is syntactically written in the following manner:

| **Syntax:** | class *name* : [public |private] *base* { *class-members* } |

The derivation may be repeated, i.e. a class may be derived from an already derived class (Example 105).[1]

```
class A {};              // base class
class B : public  A {};  // derived with public base
class C : private B {};  // derived with private base
```
(105)

All members and methods of the superclass are inherited by the subclass. The keywords **public** and **private** control the accessibility of base class features in the derived class; these topics are discussed next.

12.2   Base Class Access

A class can be declared as a base class of another class in basically two different ways. The base class can either be **public** or **private**. A new keyword **protected** is introduced for class members in addition to **public** and **private**. With respect to multiple inheritance, base classes can also be declared virtual; we will not discuss this kind of derivation here.

If the base class is declared with the access specifier **private**, the public and protected members of the superclass become private members of the derived class. If the declaration of a public base class contains protected members, these same members in a derived class are protected as well. Private members

---

[1]It is, however, illegal to have a circular sequence of derivations.

of a base class are non–accessible in their derived classes. The only possibility
to provide access to private members is by using friends (Sect. 15.4).[2]

base class	base	
members	public	private
private	no access	no access
protected	protected	private
public	public	private

Table 12.1 Access rules of base class members inside the derived class

These rules for accessibility are summarized in Table 12.1. The base class
members get new access rights in a derived class depending on whether the
base class is private or public. This is of particular importance when another
class is derived from an already derived class. Also, private parts of the base
class can be excluded from access by using private derivations (Table 12.2).

base class	base	
members	public	private
private	no	no
protected	no	no
public	yes	no

Table 12.2 Access rules from outside

Public derivation provides the natural way of refining concepts from the general to the more specific. Private derivation has a more technical application
(see the examples in [Str91a]). Public base classes are by far the more frequent
case and in the following are the only kinds of base classes used.

As can be seen from Example 106, the same name can be used for data and
function members in both the derived and base classes. The name referenced
to will always be the "closest" matching name.

---

[2]If in the base class the derived class is explicitly declared as a friend, access to private
members is granted. There are however only very rare cases where this construction makes
sense.

```
class A              { public: int i,j; void f(); };
class B : public A { public: int    j; };
class C : public B { public: int i  ; void f(); };

B b; C c;        // Objects
b.i;             // from base A
b.j;             // B's j
c.j;             // B's j
c.i;             // C's i
```
(106)

We now outline a small hierarchy of classes for geometric objects which is graphically depicted in Figure 12.1. The translation to C++–code is shown in Example 107; declaration of methods and member variables are left as an exercise.

```
class Shape { };
class Rectangle : public Shape    { };
class Triangle  : public Shape    { };
class Circle    : public Shape    { };
class Square    : public Rectangle { };
```
(107)

12.3   Construction and Destruction

The declaration and definition of a class must provide the capability of construction and deletion of an object. The constructor of a class, which is derived from a base class, first calls the constructor method from the superclass. If the base class constructor needs some arguments, then they must also be provided. Constructors are overloaded functions. The choice of the constructor depends upon the types of the constructor's arguments. In C++ it is necessary to make the names of a base class constructor's arguments explicit. The construction of class objects is done from the top down in the inheritance

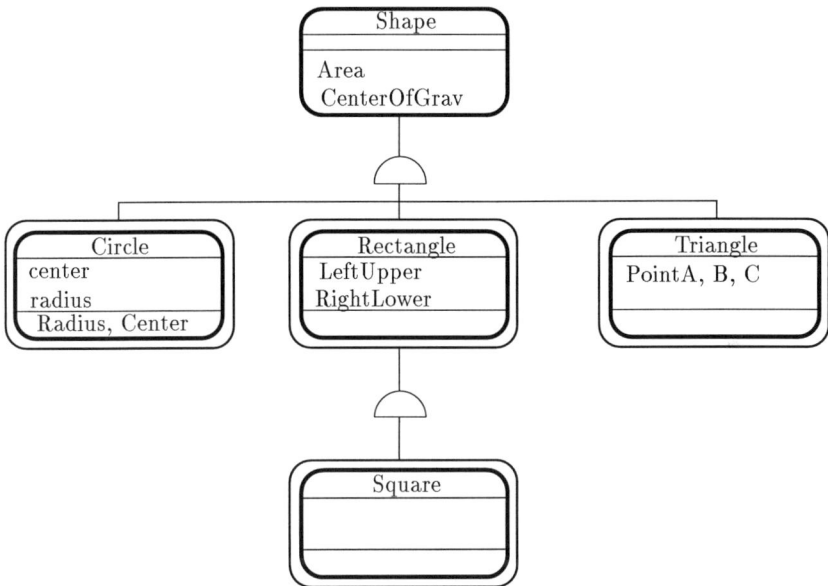

Figure 12.1 Small hierarchy of geometric shapes

graph. First, the base class constructors are called, then the constructors for member variables, and finally the derived class itself.

An example of a base class for geometric shapes is given in Example 108.

```
class Shape {
public:
    Shape();            // constructor 1
    Shape(int);         // constructor 2
    ~Shape();           // destructor
};
```
(108)

The definition of a base constructor in a derived class is shown in Example 109; like the constructors for members, the base class constructor and its arguments is given after a colon.

```
class Circle : public Shape {
public  :
   Circle() : Shape() {}  // will use constructor 1 of base class
   ~Circle()          {}  // destructor
};
```
(109)

The destructor of a class deletes an object from the main storage. In a hierarchy of classes, the destructor of the base class will be called after the destructor of a derived class, i.e. the execution of destructors will be in the opposite order of the constructor calls.

12.4   Pointer to Objects

It is necessary for pointers or references to specify the type of objects they reference. This regulation is slightly relaxed for classes which are related by inheritance. A pointer to an object of a particular type found in a base class can point to an object of another type found in a derived class, if the base class is declared *public*.[3] Nevertheless, a pointer to an object of a derived class cannot be used as a pointer to an object in a base class; if such an assignment is required, a pointer cast has to be used. Identical rules are applicable to references.

Example 110 shows pointers to objects. The cast in the last statement is required since not every rectangle object is a square. This cast can be disastrous if the object passed to foo is *not* a square (Example 111).

---

[3]If this were allowed for private base classes, a cast might circumvent the access restrictions (Table 12.1). Explain why and how!

```
void foo(Rectangle & r)
{   /* Shape -> Rectangle -> Square */
    Shape      * sp;
    Rectangle * rp;
    Square     * qp;
    rp = &r;                // natural
    sp = &r;                // ok. every square is a rectangle
    qp = (Square*) &r;   // cast required
}
```
(110)

```
void foo1()
{
    Rectangle r;
    Square    s;
    foo (s);   // ok
    foo (r);   // cast in foo will be wrong!
}
```
(111)

We now inspect the functions f() in Example 106 with respect to pointers to objects. It is determined *at compile-time* from the pointer's type which function f() is called, similarly to the data member access in Example 106. Example 112 shows these language features.

```
void Foo(C & c)
{   /* A -> B -> C */
    A * ap = &c;
    C * cp = &c;
    c.f();                  // call C::f()
    ap->f();                // call A::f()
    cp->f();                // call C::f()
}
```
(112)

12.5   Virtual Functions

Virtual functions allow the realization of dynamic binding. Functions can be declared virtual using the following syntax inside the class declaration:

| Syntax: | <u>virtual</u> *type function* <u>(</u> *arguments* <u>)</u> <u>;</u> |

If a function is defined to be a virtual function in the base class, a function with the same name and the same type of arguments declared in the derived class will also be virtual. Virtual functions allow the overriding of a definition of the base class function, i.e. if a virtual function is called via pointer to an object, the function associated with the object will be invoked, no matter whether the pointer is to a base object or to the actual object.

If the virtual function in the base class and implemented functions in the derived classes are not of the same type, no override mechanism will be invoked. The described override mechanism implies that virtual functions have to be declared as non static member variables. They cannot be declared as global non–member functions.

If in Example 108 the function `f()` was declared virtual, the calls in Example 112 would in all three cases call the same function. The function to be used is determined *at runtime* by the actual type of the object to which the method is applied.

A virtual function in a derived class may not redefine another return type for the same virtual function in the base class (i.e. a function with the same name and the same argument list). A virtual function in a derived class which differs from one in the base class with specification `const` is considered a different function! As outlined in Sect. 10.7, the compiler will choose the function marked `const` for constant objects.

Destructors may be declared virtual. The use and syntax of this idea is shown in Example 113. If the destructor were not virtual, the last line of the function `foo()` would not call the destructor of the derived class. Instead, due to the type of the pointer `Bp` only the base class destructor would be called.

```
class base              { public: base(); virtual ~base(); }
class derv : public base { public: derv(); virtual ~derv(); }

void foo()
{
   { base(); }          // ~base() will be called
   { derv(); }          // ~derv(), then ~base() will be called
   base * bp = new base();
   delete bp;           // ~base() will be called
   base * Bp = new derv(); // watch this!
   delete Bp;           // ~derv(), then ~base()
}                       // will be called
```

⑴⑴⑶

12.6   Abstract Classes

Many classes provide a common abstract structure where no instances of objects can exist. Classes where no concrete implementations can be made are called *abstract classes*. These classes are only useful for structuring a class hierarchy. We did so already in Figure 12.1. For example, we can easily define a class for lines. The methods in this class depend on the concrete representation of the line and therefore must be implemented in derived classes. For each line, for instance, a method should exist, which returns the length of a line. In order to declaring such a function in an abstract class line where no length can be computed (since the explicit representation of the line is unknown), the concept of *pure virtual functions* is required.

We can forced the redefinition of a virtual function by the use of *pure virtual functions* in the class definition part. A virtual function becomes pure virtual, if the function is initialized by = 0. No other definition is allowed then.

Syntax: virtual *type function* (*arguments*) = 0;

```
class Shape {
public:
   virtual void rotation() = 0; // pure virtual function
};
```
(114)

In Example 114 the pure virtual function for the rotation of geometrical objects in general is shown. Since the class for geometric shapes is an abstract class, no instances can be generated and no concrete implementation of the method rotation is possible. No implementation of this function can be programmed. For this reason, we declare the method pure virtual. If the function is not declared to be pure virtual, an explicit definition of this function has to be provided (see Example 115).

```
class Rectangle : public Shape {
public:                       // concrete class
   virtual void rotation();   // has to define the virtual function
};
void Rectangle::rotation() { /* ... */ }
```
(115)

12.7   Image Class Hierarchy

In Chapter 11 we saw different classes for images. Gray level images (section 11.3) and color images (section 11.6) both need the members for their size and the camera parameters. It is therefore natural to create a common base class Image and put all the shared information there (Example 116).

```
class Image {
    unsigned short xsize, ysize;    // filled by the constructors
    float focus;                    // filled by the constructors
protected:                         // abstract class
    Image();                       // all methods can be used in the
    Image(int,int,float);          // derived classes
    // ops's etc.
};
```

(116)

The base class declares all methods as "protected"; no object of class `Image` can thus be directly created, since no operations could be performed on it. This is another way of creating an abstract base class. Color images, and gray–level images are derived from this common base class (Example 117) and construct the common base class.

```
class GrayLevelImage : public Image {
    Matrix<byte> image;
    // op's
};
class ColorImage : public Image {
    Matrix<byte> r_image, g_image, b_image;
    // op's
};
```

(117)

In the following chapters we will derive more new image classes from class `Image`. The class sub–tree for images is shown in Figure 12.2.

12.8 Multiple Inheritance

The problems concerning multiple inheritance were already mentioned in section 9.8. A class can be derived from two or more classes; the superclasses can be declared public or private. Assume all super classes have member functions

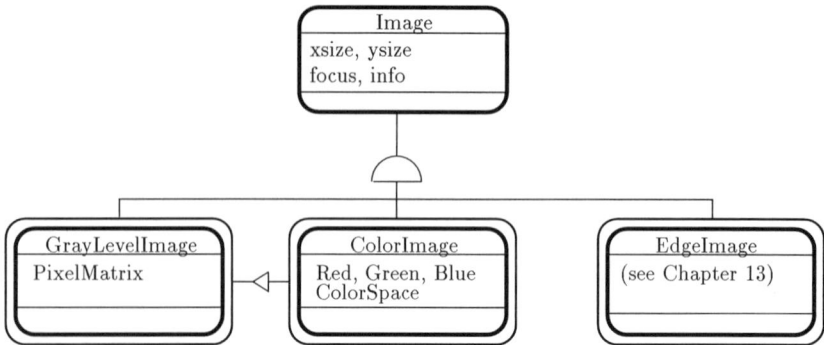

Figure 12.2 Hierarchy of image classes

with the same name. When those functions are used, they have to be disambiguated by calling the function only related with the class name it belongs to.

New aspects of a given idea can be programmed by multiple inheritance. Imagine a class `visible` which adds display capabilities to a graphics device. The interface to graphics routines can be inherited on top via inheritance from general to specific classes (Example 118). In the constructor definition, the constructors for all bases have to specified.

```
class visible {
public: void display();
       visible(int color);
};
class Rectangle: public Shape, public visible {
public:
   Rectangle() : Shape(), visible(3);
   ~Rectangle();
};
```
(118)

Sometimes a base class is reached by more than one path in the inheritance graph. This will result in multiple instances of the base object. If this is not desired, a base class can be declared as `virtual`. Casting of pointers as in Sect. 12.4 is much more complicated when multiple inheritance is used. Further information about multiple inheritance can be found in the manual [Str91a]; in the following we will use single inheritance only.

12.9 Implementation Issues

The most difficult problem in object–oriented software design is the mapping of the structures and dependencies of the objects in the problem domain. First, natural dependencies of objects and classes have to be formalized. Always have in mind whether two different classes relate to each other in terms of inheritance or with respect to clients. For example, gray–level images are represented using a matrix of internal representation; matrix and images are not related by inheritance, however.

The development of a class hierarchy should be planned very carefully. For all object–oriented systems it is the basic step in the software development stage.

The goals of object–oriented software design are the development of compact, readable programs. The programs should be easy to understand and easy to modify. For users of your programs which are not interested in algorithmic details, an abstract and well documented interface should be provided. Furthermore, the algorithms have to be implemented in an efficient manner. Often it is not easy to implement algorithms efficiently and at the same time to satisfy the needs of concepts like modularity and readability. The implementor has to find a compromise among these obviously conflicting goals.

Virtual functions are treated by the compiler in a defined way from non–virtual functions according to the manual [Str91a]. A function table is generated for every class having virtual functions. Virtual functions are called indirectly from this table. The table is constructed by the compiler in certain modules which define constructors. It is thus a wise idea *not* to use inline constructors since some compilers will then have to create many tables for one class instead of only one.

A general guideline is that destructors should be virtual when there are virtual functions in a class.

Exercises

1. Implement a template class for matrices! Discuss which members and which methods are needed or seem to be useful.

2. Define a multiplication of matrices with vectors. Which problems concerning the access of member variables may appear?

3. Formalize an abstract class for lines in C++ using the concept of pure virtual functions.

4. Extend exercise 3 in Chapter 11 using Example 116. Provide an image constructor for sub–images referring to another image. Introduce a reference count in the image class and release the memory for the image matrix only if no sub–image classes exist.

13 Edge Detection and Edge Images

This chapter gives a summary of edge detection methods in gray–level images based on [Brü90]. We also introduce unions and bit–fields in C++.

13.1 Motivation

Indications exist that lines, vertices, and other features based on lines, are very important for perception (see chapter 5). A typical part of image segmentation is the detection of edges (see Sect. 5.5). The automatic detection of line features in images usually requires several processing stages. Edge detection operators are applied to every pixel in the image. These operators check the local neighborhood for evidence of an edge. They return a measure for the likelihood of an edge at this point of the image as well as a guess of its orientation. The result is called an "edge image" (Sect. 13.8). In Chapter 22 we will further process edge images to obtain lines. This will transform edge images into more abstract geometric objects (section 5.5).

13.2 Strategies

The basic idea behind edge detection is to localize discontinuities of the intensity function in the image. Figure 13.1 shows a cross section, i.e. a one–dimensional function of an edge in an image. Figure 13.2 shows a plot of the gray–level function in the neighborhood of an edge in a real image.

Several types of edge detectors can be found in the literature:

- derivatives of the intensity function (discrete approximation),

- edge masks,

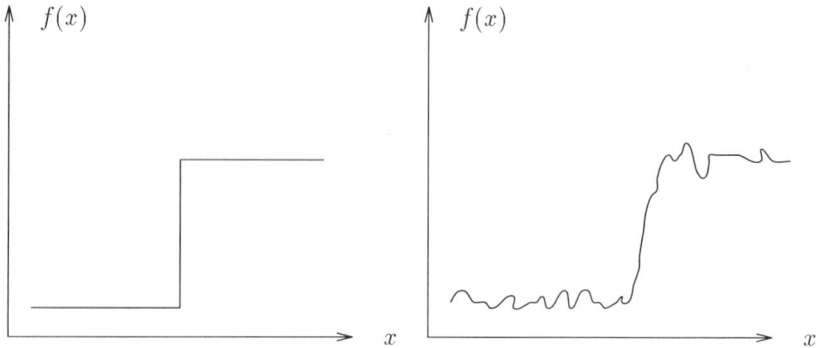

Figure 13.1 Ideal step edge (a) and real edge (b), where the x–axis is perpendicular to the edge.

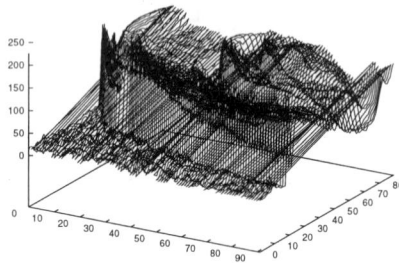

Figure 13.2 Intensity function in a real image in the neighborhood of an edge. On the left: gray–level image; on the right: 3D plot of the intensity.

- parametric models for edges,

- combinations of the above.

The first two strategies work with local masks; the first derivative will be treated in section 13.3. The second derivative, edge masks, and parametric models are part of chapter 21. Most mask operations can be computed very efficiently.

Examples for combined methods which localize edge candidates using the first derivative after a smoothing operation are the *Canny-Operator* [Can86], the *Deriche-Filter* [Der87, Der90], and the *Shen and Castan* operator [She86, She88, Cas90], which are described in Sect. 22.8.

In the following sections, we introduce a common edge image class which will be used for the representation of arbitrary edge operators. These edge images can then be further inspected and lines can be segmented within them (chapter 22).

13.3   Discrete Derivative of the Intensity

Many approaches to edge detection are based on the idea that rapid changes and discontinuities in the gray–level function can be detected using maxima in the first derivative or zero crossing of the second derivative. Figure 13.3 shows cross–section of step edges and the corresponding derivatives.

As described in section 1.7, we assume a quantized image of a fixed size — $N \times M$ — which corresponds to an intensity function $f(x, y)$ that is defined at discrete points (i, j), where $i \in \{0, 1, \ldots, N-1\}$ and $j \in \{0, 1, \ldots, M-1\}$. The more rapidly the gray–level function changes on small changes of the location, the more likely is an edge at this location. A measure for this indication of an edge is called the *edge strength*. The direction of an edge at a certain point in the image is called the *edge orientation*. These values are computed by the discrete derivative of the intensity function which calculates the gradient of the intensity function.

The *gradient* of a continuous function $f(x, y)$ is defined as the vector

$$\nabla f(x, y) = \begin{pmatrix} f_x(x, y) \\ f_y(x, y) \end{pmatrix} = \begin{pmatrix} \dfrac{\partial f(x, y)}{\partial x} \\ \dfrac{\partial f(x, y)}{\partial y} \end{pmatrix} \tag{13.1}$$

consisting of the partial derivatives of the intensity function in horizontal and vertical direction. The gradient in a position (i, j) points to the steepest ascent in its neighborhood. Discrete approximations use central differences instead of differentials for the computation of f_x and f_y (13.2).

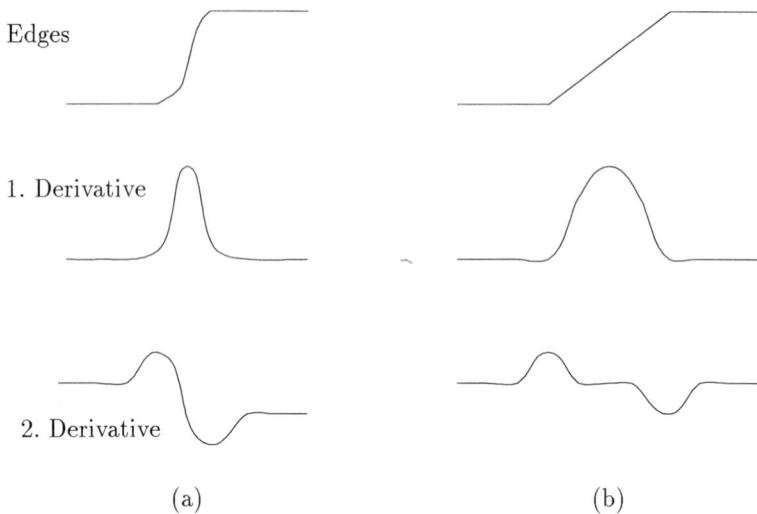

Figure 13.3 Edges and their derivatives in a cross–section. (a) steep ascent — called a step edge, and (b) subtle change — called a ramp.

$$f_x(i,j) = f(i+1,j) - f(i-1,j) \quad \text{and} \quad f_y(i,j) = f(i,j+1) - f(i,j-1) \quad (13.2)$$

Figure 13.4 shows an interpretation of equation (13.2) as a mask. The derivative can be computed by a discrete convolution of the image with the mask, i.e., the mask is centered around a point P, the neighboring pixels are weighted — multiplied — with the entries in the mask and summed up to the final result.[1]

Edge strength (13.3,13.4) and *edge orientation* (13.5) can now be calculated from the gradient using vector calculus. The edge strength is computed as the length of the gradient vector. It is often convenient to use the sum of absolute values (13.4) instead of the root of the squares (13.3) since it is

---

[1]This means that derivatives of the intensity function can be computed with a linear filter, Chapter 19.

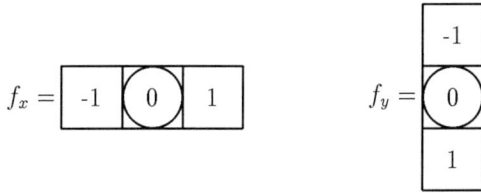

Figure 13.4 Masks for computation of the central differences in a point $P = (i, j)$ — marked by a circle.

normally not the exact value that is important, but the value in comparison to the neighborhood.[2]

$$s = \sqrt{f_x^2 + f_y^2} \tag{13.3}$$
$$s' = |f_x| + |f_y| \tag{13.4}$$
$$r = \arctan(f_y/f_x) \tag{13.5}$$

Using definition (13.5), the gradient intensity can be computed from the orientation by a rotation of 90° (Figure 13.5).

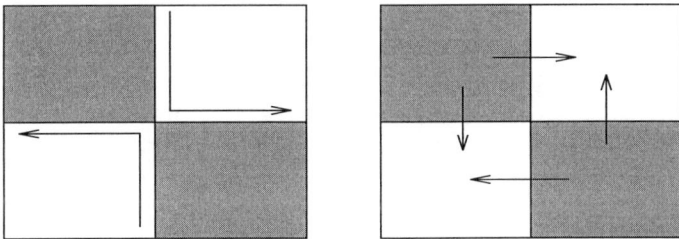

Figure 13.5 Definition of the edge orientation (left) and gradient (right)

---

[2]The values for f_x, f_y, s', and r can then be calculated using integer arithmetic which is usually much faster than floating point arithmetic which is required for the square root function.

13.4   Sobel and Prewitt Operator

Only a few pixels are taken into consideration when the discrete differential is computed using the simple operators in section 13.3. As a consequence, these operators are very sensitive to noise. The usual cure for this problem is to apply a low pass filter before the derivation is calculated. Alternatively, a larger neighborhood can be taken into consideration for the computation of the derivates, which then includes an average operation on several values of f_x and f_y.

Well known operators of this type are the Sobel operator ([Dud72]) and the Prewitt operator [Pre70], which are shown in Figure 13.6. In [Dan90] it is shown that the Sobel mask is an approximation of the first derivative.

-1	0	1
-2	0	2
-1	0	1

-1	-2	-1
0	0	0
1	2	1

(a)

-1	0	1
-1	0	1
-1	0	1

-1	-1	-1
0	0	0
1	1	1

(b)

Figure 13.6 Masks for Sobel (a) and Prewitt (b) operator. Masks on the left: f_x, masks on the right: f_y. Note that these masks may be flipped with respect to other literature since we choose the origin of the coordinate system on the left top.

The more pixels are taken into account in the computation, the lower is the sensitivity to noise. Small edges may however be missed by large operators. This trade–off situation is sometimes called the "uncertainty relation" of edge detection.

13.5   Bit Fields in C++

The application of the Sobel operator on a gray–level image yields two values for f_x and f_y. The steepest possible edge in a gray–level image is the change of 0 to 255. The values for f_x and f_y can thus be in the range of $-1024 \ldots 1024$. The edge strength will therefore be in the range of $0 \ldots 2048$ for this operator. Other operators have similar behavior. This range can be represented using two bytes (usually a `short int`, see section A.3).

The computation of the edge direction uses the function `atan2` which computes the $\tan^{-1}$ function and treats the four quadrants properly. The result is a `double` value which has to be quantized.[3] 144 directions of $2.5°$ seem to be more than sufficient. This number has the advantage that directions of 5, 10, 30, 60, … degrees can be represented as integers. 144 values can be represented in one byte (an `unsigned char` in C++).

One implementation could use a structure containing a `byte` and a `short`. Since the size of a `short` may vary between machine architectures, it is better to request exactly 16 bits. The language construct in C++ and C is a so called *bit field*. Inside a structure the number of bits for a field may be specified. An example is shown in Example 119.

```
struct edge_0 {
    unsigned int strength : 16;    // ask for 16 bit
    unsigned int orient   : 8;     // request 8 bit
};
```
(119)

---

[3]The function `atan2` has to do floating point arithmetic which tends to be slow on most computers. Since run time efficiency is a great issue for image processing (section 3.7), this computation should be done with a table lookup (see exercise 3).

Depending on compiler or hardware restrictions, there may be limitations on the number of bits which can be requested in bit fields.

13.6   Unions in C++

Another language feature in C/C++ is called a union. Inside a union, several fields can be specified. The syntax looks exactly like the syntax for structures. Fields declared inside the union are accessed just like the fields inside a structure. Similarly, methods can be declared inside unions as with structures and classes of C++. One syntactic difference with respect to inheritance between unions and structures is that unions can be derived from structures but nothing can be derived from unions, i.e. unions are always leaves of an inheritance tree.

| Syntax: | union [sname] { declaration* } [vdef] ;

In contrast to structures, all the fields in a union share the same location in memory and can be used alternatively.[4] The overall memory requirement is calculated from the longest entry. In Example 120 the size will be based on the length of the double field. There is no compiler generated run time information about which field is used and how many bits are valid.[5] If such information is required, it has to be coded explicitly.

```
union numbers {
    long a;
    double b;
    char c;
};
numbers n;
```
(120)

---

[4]The fields in structures can be used simultaneously!

[5]In Example 120 one can create illegal bit patterns for the double field when the union is written with the long field and then read using the double field.

13.7 Edge Class

A combination of the new techniques introduced in section 13.6 will give the second implementation of an edge as shown in Example 121 and 122. The methods hide the internal implementation of the data structure.

```
const int   orient_num = 144;
const float orient_dunit = 360 / float(orient_num);
const float orient_runit = 2 * M_PI / float(orient_num);
class Edge {
   union {
       unsigned int all;
       struct {                          // need no name
           unsigned int f_strength : 16;
           unsigned int f_orient   : 8;
       } fields ;                        // use member directly
};
public:
    Edge()                { all = 0; }   // clear
    inline Edge(unsigned s, unsigned o); // set strength and
                                         // orientation
    unsigned strength() const { return fields.f_strength; }
    // etc.
};                                                            (121)
```

We define constants for the number of orientations and for the quantization unit (Sect. 13.6). In Sect. 14.4 we will see how these extra global names can be avoided. Example 122 shows the inline definition of a constructor for edges. Since we do not derive this simple class from any other base class, inline construction is useful — in contrast to the hints given in Sect. 12.9.

```
inline Edge::Edge(unsigned s, unsigned o)
{
   fields.f_strength = s;
   fields.f_orient = o;
}
```
(122)

The structure Edge will require four bytes in memory on most computers even if we only ask for 24 bits;[6] we might as well use the remaining bits for further information. We will later need some features for each edge element. In section 22.1 we will extend the definition and introduce other fields in the union.

13.8   Edge Images

The application of an edge operator on every pixel of a gray–level image will produce an *edge image*. Like the images classes in the previous section, edge images share the information of the class Image (Example 116) by inheritance. Edge images can thus extend the image hierarchy shown in Figure 12.2. A code fragment is shown in Example 123. The operator [] maps the access operation to the matrix object by delegation.

```
class EdgeImage : public Image {
   Matrix<Edge> image;
   unsigned short max_s;   // maximum strength in the edge image
 public:
   EdgeImage(int,int);
   Edge* operator[] (int);
   // etc.
};
```
(123)

---

[6]Try this on your machine with the sizeof operator!

Since different operators create edge images with different ranges for the edge strength, an entry `max_s` can be useful. It is, however, difficult to guarantee a consistent value for this slot.

Visualization of edge images is shown in Figure 13.7; the range of the edge–strength is histogram equalized to 256 bit, i.e. a gray–level image, using the algorithms described in section 7.9. The edge orientation can be directly coded as gray–levels in the range of zero to 144 (Figure 13.7, right).

Figure 13.7 Gradient image computed with the Sobel operator on the image shown in Figure 11.2.

13.9 Color Edge Operators

Edge detection is possible on color images as well as gray–level images. The central differences (13.2) or the Sobel operator can be generalized for several channels. We can reorganize the definition in Figure 13.6 as a three–fold weighted (factor 1,2) sum of differences (one to the left/up subtracted from one to the right/down).

For the implementation of edge detectors we therefore need a scalar difference value for color vectors. According to [Shi87] the following differences of color pixels $f_1 = (r_1, g_1, b_1)$ and $f_2 = (r_2, g_2, b_2)$ can be used:

$$D_1(f_1, f_2) = \{(r_1 - r_2)^2 + (g_1 - g_2)^2 + (b_1 - b_2)^2\}^{\frac{1}{2}} \quad (13.6)$$

$$D_2(f_1, f_2) = |r_1 - r_2| + |g_1 - g_2| + |b_1 - b_2| \quad (13.7)$$

$$D_3(f_1, f_2) = \max\{|r_1 - r_2|, |g_1 - g_2|, |b_1 - b_2|\} \quad (13.8)$$

The disadvantage for our purpose is that these differences are all positive. In order to compute the edge direction properly, we need negative values as well. One simple possibility used in [Pau93] is shown in equation 13.9; the different channels can be weighted with $\omega_r, \omega_g, \omega_b$.

$$D_0(f_1, f_2) = \omega_r(r_1 - r_2) + \omega_g(g_1 - g_2) + \omega_b(b_1 - b_2) \quad (13.9)$$

The gradient image can now be calculated using (13.9). The resulting edge image can be further processed with the same programs as edge images resulting from gray–level images or other edge operators. The result of (13.9) on the image in Figure 11.2 (left) is shown in Figure 13.8

Figure 13.8 Gradient image computed with the color Sobel operator on the image shown in Figure 11.2.

Exercises

1. Show how the second derivative may be computed using equation (13.2) twice.

2. Create a program which has an edge image as an input and creates a gray–level image as an output. Use histogram equalization to transform the edge strength to 256 gray–levels.

3. Implement a program which generates a table for the tan^{-1} function of the 144 discrete direction values. The number of directions should be a parameter of the program. This will increase the efficiency of the computation. You may either use the program awk[7] or write a C++– program.

4. Create a program which has a color image as an input and creates an edge image as an output. Use a color Sobel operator with the difference D_0 in equation (13.9).

---

[7]Consult your computer manual. You may also use the GNU version of awk.

14 Class Libraries

The implementation of large software systems and class hierarchies using C++ obviously implies the development of a standard class library whose implemented classes are useful, convenient, and necessary for a majority of applications. These class libraries, however, are not a standard part of C++. In this chapter we give an overview of the nihcl class library. This software package is in the public domain and satisfies the requirements of a *general purpose* C++ class library. We describe the basics in simplified form — just to enable the use of the use of the library. Details of nihcl can be found in the book of K. Gorlen et al. [Gor90].

We discuss abstract and very general classes, which are the super classes of all classes which are implemented in the system. The input and output capabilities of the C++ standard library and nihcl are described in this chapter as well. The concepts needed for that purpose are streams, which are described in [Str91a]. We also introduce static class members for C++.

14.1 Stream Input and Output

Input and output operations like reading or writing data from a file are necessary for many programs. In C++ we implement input and output operations on objects which are themselves instances of user–defined classes. The programming language C++ does not directly provide the facilities for input and output of built–in objects. Nevertheless, those operations can easily be implemented in an object–oriented environment using so called *streams*. Streams a part of the C++ library definition that comes with the language definition. The resulting function calls for I/O–operations using streams are made simpler and easier to read.

The implemented classes for input and output streams are `istream` for handling the input of abstract data types and `ostream` for the output of objects. Predefined global static objects are `cerr`, `cout`, and `cin` which are attached to standard error, standard output and standard input respectively. The described C++ classes become available when the header file `iostream.h` is included. The class `ostream` has an overloaded operator `>>` which writes an object to a stream. Analogously, `istream` provides overloaded methods `<<` for reading data. The following Example 124 shows a simple program which reads an integer and writes it to standard output. If the value of the given integer is negative, an error message will be written to standard error instead.

```
#include <iostream.h>

main()
{
   int  i;              // integer to be read from standard input
   cout << "Please, type a nonnegative integer!\n";
                        // write to standard output
   cin >> i;            // read i from standard input
   if (i >= 0)          // input correct
    cout << "Your number is: " << i;
   else                 // wrong input, type error message
    cerr << "Your number is a negative integer!\n";
}
```
(124)

The definition of operators `<<` and `>>` for built–in abstract data types can be extended in the following way: assume you want to write the member variables of the given class `Image` to stdout or some other stream. For that purpose, you have to define an operator `<<` as shown in Example 125.

```
ostream& operator<<(ostream& strm, Image i)
{
   strm << "focal length: " << f << "\n";
   strm << "image size  : " << i.getxsize() << ","
        << i.getysize() << "\n";
   return strm;
}
```
(125)

Now the operator **<<** can be used in an adequate manner for the output of image objects. This operator maps the arguments to the overloaded virtual function **put**, which — depending on its arguments — stores the given data to the output stream. The input function can be defined analogously. These mechanisms have to be extended for object–oriented programming; this was one key issue of nihcl. Thus, we do not provide any other information about C++–streams and refer the interested reader to the manual [Str91a]. We rather introduce the ideas of object input and output in nihcl.

14.2   National Institutes of Health Class Library

The ideas of Smalltalk [Gol83] should be familiar to everyone who wants to do object–oriented programming. Simula [Bir83] and Smalltalk can be seen as the 'parents' of object–oriented programming. Both language definitions describe the syntax and provide extensive class libraries for various applications. C++ — as defined in [Str91b] — provides no such environment as Smalltalk. The nihcl class hierarchy re–implements some of the Smalltalk ideas for C++. It uses the same identifiers for methods and classes.

Figure 14.1 shows the important classes of the nihcl–class tree which are outlined shortly in this chapter. This tree shows that concrete classes can exist (**Set**) which have derived classes, i.e. not every class having sub–classes must be abstract.

Conceptually, the most general class in nihcl is the class **Object**. For technical reasons, a class **NIHCL** is put on top of the hierarchy, i.e. class **Object** is derived from **NIHCL**. **NIHCL** is the base class of all the built–in classes in the hierarchy. Of course this general class has to be an abstract class itself if it provides the general member functions. The member functions are implemented in the derived classes, where the explicit representation of an object is known. The general member functions of the class **Object** can be divided into three main categories: functions for identifying and testing the class of an object at run–time (like **isA**), functions for comparing objects (like **isEqual**), and finally functions for input and output operations of objects (like **storeOn**). A comfortable interface to input and output of objects (OIO) is provided by abstract classes (**OIOin** and **OIOout**); derived classes specify possible sources and destionations and data representation as binary or ascii.

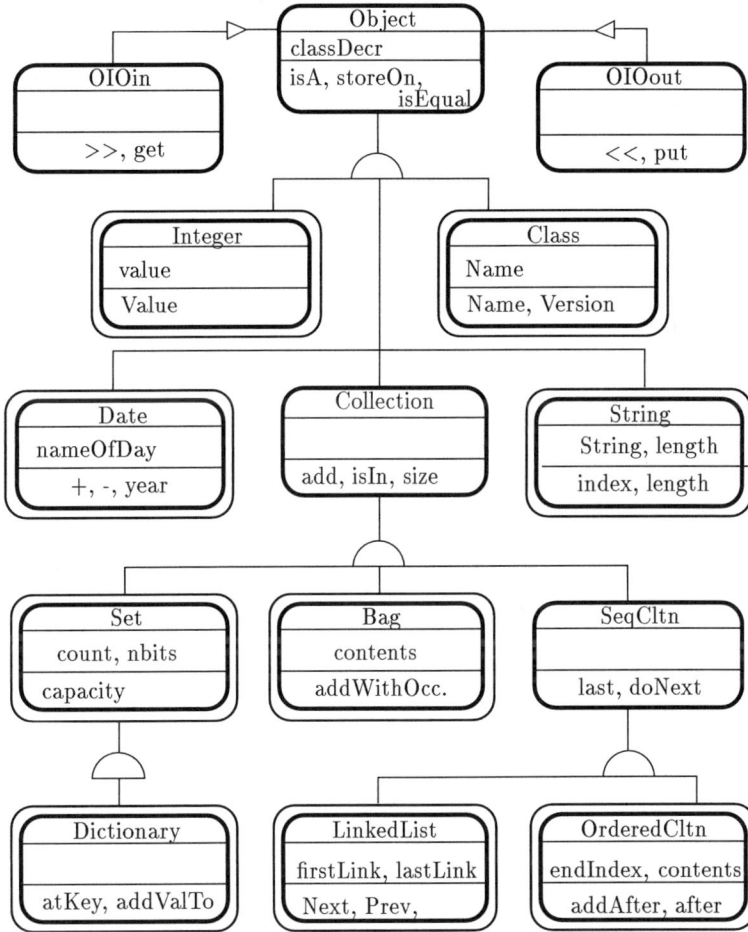

Figure 14.1 Essential classes of the nihcl class tree. Method names are abbreviated.

The implementation of a descendent class of the class `Object` must include the declaration and definition of about 20 functions of the above mentioned three categories to be compatible with other nihcl classes. Nevertheless, the implementation of these functions is elementary and fairly easy. nihcl provides some macros which support the declaration and definition of these functions.

14.3 Dynamic Class Descriptions

In many situations it is advantageous to have the capability to check the type of a given object, i.e. to determine the class which the object belongs to. For that purpose, Smalltalk provides a "meta class". In nihcl a class Class is implemented, which allows to get run–time information of the involved objects. The information contained in the class Class is the name of the class the object belongs to, the classes of the member variables, the size of its instances, and the version number. To ensure that all classes supply this information, a virtual member function isA() in the class Object is declared, which returns a pointer to a member variable classDesc of the class Class.

A simplified version of a class Class is shown in Example 126.

```
class Class {
   char * className;
   int version;
public:
   Class(char *, int);
   const char * ClassName() const { return className; }
   int Version() const { return version; }
};
```
(126)

14.4 Static Class Members

Since the member variable classDesc is equal for all instances of one class it can be shared by these instances. It is not necessary that each object of the class has its own copy of this member variable. For that purpose, C++ provides the declaration of static members, where all instances of the class

share those static variables; i.e. the keyword `static` indicates to the compiler
that this member is allocated *once* for every *class* — not for every object.
Such variables are called *class variables* in Smalltalk – in contrast to *object
variables*. Example 127 outlines this idea in a simplified form.

```
class Object {                    // root of the object
                                  // tree NIHCL
   static Class classdesc;        // once in the program
public:                           // enquire class membership
   Object();                      // default constructor
   virtual const Class* isA() const; // { return & classdesc; }
   virtual void storer(OIOout&);  // external representation
   // etc.
};                                                        (127)
```

Class variables are like regular data members and obey the visibility and
scoping rules (see section 4.5). The only difference is that they exist only
once and that they have to be initialized *once* (Example 128) in the program.
The C++ run time system will guarantee that such objects are created before
the function **main** starts.

```
const Class* Object::isA() const { return & classdesc; }
Object::Object() {};
Class Object::classdesc ("Object",0);                     (128)
```

Every nihcl class redefines `isA` and defines its own `classdesc`, i.e. there
exists exactly one class description per class. The different static variables
`classdesc` can be accessed by the prefix e.g. `Time::` (Example 129).

```
class Time : public Object {      // one typical example
   static Class classdesc;        // again, one object
public:                           // isA() looks similar
   virtual const Class* isA() const; // { return & classdesc; }
   Time();
};

Time::Time() {};
const Class* Time::isA() const { return & classdesc; }
Class Time::classdesc ("Time",0);                                    129
```

Since all classes which use nihcl have to define these members and methods, and since all these definitions are textually identical, nihcl provides macros for their definition. Again, a simplified version is shown in Example 130;[1] the real macros in nihcl have more parameters. The definition for `readFrom` is a dummy function in this example.

```
#define DECLARE_MEMBERS(c)                                       \
  private: static Class classdesc;                               \
  public:  static c * readFrom(OIOin&);                          \
  public:  virtual const Class* isA()  const;                    \
  public:  virtual const char* ClassName() const;                \
           virtual void storer(OIOout&);                         \
  private:
#define DEFINE_CLASS(c,v)                                        \
  const Class* c::isA() const { return & c::classdesc; }         \
  const char*  c::ClassName() const                              \
    { return c::classdesc.ClassName(); }                         \
  c* c::readFrom(OIOin&) { /* complicated */ return NULL; }  \
  Class c::classdesc(#c,v);                                       130
```

In cases as in Example 130, macros are required, or at least simpler than templatates. The token `#c` expands to a string containing the macro argument, if

---

[1] Mult–line macros use a backslash to continue on the next line, cmp. Sect. 2.8

an ANSI preprocessor is used. The first macro is used in the class declaration. The second macro is used in the module which defines the methods.

The methods `readFrom` and `storeOn` referenced the `OIO` classes. These classes are special *streams* for input and output of objects in an object–oriented environment. The virtual function `storer` is called from `storeOn` declared in class `Object`. We will introduce these streams next.

14.5 Input and Output for Objects

nihcl extends the notion of streams and adds methods for storing arbitrary objects (with `storeOn` resp. `storer`) and construction from streams. The abstract base classes for object input `OIOin` and output `OIOout` are shown in Figure 14.1. The major difference to standard C++ streams is that these streams automatically recognize type and version of the object during a read operation. Multiple occurences of the same object in a collection will be recognized upon write and only one copy will be stored. This will also be recognized, when a collection is being read in. Using this mechanism, object *references* can be stored and restored.

Here, we only give an overview of the interface allowing the user to store and read objects in nihcl.[2] nihcl uses two types of streams one of them uses binary and one uses textual representation of objects. The usage is basically the same; we describe binary storage, since images and speech data has to be stored in binary format to save space.

Objects are stored via the `storeOn` method which has to be defined for each class. Arbitrary objects can be read using `readFrom`; this function is defined by the `DEFINE_CLASS` macro. The actual code for reading has to be provided in a constructor which has an input stream as an argument.[3] Clearly, when an object is read, its base class has to initialized as well. This is simply done by the base class constructor which is executed before the object is initialized. An example is shown in Example 131.

This automatic mechanism is not available for the opposite direction, the storage operation by the method `storer`. The `storer` method of the base class has to be explicitly called; this is done using the name of the base as a

---

[2]Again, the reader is referred to [Gor90] for details.

[3]A tricky mechanism is used to call a constructor from the `readFrom` function.

prefix. It is convenient to define a macro for the actual class name and base (Example 131).

```
#include "OIOnih.h"
#include "Image.h"
#define THIS Image
#define BASE Object
THIS::THIS(OIOifd& strm) :
    BASE(strm)
{
    strm >> f >> xsize >> ysize;
}
void THIS::storer(OIOofd& strm)
{
    BASE::storer(strm);
    strm << f << xsize << ysize;
}
```
(131)

The class Object's input and output functions provide consistency checks and version control. In addition, the class name is stored; thereby, arbitrary objects can be read from a stream without exactly knowing in advance which object will be read.

In Sect. 15.9 we derive special classes for object input and output from the nihcl classes. We will show there how to open a stream and how to close it.

14.6   Strings

Strings are frequently used structures and string manipulations on character pointers in C++ as well as C is error prone, since explicit requests and releases of memory are required. nihcl provides handy classes for dynamic strings including access and manipulation.[4] As in Smalltalk, these classes are called String and SubString. The methods available for objects of the class String are for example concatenation, comparison of strings, the selection of one

---

[4]Compare Example 83 and exercise 2 on page 138.

character of a given string, or methods for determining the length of a string. The class Substring supports some manipulation of parts of a string. For example, a constructor is defined for declaring a substring of a specified length of a known object of the class String. To make the private member variables and function accessible to the class String, they are declared to be a friend (Sect. 15.4) of the class Substring.

Some applications are shown in Example 132. Individual characters can be accessed by an overloaded index operator. Allocation and release of the memory for the strings is managed automatically during construction and destruction.

```
String S1="string 1";    // define and initialize
String S2("string 2");   // alternative construction
S1[7]= '2';
S2[7]= '1';
cout << S1 << "\n";      // prints "string 2"
cout << S2 << "\n";      // prints "string 1"              (132)
```

14.7   Container Classes

In many applications, facilities for construction and manipulation of complex data structures are desirable. Examples for frequently used data structures are linked lists, stacks, or sets. The types of the elements of those complex data structures should be parameterized. In nihcl the general super class Container holds instances of nihcl classes. The methods of the abstract class Container are functions for comparing instances of the Container class, adding objects, removing objects, converting containers, the "element of" relation, or a function for determining the cardinality of an object. Container classes are defined with variable objects. This polymorphic implementation guarantees that the code is useful for a wide range of applications. Examples for derived classes are the already mentioned classes Set, Stack, and LinkedList with their customary meanings. A sub–class Bag can contain multiple occurences of one object, or several objects which are equal. In addition to the high degree of reusability of the polymorphic container classes, they also allow the definition of recursive data structures. For example, the elements of a set can also be sets and so on. Most of the problems concerning the use of container classes is due to the fact that container classes hold pointers to objects and do not represent the objects explicitly, i.e. they hold no explicit copy of objects, only references. Therefore, the programmer should take care and pay attention to correct memory management. In particular, we must be very careful about the lifetime of the objects which are parts of containers.

Some applications of sets and collections are shown in Example 133. Elements can be added to and removed from collections. When an element is added to a set, the existing objects are compared for *equality* with the new object. The contents of s will be {"Jack", "Joe"} when it is printed. The collection o will contain {"Joe", "Jack", "Peter", "Joe"}.

```
Set s;                    // define an empty set
OrderedCltn o;            // objects will be sorted
String s1="Peter";        // define and initialize
String s2("Jack");        // other initialization
String s3= "Joe";         // s3 and s4 will be
String s4= "Joe";         // equal, but not the same
s.add(s1);                // add several strings
s.add(s2);                // to the set s
s.add(s3);                // here comes joe
s.add(s4);                // will have no effect
s.remove(s1);             // remove element
o.add(s3);                // now add strings
o.add(s2);                // to the ordered
o.add(s1);                // collection
o.add(s4);                // joe will go in twice!
cout << "s:" << s << endl; // print contents of s
cout << "o:" << o << endl; // print contents of o   (133)
```

An attempt to remove an element which is not in the collection, is an error. nihcl also provides macros for iteration over all elements in a collection as in a loop.

Example 75 showed a simple class declaration of an "association" data type between a string and an integer. nihcl provides a more elaborate version of associations using a key–object and a value–object. The String class is often used for the key and an arbitrary Object as value. For example the key can be an English word and the value object is a list of all possible German translations of this word. A collection of these associations are called a `Dictionary`, if every key occurs only once. The class name `Dictionary` is obvious with respect to the above example. An application is shown in Example 134.

```
Dictionary d;
String word1("time");
String word2("date");
d.addAssoc(word1,word2);
cout << d << endl;          // print d
```
(134)

14.8   Time and Date

nihcl provides classes for the access and manipulation of the time and date. As in Smalltalk, the classes are called `Date` and `Time`. In these classes the complexity of calendars is encapsulated. In application programs Time and Date objects provide arithmetical manipulations of this data. The programmer can handle those objects as they were ordinary numbers. For instance, the date can be compared with another one or you can add some days and will get the new resulting date. Some applications are shown in Example 135.

```
Date bdpa(9,"April",59);
Date bdho(10,"August",67) ;
int year= bdho.year();      // select the year
Time t(bdho,                // date
       8,                   // hour
       12,                  // minute
       0);                  // second
cout << bdho - bdpa << "\n"; // difference
```
(135)

14.9   More Classes

For graphical applications, nihcl provides classes for simple geometric objects
like points or rectangles (classes `Points` and `Rectangle`). Similar data structures with enhanced features are needed in image analysis and introduced
in chapter 15. We use different names for the classes.[5] For image processing
applications, this small class hierarchy will not be sufficient. In Chapter 15 a
class hierarchy for image processing and analysis will be described.

```
Point  p(108,67), q(123,68); // two points (x,y)
Rectangle r(p,q);            // corner points
cout << r << " " << r.area() << "\n";
```
(136)

Applications in [Gor90] include the definition of the class `Line`, `Triangle`,
`Circle`, and the class `Picture`. These classes are all derived from the abstract
class `Shape`.

Numeric data in C++ is represented as in C as standard predefined data type.
No object–oriented programming is possible with these data types. nihcl defines the classes `Integer` and `Float` which can be accessed as *objects*. Thereby,
they can for example be stored on object streams. Arithmetic methods are
available, operation is however slow in comparison to standard data types.

Exercises

1. Implement the class `Image` using the class `Class` for run–time information
   about the objects.

2. Extend the implemented classes with respect to input and output facilities using streams.

3. Discuss the problems concerning the pointers to objects in container
   classes.

---

[5]Compilation of nihcl with X11 may as well cause problems since Point, Line, etc. are
defined there as well.

4. Implement a String and SubString class compatible with Example 83.

5. Implement a Date and Time class compatible with what you saw in Example 135.

6. Extend the class definition in Example 121. Make the global constants for quantization *constant* static class members and initialize them properly, e.g. as

```
const int Edge::onum = 144;
```

Do some experiments, how `public:` and `protected:` affects the accessibility of these constants from outside.

15 Hierarchy of Picture Processing Objects

The object–oriented programming system ἵππος[1] for image analysis was introduced in [Pau92b]. In this chapter we outline the ἵππος–system in general. We describe the concepts of lines, their representations as classes, and the implementation in C++ in detail. We also introduce the enumeration type, scope resolution, and friends for C++.

15.1 General Structure

The overall structure of ἵππος is described in [Pau92c, Pau92b, Pau92a]. Here we can only give an overview of selected classes and methods. The classes described in this book and in the appendix are a trimmed down subset of the corresponding classes in the ἵππος system. Algorithms and programs using these smaller classes can be compiled and run with very few changes in the complete system. A small but complete sub–system for 2D segmentation will be introduced in Part III.

The system consists of a large class tree with the top node class `HipposObj` (Sect. 15.2) which is directly derived from the nihcl–class `Object` (Sect. 14.2). All classes required for image segmentation are derived from this class; they inherit the basic functionality for image processing.

Some other classes in ἵππος are derived from other branches of the nihcl–tree. This is done for concepts which are not directly related to image processing. Parametric classes for matrices are defined and derived in a matrix–subtree. The persistent storage of objects as implemented in nihcl can be in a machine dependent binary format or in a machine independent ASCII format (Sect. 14.5). A machine independent efficient storage scheme for nihcl and ἵππος is introduced in Sect. 15.9 using the XDR–classes.

---

[1] **HI**erarchy of **P**icture **P**rocessing **O**bject**S**, see Sect. 3.9

Visualization is decoupled from algorithmic structure for all these classes by using a class for image display that interfaces with several devices. Similarly, images are input from a camera class and will be described in Sect. 17.4.

A top level view of the ἵππος–hierarchy and the related classes is shown in Figure 15.1. The classes above the dotted line are nihcl–classes (cmp. Figure 14.1); the classes below belong to ἵππος.

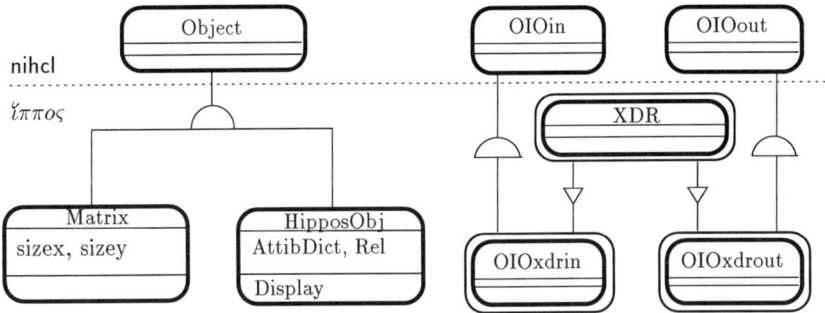

Figure 15.1 Interface of nihcl and ἵππος

15.2   Hippos Object

The ἵππος tree is dedicated to the *representation* of data which is computed during image segmentation. The representation is general enough to include all known segmentation algorithms. These classes are united in a subtree under the abstract class HipposObj. Its basic purpose is to bundle all the derived classes for image processing and analysis and to provide the basic functionality of every object of this application area.

A top level view is shown in Figure 15.2. All image types are derived from the abstract Image class. The Representation subtree contains classes for the results of various line–based or region–based algorithms. Geometric objects provide a more abstract interface to these representations (Sect. 15.7). Relational objects RelObj will be needed in Sect. 15.8.

Three major features can be found for all imaging objects:

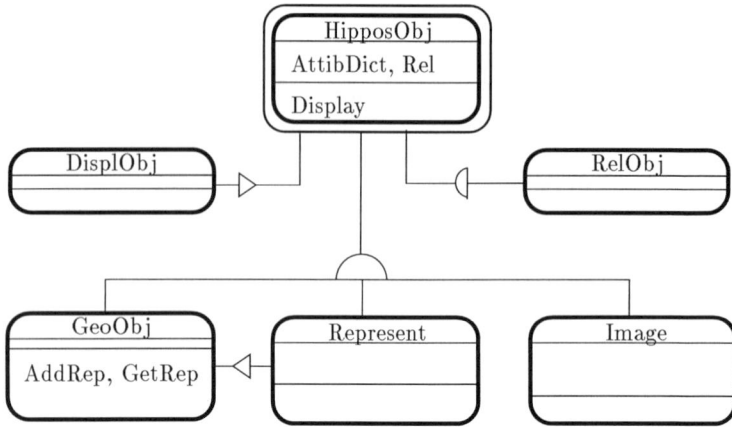

Figure 15.2 Top of image processing class hierarchy

- Image processing objects usually reflect some sort of visual information. They can commonly be displayed on an appropriate graphics display.

- In order to specify a mainly problem independent control strategy for knowledge based image analysis (Sect. 5.4), it is essential that every segmented object is attached with a judgement or quality measure (see Sect.5.5).

- In addition to fixed members, image processing objects often have varying additional information which may be useful in one application but not required in another. Examples are the mean contrast along a segmented line which may be computed by a line finding algorithm but ignored in the following steps.

These features are translated to C++ in a straightforward way. The displaying feature is taken into account by a pure virtual `Display` function which passes the graphics information to its argument which is another object derived from the `HipposObj` called a "virtual frame buffer" `DisplObj` (Figure 15.2). This object can be mapped to an arbitrary physical device (Sect. 17.4).[2]

---

[2]In the ἵππος implementation this is decoupled from the imaging objects. The display information is passed from the virtual frame buffer to a graphics server using remote

The varying information on attributes is stored in an nihcl–Dictionary. The judgement is a floating point value that is inherited by every object in the hierarchy. A basic implementation of this class is shown in Example 137.

```
#include "Dictionary.h"
class DisplObj;                        // Need not care about it here
class HipposObj : public Object { // Abstract class, no public part
    DECLARE_MEMBERS(HipposObj)
    Dictionary attributes;
    float judgement;
protected:
    HipposObj(float r=0.0);
    const Dictionary & Attributes()  const;
    float              Judgement() const;
    void setAttrib(const char *, const Object *);
    virtual int Display(DisplObj&) = 0;   // pure virtual
};
```

(137)

15.3   Images and Matrices

Images were introduced as classes in chapter 11; this class is now integrated in the image processing hierarchy. Several classes for images are derived from a common abstract base class Image in ἵππος. Stereo images, range images, color images, gray–level images, binary images, edge images, etc. are available for programming together with their appropriate operations.

Sub–images as described in Sect. 11.7 are available for any image class. Stereo images may be either gray–level images or color images.

Pixels are naturally stored in matrix objects. A matrix class tree was created for parametric matrix classes. Those matrices with numeric elements declare mathematical operations like addition, multiplication, transposition, etc. Other matrices — e. g. those containing edge elements — only provide

procedure calls. The server then invokes the required display routines, for example on an X11 device. This means, that the programs do not have to compile and link in any X11 routines!

basic access and input–output functions. Since these matrix classes do not
directly refer to image processing, they are not derived from the HipposObj.
Thereby they are available to speech processing or any other non–image processing purposes without linkage of the ἵππος class library.

In this book we use three image classes:

- gray–level images (GrayLevelImage),

- color images (ColorImage), and

- edge images (EdgeImage).

These classes are derived from the abstract class Image which itself can contain additional textual and numeric descriptions, like the camera used and its
parameters (lens, focus, aperture, exposure time, etc.) similar to the simple
hierarchy shown in Example 117. A basic definition for a gray–level image is
given in Example 138.

```
#include <HipposObj.h>
#include <Matrix.h>
class Image : public HipposObj {  // extend as outlined in the text
    int x,y;
 public:
    Image (int xs,int ys) : x(xs), y(ys) {}
    int getxsize() const { return y; }
    int getysize() const { return x; }
};
class GrayLevelImage : public Image {
    DECLARE_MEMBERS(GrayLevelImage)
    Matrix<byte> img;
 public:
    GrayLevelImage(int x,int y) : Image(x,y), img(x,y) { };
    byte* operator[] (int i) {return img[i];}
    virtual Display(DisplObj&);
};
```
(138)

The next step in segmentation (in the sense of Figure 5.5) is to detect geometric objects in a representation close to the pixel data.

15.4 Chain Code Class

The chain code representation is a very common representation for lines very close to the pixel raster data. This representation uses the start point of a line and a sequence of numbers from the interval $0 \ldots 7$ which indicate the next point in the line, called *links*. This is exemplified in Figure 15.3. The information about the intensity of a line along a chain code is lost.[3]

Chain codes are very common in the first stages of image segmentation since they are a compact representation with a nice set of simple operations (see Chapter 23, [Fre80]). The program in Example 26 in Sect. 4.6 is also used for chain codes (see exercises).

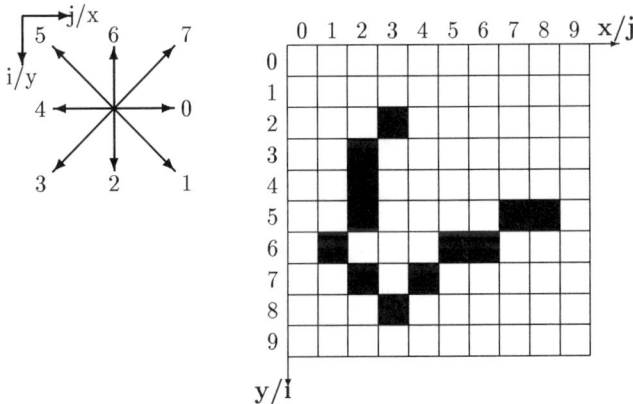

Chain Code:
Start (x,y) = (3,2)
Direction: 3,2,2,3,1,1,7,7,0,7,0

(a)   (b)

Figure 15.3 Definition of the directions in a chain code (a) and example for a line represented by a chain code (b)

---

[3]We will however record the mean intensity difference — the so called contrast — along the line in an attribute of the base class `HipposObj` (Sect. 15.2).

For the implementation of a class for chain codes, we first introduce a helper class ChainSeq (Example 139) to represent sequences of links. This class will be usable only by the class Chain (Example 143) which is a *friend* of the class ChainSeq. This language feature of C++ grants access to private parts of the class without any restrictions, but only to those classes or functions which are declared as friends.

```
class ChainSeq {              // No public part
    friend class Chain;       // grant access to internals
    byte * seq;               // actual chains
    unsigned len;             // number of bytes allocated
    unsigned act;             // number of bytes used
    ~ChainSeq();              // destructor releases seq
    ChainSeq(unsigned);       // pre allocate
    ChainSeq(const ChainSeq&);
    int length() const { return len; }
    void append(byte);        // appends to the sequence seq
    byte & at(unsigned i) { return seq[i]; }  // access
};
```
(139)

Friends should generally be used rarely, since they disturb modularity and data abstraction. In this example the contrary is the case; the dependencies are clear and both classes can be in the same module. So this is, in effect, a useful application of the friend concept.

The method ChainSeq::append appends a byte to the sequence. If there is no more space available in the vector seq, i.e. len == act, then the object has to reallocate memory with len increased by a factor (e.g. with factor 1.5). The class Chain will be defined after the introduction of two new language features in C++.

15.5   Enumerations and Scope Resolution

Enumeration data types allow integer data with a very small range to be explicitly named. They are a handy feature to use to associate several constant values with their own name.

Consider again the class for edges (Example 121). We now store with each element whether we consider it part of an edge, part of a closed line, start or end of a line, etc. We use an *enumeration data type* for the symbolical description of these features. The syntax is as follows:

Syntax: <u>enum</u> [*typename*] <u>{</u> *name* [<u>=</u> *int_value*] * <u>}</u> [*vdef*] <u>;</u>

Variables can be defined using the *typename*. If no initialization is specified with the *int_value*, the next free integral value is chosen by the compiler.[4]

```
enum A { i = 1, j = 2, k, l};  // k = 3, l = 4
A a;
```
(140)

Enumerations as in Example 140 introduce many global names. This is generally not good software practice. Enumerations should therefore be used within a class scope (Example 141). The names are now visible only inside the structure or class. They can still be used from the outside by the *scope resolution operator* "::".[5] We now see that the function name in the method definition in Chapter 10 fits logically into this concept (e.g. `rational::set` in Example 74); the class name prefix is a scope resolution which uniquely determines the name space where the function name has to be searched for by the compiler.

Type declarations inside class obey the rules of visibility (Sect. 10.3, Table 12.2). The enumeration type `edge_type` in Example 141 can be used outside the class since it belongs to the public part of the structure.

---

[4]It is even possible to assign the same value twice to different names with explicit initialization.

[5]Another application of this operator is to access a name which was overwritten by the same name in a closer block, as in Example 106. Various other sophisticated applications of this operator are possible but not treated in this book.

```
struct edge_1 {
    enum edge_type { start = 0, end = 1, closed = 2 };
    unsigned int strength : 16;
    unsigned int orient   : 8;
    edge_type    features : 3;      // can use enums in bit fields
};
int test_access = edge_1::start;  // use scope resolution
```
(141)

Chain codes are a special case of a representation for lines. Other representations exist. We introduce an abstract base class for line representations in Example 142. It contains the general interface for lines including access to start and end, predicates for closed lines, etc., and separates these representations from those for regions.[6] This class utilizes the class `PointXY` (Example 81, exercise 3 on page 138).

```
#include "PointXY.h"
class LineRep : public Represent {
    DECLARE_MEMBERS(LineRep)
    PointXY start;
public:
    LineRep();
    LineRep(const PointXY&);
    LineRep(const LineRep&);
    virtual double length() const;
    virtual PointXY End() const;
    virtual const PointXY& Start() const;
    int isClosed() const ; // e.g. { return start == End(); }
};
```
(142)

We can now completely declare the class `Chain`. We also define an enumeration data type inside the class for symbolic description of the chain directions. Also note the constant static variable for the default allocation length declared in class scope.

---

[6]In ἵππος, this class is actually separated into a class for three dimensional lines and one for lines in two dimensions.

```
class Chain : public LineRep {
    DECLARE_MEMBERS(Chain)
    ChainSeq chain;
public:
    enum ChainDir { east = 0, se = 1, south = 2, sw = 3,
        west = 4, nw = 5, north = 6, ne = 7};
    static const int DefaultLen; // default chunk length for chain
    ~Chain();
    Chain();
    Chain(PointXY &, int = Chain::DefaultLen);
    Chain(const Chain &p);
    int number() const { return chain.act + 1; }
    void append(byte b)  { chain.append(b); }
    virtual int Display(DisplObj&);
};
```
$\left(143\right)$

Examples 144 and 145 show the implementation of some of the methods.

```
DEFINE_CLASS(Chain,0)
const int Chain::DefaultLen = 8;
Chain::Chain() : chain(DefaultLen) {}
Chain::Chain(PointXY & p, int l) : LineRep(p), chain(l) {}
Chain::Chain(const Chain &c)      : LineRep(c.Start()),
                                    chain(c.chain) {}
```
$\left(144\right)$

The destructor of the helper class releases the memory which was allocated for the links. This destructor is called implicitly when a Chain is deleted.

```
ChainSeq::~ChainSeq() { delete  [] seq; }
Chain::~Chain() { }
ChainSeq::ChainSeq(unsigned l)
{
    act = 0;
    len = l;
    seq = new byte[l];
}
```
(145)

As will be described in Chapter 22, edges will be connected and chain codes can be extracted from an edge image. It is a useful extension for edges to add a possible successor to an edge element that points to any of its eight neighbors. This can naturally be done with a chain code, i.e. with the enumeration inside the class Chain. Since we made this definition public, we can use it in an extended edge class. The class for edges (Example 141) still has five extra bits which can be used; these bits are filled in Example 146.

```
struct edge_2 {
    static const int ONUM;          // will be defined as 144
    enum edge_type { start = 0, end = 1, closed = 2 };
    unsigned int    strength : 16;
    unsigned int    orient   : 8;
    edge_type       features : 5;   // for later extension
    Chain::ChainDir succ     : 3;   // use Chain definition
};
```
(146)

The constant class variable edge_2::ONUM will have to be initialized as the Chain::DefaultLen in Example 144.

15.6 Polygonal Representation

Polygons are a line representation by a sequence of straight line segments. These segments can be described by a sequence of points. An example of a segmentation of a gray–level image into a set of polygons (a segmentation object) is shown in Figure 15.4. Polygons may be computed from a line segmentation in chain codes (see Sect. 23.7). A simple algorithm for polygonal approximation is left as exercise 2.

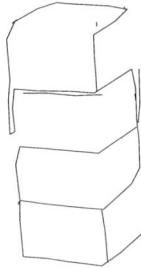

Figure 15.4 Polygon–approximation of a chain code segmented from the red channel of Figure 11.2 (left).

Polygons — like chain codes — are derived from the line representation class. A basic declaration is given in Example 147. The sequential collection (OrderedCltn) of nihcl is used to store the sequence of points.

```
#include "OrderedCltn.h"
class Polygon : public LineRep {
    OrderedCltn points;    // sequence of points excluding start
public:
    virtual double length() const;
    // ...
};
```
(147)

15.7   Atomic Objects

Various representations can be found in the literature for lines in addition to chain codes and polygons. A common abstract base class for line representations LineRep was introduced which bundles the similarities of the known representations, like the feature that a line has a start and an end that are point objects.

Several representations of one line in an image (or in the scene) may even exist simultaneously. These representations are stored in an object of class AtomLine. The same holds for regions which may have several representations. A AtomLine and a AtomRegion are derived from the class GeoObj which bundles the subtree for geometric objects. The class AtomObj is introduced which separates compound objects (e.g. a collection of lines forming a rectangle) from those which contain only one instance of a given type. Compound objects are called *segmentation objects* and will be introduced in Sect. 15.8. The class hierarchy of these classes is shown in Figure 15.5.

Basic implementations of geometric objects and atomic objects are given in Example 148, 149, and 150. In Example 148 we define the abstract base class for this part of the hierarchy.

```
class GeoObj : public HipposObj {
   DECLARE_MEMBERS(GeoObj)
protected:        // abstract, no public parts
   GeoObj();
   virtual int Display(DisplObj&);
};
```
(148)

Atomic objects are derived from class GeoObj; this class is abstract as well (Example 149). The method getRep will return a representation of a class indicated as an argument. If a representation is requested which is not currently stored in the set of representations, a conversion method in the class Represent is used to produce such a representation.

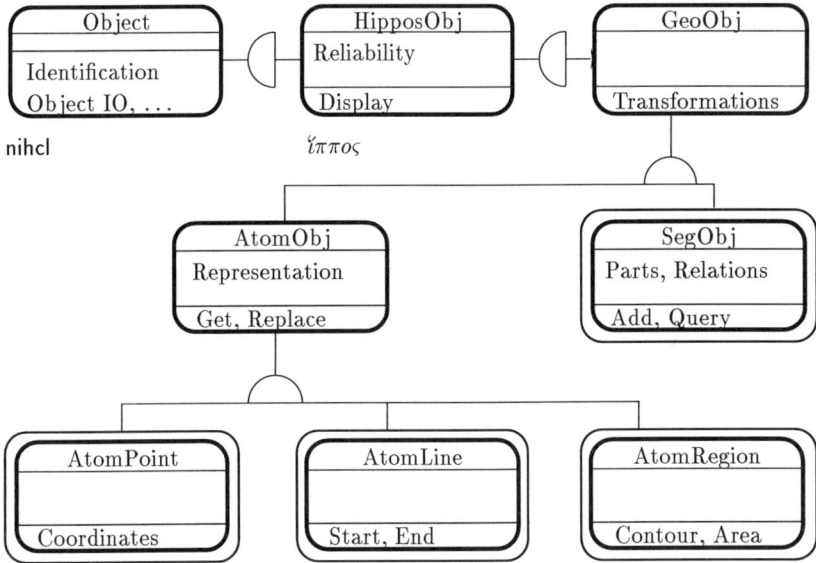

Figure 15.5 Hierarchy for geometric objects and segmentation objects

```
#include "Set.h"
#include "Represent.h"
class AtomObj : public GeoObj {
   DECLARE_MEMBERS(AtomObj)
   Set representations; // will always be nonempty
protected:
   AtomObj();
   virtual addRep(const Represent&) = 0;
   Represent * getRep(const Class&);
};                                                    (149)
```

Objects can be created from the class AtomLine which is derived from the abstract base AtomObj.

```
class AtomLine : public AtomObj {
   DECLARE_MEMBERS(AtomLine)
public:
   AtomLine();
   AtomLine(const Represent&);
   virtual addRep(const Represent&); // will add a
                                     // line representation
};
```

(150)

15.8   Segmentation Objects

It is very important to represent intermediate results of image segmentation
in a common format which can be used by many segmentation programs.
Generally, a so–called *segmentation object* consists of a set of parts and the
relations between those parts. In most applications, these parts are geometric
objects which cannot be further split, i.e. the atomic objects (Example 149).
Occasionally, segmentation objects may be recursive and include other segmentation objects, i.e. compound objects.

```
#include "Set.h"
class SegObj : public GeoObj {
    DECLARE_MEMBERS(SegObj)
    Set parts;   // set of GeoObj (!)
    Set rels;    // set of RelObjs
public:
    SegObj();
    void add(const GeoObj &s);
    virtual int Display(DisplObj&);
};
```

(151)

Segmentation results are represented in a common interface class called the
SegObj (Figure 15.5). Example 151 shows a basic implementation. This class

is also derived from the class GeoObj and provides compound segmentation data. Parts may be added which are of the class GeoObj, i.e. either atomic objects or geometric objects. Since sets of objects of nihcl are used, efficient functions for comparing objects have to be provided for geometric objects.

This very powerful class is the central class of the ἵππος system. Since segmentation objects may contain other segmentation objects, special care has to be taken that no circular structures will be created. The implementation of the method add guarantees that parts may only be included in the object if this will not create an inconsistent *part–of* relation. Further restrictions improve the safety of this representation scheme (see [Pau92b] for details).

Several features not shown in Example 151 are implemented in ἵππος. Parts of segmentation objects may be related in various ways to each other. For example, lines may be marked as parallel. This is represented in relations (in the mathematical sense) which we also provided as classes (see RelObj in Figure 15.1). These relational features are stored in the set rels. Vertices (see for example Figure 5.4) are special segmentation objects defined by the intersection of at least two lines.

15.9   External Representation

The nihcl–system introduces streams for persistent objects (i.e. permanent storage of objects, Sect. 14.5). In ἵππος this concept was extended to machine independent binary storage using XDR (eXternal Data Representation, [XDR88]), which is available on almost any computer by the SUN network file system (nfs). A class XDR was introduced for this purpose [Pau92b]. This enables a portable and highly efficient data transfer between different computer architectures. All nihcl–objects can be stored and retrieved from XDR–streams using their storeOn and readFrom methods on the derived streams. No changes are required for nihcl.

This is a nice example of the power of virtual functions. Existing class libraries can be extended by inheritance and existing functionality can be overwritten with new virtual functions. A new class OIOxdrout is derived from the nihcl–class OIOout. The overloaded virtual functions put declared for the nihcl–class (Sect. 14.5) are redefined and mapped directly to the xdr functions. The method OIOxdrout::put(int i) for example uses the xdr_int function. This derivation scheme is shown in Figure 15.1 on the right.

Without any modification or re–compilation, nihcl–objects can now be stored to `OIOxdrout`–streams . Their methods `storeOn(OIOout&)` will be simply used. The same holds for the new class `OIOxdrin` which is derived from the nihcl–class `OIOin`.

```
#include "OIOxdr.h"
#include "HipposObj.h"
DisplObj display;
main(int argc, char **argv)
{
    OIOxdrin if(*++argv);
    OIOxdrin of(*++argv);
    HipposObj * o = HipposObj::readFrom(if);
    o->Display(display);
    o->storeOn(of);
}
```

$$\left(152\right)$$

Example 152 provides a good example of object–oriented programming. The main program just reads an object, which can be of any class derived from `HipposObj`, and displays it using the virtual function `Display`. When a new class is added to the image processing hierarchy, this program will just have to be linked again in order to know about the new possible objects and their display methods.

Exercises

1. Use the algorithms for line detection in Chapter 13 to fill in the classes for chain codes with data.

2. Invent a simple algorithm to convert a chain code into a polygon. Iterate along the chain code and approximate the current segment by a straight line. Whenever the approximation error exceeds a threshold, start a new line segment. Write a program which does this conversion from one segmentation object to another; the threshold should be given as command line argument.

3. Complete the definitions for the classes `Chain` and `ChainSeq` (Example 143 and 139).

4. Complete the switch in Example 26 for use in a chain code class.

5. Implement simple classes `OIOxdrin` and `OIOxdrout` to store and read data. Do not try to re-implement nihcl, just provide sufficient functionality to be able to read and write images.

16 Spectral Features and Speech Processing

In the field of image processing a sampled continuous signal usually serves directly as input data for extraction algorithms of geometrical features and segmentation (Chapter 22).

In speech recognition it is also necessary to derive a set of features which are convenient for the subsequent processing steps. There are a lot of parameters to represent a speech signal. For example, you can take the waveform of the speech and compute features like the zero crossing rate, the energy of the signal, or others [Nie90b, Rab88]. Usually, the features are not computed in the spatial domain, but in the frequency domain of the signal. Those features have some characteristics which are not directly evident in spatial data [Dud73]. Therefore, it has proven advantageous to do a spectral analysis of given speech signals.

In this chapter we will give an introduction to the computation of Fourier transforms and the determination of features of the frequency domain for speech signals. Classification techniques based on dynamic programming (DP) [Big89] and Hidden Markov Models [Hua90, Rab88, ST95] will be introduced including suggestions for an implementation in C++ of these algorithms.

16.1 Fourier Series and Fourier Transform

The basic idea of using the frequency domain of speech signals is founded on the mathematical result, that an arbitrary 2π–periodic function $f(t)$ can be approximated by a Fourier series, i.e. a superposition of sine and cosine terms.

$$f(t) \quad = \quad \frac{a_0}{2} + \sum_{k \geq 1} a_k \cos(kt) + b_k \sin(kt) \quad . \qquad (16.1)$$

The convergence properties of this infinite were developed by Dirichlet and can be found in [Bro85]. The cosine function is an even function and the sine function is symmetrical with respect to the origin of the coordinate system. The approximation of odd functions includes only summands of sine functions and analogously, even functions are a superposition of cosine terms. Figure 16.2 shows an example how the even step function

$$f(t) = \begin{cases} 1, & \text{if } 0 \leq t < \frac{\pi}{2} \\ -1, & \text{if } \frac{\pi}{2} < t < \frac{3\pi}{2} \\ 1, & \text{if } \frac{3\pi}{2} < t \leq 2\pi \end{cases} \qquad (16.2)$$

is successively approximated by cosine terms.

It should be clear to the reader, that if a finite sum of sine and cosine functions approximates a function without any errors, the function can be exactly recomputed, if the discrete values a_k and b_k of the occurring frequencies of sine and cosine terms are known. This observation constitutes the basis for the sampling theorem of Sect.1.7.

Let the function $f(t)$ be a given 2π–periodic function. Now the question arises, how the coefficients a_k and b_k for $k \geq 0$ of (16.1) can be computed.

We multiply both sides of (16.1) with $\cos(lt)$ and determine the integral over the interval $[-\pi, \pi]$ of the resulting function. Using the orthogonality of the trigonometric sine and cosine functions, we get

$$a_k = \frac{1}{\pi} \int_{-\pi}^{\pi} f(t) \cos(kt)\, dt \quad . \qquad (16.3)$$

By a multiplication of equation (16.1) with $\sin(lt)$ and subsequent integration we have

$$b_k = \frac{1}{\pi} \int_{-\pi}^{\pi} f(t) \sin(kt)\, dt \quad . \qquad (16.4)$$

Let us compute the Fourier series for the step function (refstep:function) Figure 16.2 shows an example how the even step function is successively approximated by cosine terms. We conclude $b_k = 0$ for all k. The coefficients a_k are computed by the evaluation of (16.3). The occurring integrals over cosine functions are fairly easy to compute and we get:

$$a_k = \begin{cases} 0, & \text{if } k \text{ is even} \\ \frac{4}{k\pi}, & \text{otherwise} \end{cases} \qquad (16.5)$$

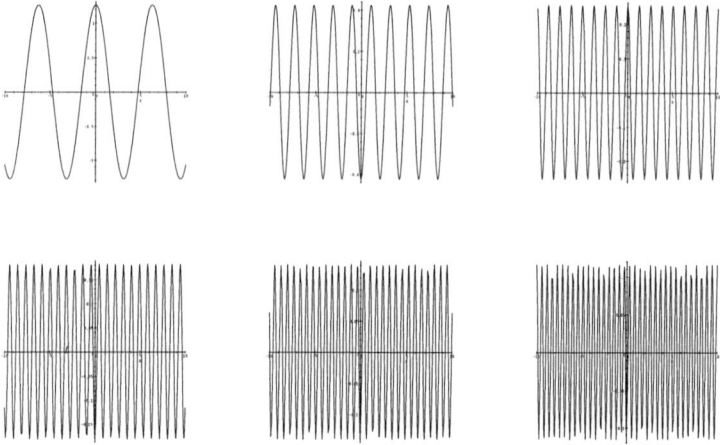

Figure 16.1   First 6 summands of the Fourier series for the function (16.2)

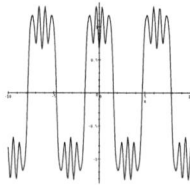

Figure 16.2   Superposition of the functions in Figure 16.1

Figure 16.1 shows the first summands of the resulting Fourier series and Figure 16.2 illustrates the superposition of these functions, which demonstrates that the Fourier series will converge against the step function.

Fourier series can also be written in complex form. By the use of the Eulerian formula

$$e^{\pm i\phi} \;=\; \cos\phi \pm i\sin\phi \quad, \tag{16.6}$$

the trigonometric functions can be written in terms of exponential functions.

$$\cos(kt) \;=\; \frac{1}{2}(e^{ikt} + e^{-ikt}) \tag{16.7}$$

$$\sin(kt) \;=\; \frac{1}{2i}(e^{ikt} - e^{-ikt}) \tag{16.8}$$

Consequently, we can approximate the function using a complex series.

$$f(t) \;=\; \frac{1}{2\pi} \sum_{k=-\infty}^{+\infty} c_k e^{ikt} \quad, \tag{16.9}$$

where

$$c_k = \left\{ \begin{array}{ll} \pi(a_k - i\,b_k), & \text{if } k \geq 0 \\ \pi(a_{|k|} + i\,b_{|k|}), & \text{otherwise} \end{array} \right. . \tag{16.10}$$

The formula for computing the weights of each complex summand is easily shown to be:

$$c_k \;=\; \int_{-\pi}^{\pi} f(t)e^{-ikt}dt \quad. \tag{16.11}$$

Even functions have no complex parts in their Fourier series, because there are no sine terms.

Let us now assume that the interval of periodicity of the function $f(t)$ is infinite. The sum of (16.9) will become an integral and the coefficients c_k will become a continuous weight function $c(k)$ with respect to the variable k

$$c(k) \;=\; \int_{-\infty}^{+\infty} f(t)e^{-ikt}dt \quad. \tag{16.12}$$

The weight function $c(k)$ is usually called the *Fourier transform* of the function $f(t)$. In the following we will denote the Fourier transform of $f(t)$ by

$$F(\xi) \;=\; \int_{-\infty}^{+\infty} f(t)e^{-i\xi t}dt := FT(f) \quad. \tag{16.13}$$

The Fourier transform of a function represents the amplitude of each frequency. Some useful and often needed properties of this transform are summarized in Table 16.1. The proofs are elementary and left as an exercise to the reader. The symmetry character shows that the inverse of the Fourier transform is again a Fourier transform. Thus, the computational complexity of the inverse Fourier transform is identical to the calculation of Fourier transform itself.

	spatial domain	frequency domain
scaling	$f(at)$	$\frac{1}{|a|}F(\frac{\xi}{a})$
shifting	$f(t - t_0)$	$e^{-i\xi t_0}F(\xi)$
symmetry	$F(t)$	$f(-\xi)$
differentiation	$\frac{d^n f(t)}{d\,t^n}$	$(i\,\xi)^n\,F(\xi)$

Table 16.1   Some properties of the Fourier transform

One fundamental property of the Fourier transform is the *convolution theorem*. It states, that for the function

$$h(t) \;=\; f(t) \star g(t) = \int_{-\infty}^{+\infty} f(x)\,g(t-x)\,dx \qquad (16.14)$$

the Fourier transform satisfies the equation

$$H(\xi) = F(\xi)\,G(\xi) \quad , \qquad (16.15)$$

since due to the shifting property of the Fourier transform we get

$$H(\xi) \;=\; \int_{-\infty}^{+\infty} h(t)e^{-i\xi t}\,dt = \int_{-\infty}^{+\infty}\int_{-\infty}^{+\infty} f(x)\,g(t-x)\,dx\,e^{-i\xi t}\,dt$$

$$=\; \int_{-\infty}^{+\infty} f(x)e^{-i\xi x}\,G(\xi)\,dx = F(\xi)\,G(\xi) \quad . \qquad (16.16)$$

This theorem shows that the computation of the convolution of two functions can be done by the multiplication of the Fourier transform of both functions and a subsequent use of the inverse Fourier transform.

The more convenient application of the convolution theorem is the determination of the function $f(t)$ from equation (16.14), if $g(t)$ and $h(t)$ are known. One well known application of this technique is the analysis of time–invariant linear systems (see [Nie83]).

$$h(t) = f(t) \star g(t) \quad \text{-----------} \longrightarrow \quad f(t)$$

FT $\qquad\qquad\qquad\qquad\qquad\qquad$ FT^{-1}

$$H(\xi) = F(\xi)\, G(\xi) \quad\longrightarrow\quad F(\xi) = \frac{H(\xi)}{G(\xi)}$$

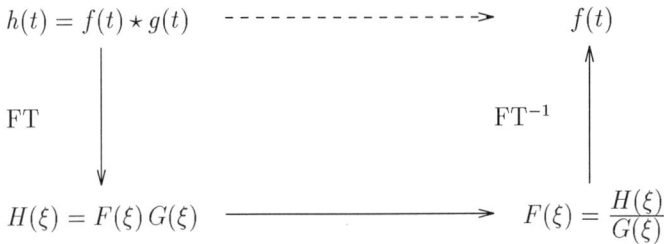

Figure 16.3 Application of the convolution theorem

The principle of this process is shown in Figure 16.3. Computations using this homomorphism are in general less complex than the direct use of the convolution theorem. This is especially the case when several convolutions have to be computed in series.

16.2 Discrete Fourier Transform

If we have to compute the Fourier transform of a recorded speech signal with the sequence of sampling values $f_0, f_1, \ldots, f_{M-1}$, we need the discrete version of the Fourier transform.

$$F_\nu = \sum_{j=0}^{M-1} f_j e^{-i2\pi \frac{j\nu}{M}} =: DFT\{f\} \tag{16.17}$$

The computation of the *discrete Fourier transform* and its inverse can easily be done, because it is a linear transform, which thus can be written in matrix form. The discrete Fourier transform F_ν is a linear combination of powers of the solutions of the equation

$$x^M - 1 = 0 \ . \tag{16.18}$$

Let $m^{j\nu} := e^{-i2\pi \frac{j\nu}{M}}$ denote powers of the solutions of above equation. We conclude $\sum_{j=0}^{M-1} e^{-i2\pi \frac{j}{M}} = 0$. Using definition (16.17) for $\nu = 0, 1, 2, \ldots, M-1$, we get the following linear system of equations for discrete Fourier coefficients:

$$
\begin{pmatrix} F_0 \\ F_1 \\ F_2 \\ \vdots \\ F_{M-1} \end{pmatrix} = \underbrace{\begin{pmatrix} 1 & 1 & \cdots & 1 \\ 1 & m & \cdots & m^{M-1} \\ 1 & m^2 & \cdots & m^{2(M-1)} \\ \vdots & \vdots & \vdots & \vdots \\ 1 & m^{M-1} & \cdots & m^{(M-1)^2} \end{pmatrix}}_{\boldsymbol{D}_m} \begin{pmatrix} f_0 \\ f_1 \\ f_2 \\ \vdots \\ f_{M-1} \end{pmatrix} \tag{16.19}
$$

The inverse discrete Fourier transform DFT^{-1} can be computed by inverting the matrix $\boldsymbol{D}_m$. Due to the fact that the components of $\boldsymbol{D}_m$ are $(\boldsymbol{D}_m)_{u,v} = m^{uv}$, we conclude

$$
(\boldsymbol{D}_m \cdot \boldsymbol{D}_{m^{-1}})_{u,v} = \left(\sum_{k=0}^{M-1} m^{uk} m^{-kv} \right)_{i,j} = \begin{cases} M, & \text{if } u = v \\ 0, & \text{otherwise} \end{cases} \tag{16.20}
$$

The inverse discrete Fourier transform is thus given by a linear mapping defined by the matrix

$$
(\boldsymbol{D}_m)^{-1} = \frac{1}{M} \boldsymbol{D}_{m^{-1}} , \tag{16.21}
$$

where

$$
\boldsymbol{D}_{m^{-1}} = \begin{pmatrix} 1 & 1 & \cdots & 1 \\ 1 & m^{-1} & \cdots & m^{-(M-1)} \\ 1 & m^{-2} & \cdots & m^{-2(M-1)} \\ \vdots & \vdots & \vdots & \vdots \\ 1 & m^{-(M-1)} & \cdots & m^{-(M-1)^2} \end{pmatrix} \tag{16.22}
$$

The properties of the Fourier transform shown in Figure 16.1 are also valid for its discrete version. The computation of the discrete Fourier transform using above matrix notation requires M^2 operations of addition and multiplication.

16.3   Fast Fourier Transform

The complexity of determining the discrete Fourier transform can be reduced to $O(M \log M)$ using the idea of Cooley and Tukey [Kro79].

The basic assumption of the fast Fourier transform is that the number of discrete sampling values is $M = 2n$. From the previous section we know that

$$F_\nu = \sum_{j=0}^{M-1} f_j \, m^{j\nu} \quad ; \qquad\qquad (16.23)$$

thus we get for $0 \leq u \leq n$ the following formulas for the values of the discrete Fourier transform divided up into even and odd indices:

$$F_{2u} = \sum_{j=0}^{n-1} (f_j + f_{n+j}) \, m^{2uj} \qquad\qquad (16.24)$$

$$F_{2u+1} = \sum_{j=0}^{n-1} (f_j - f_{n+j}) \, m^j \, m^{2uj} \quad . \qquad\qquad (16.25)$$

We conclude that for the computation of the DFT for $M = 2n$ sampling points we have to do $2n$ operations of addition, n operations of multiplication, and finally two discrete Fourier transforms of order n. By successively applying above idea, this algorithm for computing the DFT is bounded by $O(M \log M)$. Implementation details and a more detailed discussion of the fast Fourier transform can be found in [Nie83] and [Kro79].

16.4   2D Fourier Transform

The Fourier transform can be extended to arbitrary dimensions. For image processing purposes the two–dimensional Fourier transform is needed. The discrete Fourier transform for 2D signal is defined as

$$F_{\mu,\nu} = \sum_{u=0}^{N-1} \sum_{v=0}^{M-1} f_{u,v} e^{-i2\pi \frac{u\mu}{N}} e^{-i2\pi \frac{v\nu}{M}} = \sum_{u=0}^{N-1} \left(\sum_{v=0}^{M-1} f_{u,v} e^{-i2\pi \frac{v\nu}{M}} \right) e^{-i2\pi \frac{u\mu}{N}} \quad (16.26)$$

Equation (16.26) shows that the 2D DFT can be decomposed into two subsequent one–dimensional Fourier transforms. The continuous version of the two–dimensional extension is straightforward. The result of the DFT applied to an image is shown in Figure 16.4 The right image shows the real part and the right image the imaginary part of the discrete Fourier transform.

The discrete Fourier transform of an image shows so called "spatial frequencies" Many rapid gray–level changes mean high frequency in the direction of these changes. The typical cross in Figure 16.4 results from digitalization which cuts the image into rectangular pieces.

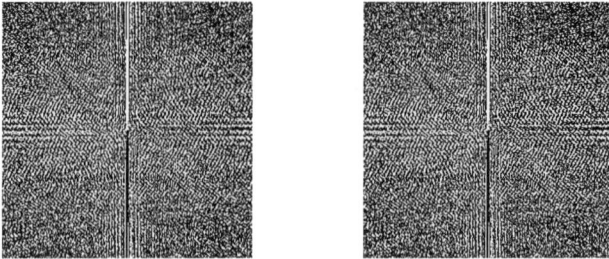

Figure 16.4 Fourier transformed image (Figure 19.1) real and imaginary part as gray values

16.5 Short time Fourier analysis

Speech signals are usually divided up into short intervals of equal length, called *frames*. The length of those intervals has to be large enough to include the typical information of the speech signal. But, the frequency should not vary too much within the chosen frame, i.e. the frame should be relatively short. In general, those windows have a duration of 10–20 ms and they can overlap. The overlapping part may be weighted with different values [Nie90b]. The Fourier transform of these short frames is called *short time Fourier analysis*.

The basic model of speech production states that a speech sample sequence results from a convolution of the excitation and the impulse response of the vocal tract in the time domain [Hua90, Nie90b]. The convolution theorem for Fourier transforms states that the convolution of two functions corresponds to a multiplication of their Fourier transforms. If the convolution kernel of the vocal tract is known the Fourier transform of the input signal can be computed by a simple division. This is, of course, also valid for the short time Fourier analysis.

Fundamental in the field of signal processing is the spectrum, which is a measure for the energy of different frequencies. Let $f(t)$ be a continuous speech signal. The energy of this signal is defined by

$$E \quad = \quad = \int_{-\infty}^{+\infty} \left(\int_{-\infty}^{+\infty} f(t) e^{-i\xi t} \, dt \right)^2 \, d\xi \quad , \tag{16.27}$$

where the argument of the outer integral is called *energy spectrum*. The computation of the energy spectrum for the complete speech signal is not useful, because changes of the spectrum within the signal include a high degree of information. Therefore, the integrand of the signal's Fourier transform is weighted by a *window function* and short time Fourier analysis is used.

$$F(\tau, \xi) = \int_{-\infty}^{+\infty} w(\tau - t) f(t) e^{-i\xi t} \, dt \quad . \tag{16.28}$$

Established window functions are the rectangular, the Hamming, and Hanning window function (see [Nie90b], p. 38 for definitions). The representation of the speech signal using $|F(\tau, \xi)|$ is called a *spectrum*. Figure 16.5 shows a speech signal and its spectrogram.

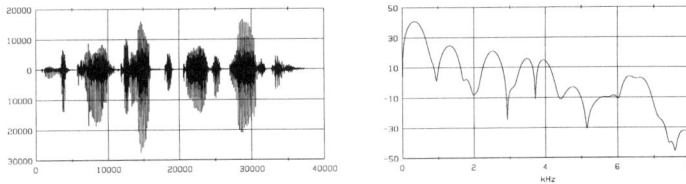

Figure 16.5 Utterance "The pan galactic gurgle blaster" and its logarithmic spectrum.

Another fundamental spectral feature is the so called *cepstrum*, which is defined by

$$T_c(f) = FT^{-1}(\log(FT(f))) \quad . \tag{16.29}$$

A more detailed discussion of different spectral features and their use for speech recognition applications can be found in [Hua90, Nie90b].

16.6   Linear Predictive Coding

Linear predictive coding (LPC) provides a complete model for speech production. The basic idea of LPC is that each discrete value of the speech sample f_n

can be approximated by a linear combination of a finite number of previous samples.

$$\hat{f}_n \;=\; \sum_{\mu=1}^{M} a_\mu f_{n-\mu} \;.$$ (16.30)

The predictor coefficients $a_\mu \in \mathbb{R}$ of the linear combination (16.30) are computed by minimizing the mean–square error ϵ of the prediction.

$$\epsilon \;=\; \sum_{n=n_0}^{n_1} (f_n - \hat{f}_n)^2$$ (16.31)

The optimization of (16.31) can be done by computing the zero crossings of the first partial derivatives with respect to a_μ. Obviously, this results in a system of linear equations for the coefficients a_μ, which can be solved using the standard techniques of linear algebra. A very efficient way to solve the resulting equations is due to Levinson (see [Nie83], p. 99).

Another, equivalent, algebraic approach for computing the prediction coefficients is based on linear regression. For all samples f_n $(n_0 \le n \le n_1)$ the linear combination (16.30) can be written in form of a matrix equation

$$\begin{pmatrix} f_{n_0} \\ f_{n_0+1} \\ f_{n_0+2} \\ \vdots \\ f_{n_1} \end{pmatrix} = \underbrace{\begin{pmatrix} f_{n_0-M} & f_{n_0-M+1} & \cdots & f_{n_0} \\ f_{n_0+1-M} & f_{n_0-M+2} & \cdots & f_{n_0+1} \\ f_{n_0+2-M} & f_{n_0-M+3} & \cdots & f_{n_0+2} \\ \vdots & \vdots & \vdots & \vdots \\ f_{n_1-M} & f_{n_1-M+1} & \cdots & f_{n_1} \end{pmatrix}}_{\boldsymbol{M}} \begin{pmatrix} a_1 \\ a_2 \\ a_3 \\ \vdots \\ a_M \end{pmatrix} .$$ (16.32)

In general, this system of equation will not be solvable. The mean–square error of the prediction gives the solution of the auxiliary system of equations, where both sides of equation (16.32) are multiplied by $\boldsymbol{M}^T$ from the left:

$$\boldsymbol{M}^T \begin{pmatrix} f_{n_0} \\ f_{n_0+1} \\ f_{n_0+2} \\ \vdots \\ f_{n_1} \end{pmatrix} = \boldsymbol{M}^T \boldsymbol{M} \begin{pmatrix} a_1 \\ a_2 \\ a_3 \\ \vdots \\ a_M \end{pmatrix} .$$ (16.33)

This new system of equations (16.33) minimizes the mean–square error (16.31) for the following reason: The matrix M defines a mapping from $\mathbb{R}^M$ into $\mathbb{R}^{n_1-n_0}$. If there exists no $a = (a_1, a_2, \ldots, a_M)^T$ which satisfies equations (16.32), we conclude that the vector $f = (f_{n_0}, f_{n_0+1}, \ldots, f_{n_1})^T$ is not element of the range of matrix M, which is a sub–vector space of $\mathbb{R}^{n_1-n_0}$. The minimization of the mean–square error is equivalent to solving the system of linear equations

$$M\,a \;=\; P\,f \; , \qquad\qquad (16.34)$$

where $P\,f$ is the orthogonal projection of f onto the sub–space for the range of matrix M (Figure 16.6). The orthogonal projection coincides with

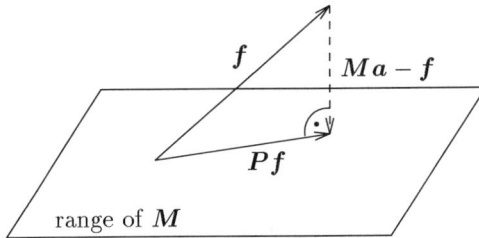

Figure 16.6   Orthogonal projection on the range of matrix M

$$(M\,a - f)\,M\,v = 0 \qquad\qquad (16.35)$$

for all $v \in \mathbb{R}^M$, which is equivalent to

$$(M^T M\,a - M^T f)v = 0. \qquad\qquad (16.36)$$

Since (16.36) has to be valid for all vectors v of the domain of matrix m, we conclude that the best parameter vector a with respect to criterion (16.31) can be computed by solving (16.33).

One common problem in using linear prediction is the question how many predecessors of f_n should be involved in the linear combination. Experience shows that the sampling rate in kHz plus 4 or 5 is a suitable number of prediction coefficients ([Nie83], p. 100).

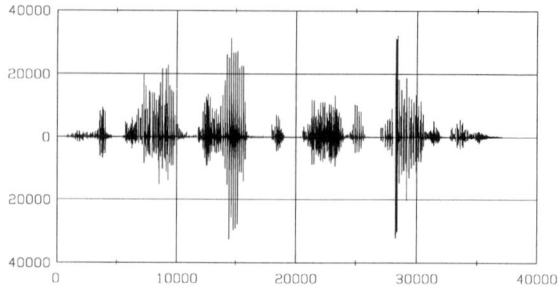

Figure 16.7 Resynthetized speech signal of Figure 16.5 using LPC with 10 prediction coefficients.

The practical use of LPC coefficients is multifarious. One common application is speech encoding. Figure 16.7 shows a re–synthesized speech signal using 10 LPC coefficients for each sample value. LPC coefficients for different speech signals differ. Thus, the vector of LPC coefficients serve as a feature vector for discriminating signals of different classes. Besides the coefficient list a, usually the mean–square error (16.31) is also used as an additional component of the feature vector. Instead of applying the discrete Fourier transform to the sample values of the speech signal we can also compute the DFT for the LPC coefficients. The result is called the *LPC spectrum* and its local extrema are important features for distinguishing vocals ([Nie83], p. 108).

16.7 Dynamic Time Warping

The classification of speech signals can be done by a comparison of an input signal and a sequence of features with a reference pattern. For that purpose, one can use for instance the sample values, cepstral features, zero crossings of the speech signal, the discussed LPC coefficients, or their spectrum. The easiest way to solve this problem is through a simple computation of the features' distances along corresponding time and accumulation. This simple distance measure has proven to be unsatisfactory for practical purposes [Nie83]. Depending on the speed of speaking, speech signals can be stretched or compressed. The accuracy of the distance measure significantly increases through the use of a non–linear mapping of the speech signal and minimizes the effect of stretching and compressing.

Let the sequence of samples of the speech signal be $f_0, f_1, \ldots, f_{n-1}$ and the samples of the reference $f_{\lambda,0}, f_{\lambda,1}, \ldots, f_{\lambda,m-1}$. The sequence of matched pairs will be denoted by the corresponding indices

$$S = ((i(0), j(0)), (i(1), j(1)), \ldots, (i(k), j(k))) \quad , \tag{16.37}$$

where k is the number of assignments between the observed pattern and the reference and a pair $(i(l), j(l))$ denotes the correspondence of $f_{\lambda,i(l)}$ and $f_{j(l)}$. In speech recognition applications the set of corresponding indices is usually restricted to special types of index pairs. This can be done by defining continuity and monocity constraints. For instance, the constraint

$$(i(l), j(l)) \quad \in \quad \{(i(l-1), k(l-1)+1), (i(l-1)+1, k(l-1+1)), \\ (i(l-1)+1, k(l-1))\} \tag{16.38}$$

is a suitable reduction of the admissible indices.

The optimization problem is the minimization of the accumulated distances for each matching

$$D_\lambda^k \quad = \quad \min_S \sum_{l=1}^{k} d(f_{\lambda,i(l)}, f_{j(l)}) \quad , \tag{16.39}$$

where $d(f_{\lambda,i(l)}, f_{j(l)})$ denotes a suitable distance measure, like for example the Euclidean distance.

An algorithm for the computation of the sequence of index pairs S, which minimizes the distance D_λ^k, results from the application of the *dynamic programming* technique [Big89]. This technique is well known in discrete mathematics and supports the efficiency in computing the non–linear mapping we are looking for. We observe that the distance (16.39) can be decomposed in the following manner

$$D_\lambda^{l+1} \quad = \quad D_\lambda^l + d(f_{\lambda,i(l+1)}, f_{j(l+1)}) \quad . \tag{16.40}$$

This additive decomposition allows the conclusion that given an optimal path $S_{i(l),j(l)}$ from the staring point $(0,0)$ to $(i(l),j(l))$, all other optimal paths for the successive index pair $(i(l+1),j(l+1))$, which should also include $(i(l),j(l))$, enclose the optimal path $S_{i(l),j(l)}$. Consequently, the search for the optimal path S avoids the evaluation of all possible paths. The combinatorial search space is drastically reduced and only the best alignments for a subsequence ending up in a special pair $(i(l),j(l))$ have to be stored.

An object–oriented implementation of the dynamic time warping algorithm should be as general as possible. There are two degrees of freedom: on the one hand the algorithm should be parameterized regarding the distance measure d for comparing two sample values; on the other hand the exchange of the needed neighborhood functions should be easily possible.

These demands can be realized by defining a class DP with the header file of Example 153.

```
class DP {
 protected:
   doubleArray reference;    // reference pattern

 public:
   DP(void);                 // default constructor
   DP(const doubleArray&);   // constructor with reference pattern
   DP(const DP&);            // copy constructor

   double distance(const doubleArray& o, int ref_pos, int obs_pos);

 protected:
   virtual double distance_measure(double a, double b);
   virtual intArray2d neighborhood (int p1, int p2);
};
```
(153)

The methods distance_measure and neighborhood are declared to be virtual functions. Changes of virtual functions can be implemented in derived classes. These modifications in the methods distance_measure and neighborhood will be transparent to the method distance of the base class DP. The implementation shown in Example 154 is straightforward using (16.39) combined with (16.40).

```
double DP::distance(const doubleArray& o,int ref_pos, int obs_pos){
  if (ref_pos<=0 && obs_pos<=0)
    return distance_measure(o[0],reference[0]);
  intArray2d neigh= neighborhood(ref_pos,obs_pos);
  double    act_val= distance(o,neigh[0][0],neigh[0][1]);
  for (int i=1; i<neigh.getysize(); i++){

    double new_val= distance(o,neigh[i][0],neigh[i][1]);
    if (new_val<act_val) act_val= new_val;
  }
  act_val+= distance_measure(o[obs_pos],reference[ref_pos]);
  return act_val;
}
```
(154)

Dynamic programming is also applied for solving image processing problems. For example, line following algorithms are based on the above introduced ideas [Bal82, Pit93].

16.8   Hidden Markov Models

Dynamic time warping, as described in the section before, is a powerful tool for the classification of speech signals. The success of speech recognition systems, however, is not based on the use of this technique. Statistical methods dealing with stochastic automata are actually a more established tool. The advantages of statistical approaches for solving classification problems are:

1. Statistical approaches can deal with uncertainties in a natural manner.

2. The classifier is trainable; a sufficient set of training samples is used to adopt the free parameters by mathematical estimation techniques.

3. The application of the maximum a posteriori decision rule leads to an optimal classification system with respect to the probability of misclassifications.

One established stochastic automaton is the *Hidden Markov Model* (HMM). This statistical model generates a set of output symbols. Each observable symbol is emitted in a state of the of the automaton with a certain probability. A measure for a sequence of observed features is therefore the probability for this ordered set of features to be an output sequence of a given HMM.

An HMM consists of states, transitions among states, and emission probabilities for elements of a given alphabet. A HMM with N states $\{S_1, \ldots, S_N\}$ is described by a triple $\boldsymbol{\lambda} = (\boldsymbol{\pi}, \boldsymbol{A}, \boldsymbol{B})$, where $\boldsymbol{\pi} = (\pi_1, \pi_2, \ldots, \pi_N)$ is the vector of probabilities, that the generation of a sequence of output elements starts at a certain state S_i, i.e. $\pi_i = P(s_1 = S_i)$. The state transition matrix $\boldsymbol{A} = (a_{i,j})_{0 < i \leq N, 0 < j \leq N}$ includes the probabilities $a_{i,j} = P(s_t = S_j \,|\, s_{t-1} = S_i)$ to change from state S_i to state S_j. The components of the vector $\boldsymbol{\pi}$ and the matrix $\boldsymbol{A}$ are probabilities and this implies

$$\sum_{i=1}^{N} \pi_i = 1 \quad \text{and} \quad \sum_{i,j=1}^{N} a_{i,j} = N \quad . \tag{16.41}$$

The third element of $\boldsymbol{\lambda}$ is either a matrix $\boldsymbol{B} = (b_i(\boldsymbol{o}_l))_{0 < i \leq N, 0 < l < L}$ describing discrete probabilities $b_i(\boldsymbol{o}_l) = P(\boldsymbol{o}_l \,|\, s_t = S_i)$ for observing an output symbol $\boldsymbol{o}_l$ in the state S_i, or a vector of density functions. The random variable $\boldsymbol{o}_l$ is in the discrete case an element of a finite alphabet $\boldsymbol{O} = \{\boldsymbol{o}_1, \boldsymbol{o}_2, \ldots, \boldsymbol{o}_L\}$.

The name "Hidden Markov Model" originates from the fact that for an observable sequence of output symbols, it is unknown which state sequence caused this. The structure may, however, be known, e.g. some transitions are impossible ($a_{i,j} = 0$). Figure 16.8 shows one example for a HMM with three states. The emission probabilities are left out in the figure.

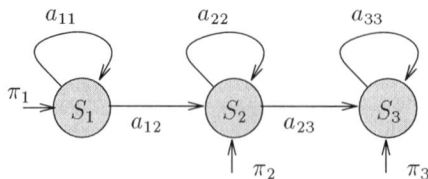

Figure 16.8 "Left right" HMM

During the training phase of an HMM, the set of parameters $\boldsymbol{\lambda}$ – including the emission probabilities, transition probabilities, and the probability of beginning at a certain state – have to be estimated. There exist different techniques for computing statistical parameters from a set of observable training samples. In connection with HMM we compute the parameters such that for all observed learning sequences O_k ($1 \leq k \leq K$) the a priori probability $P(O_k \mid \lambda)$ is maximized. This parameter estimation procedure is unsupervised, because it is not known which state sequence has generated the observable output symbols (Figure 16.9). Thus, we have to use parameter estimation techniques which can deal with such a type of incomplete data. The computation of the parameters for the HMM λ is done iteratively by

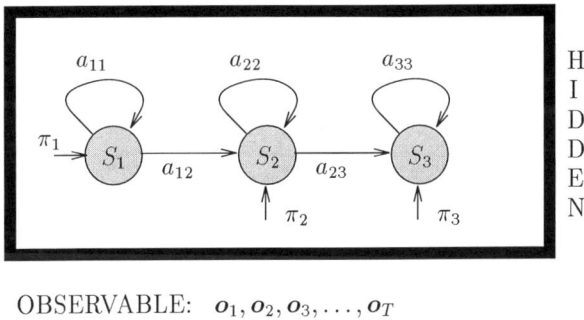

OBSERVABLE: $o_1, o_2, o_3, \ldots, o_T$

Figure 16.9 The hidden statistical processes and an observable feature sequence for parameter estimation

applying the *Expectation Maximization* algorithm (EM algorithm, [Dem77]). $\lambda^{(0)}$ is an initialization of the HMM parameters and the reestimation for the model parameters $\lambda^{(n+1)} = (\pi^{(n+1)}, A^{(n+1)}, B^{(n+1)})$ is done using the model $\lambda^{(n)} = (\pi^{(n)}, A^{(n)}, B^{(n)})$ by the *Baum Welch* formulas

$$\pi_i^{(n+1)} = \frac{P(s_1 = S_i, O \mid \lambda^{(n)})}{P(O \mid \lambda^{(n)})} \quad , \tag{16.42}$$

$$a_{i,j}^{(n+1)} = \frac{\sum_{t=1}^{T-1} P(s_t = S_i, s_{t+1} = S_j, O \mid \lambda^{(n)})}{\sum_{j=1}^{N} \sum_{t=1}^{T-1} P(s_t = S_i, s_{t+1} = S_j, O \mid \lambda^{(n)})} \quad , \tag{16.43}$$

$$b_i^{(n+1)}(o_j) = \frac{\displaystyle\sum_{t \in \{t \mid o_t = o_j\}} P(s_t = S_i, O \mid \lambda^{(n)})}{\displaystyle\sum_{t=1}^{T} P(s_t = S_i, O \mid \lambda^{(n)})} \; . \tag{16.44}$$

The theory of the EM algorithm [Wu83] ensures the convergence of this reestimation technique and states

$$P(O \mid \lambda^{(n)}) \leq P(O \mid \lambda^{(n+1)}) \; . \tag{16.45}$$

The iterations terminate if the identity in (16.45) is satisfied or $P(O \mid \lambda^{(n)}) - P(O \mid \lambda^{(n+1)}) < \epsilon$, for a sufficient small threshold ϵ.

A detailed derivation of above training formulas can be found in [Bau67]. Nevertheless, the EM iterations provide only convergence against a local maximum. Thus, the initialization of the model parameters $\lambda^{(0)}$ is crucial for a successful training. See for example [Rab88] for a discussion of this initialization task.

The Bayesian decision rule is used in the recognition stage, i.e. the a posteriori probability $P(\lambda \mid O)$ for an observed feature sequence O has to be computed, in order to find out which of a given set $\{\lambda_1, \lambda_2, \ldots, \lambda_k\}$ of HMMs most likely created the feature sequence. The decision rule for recognition depends on the computation of

$$\max_l P(\lambda_l \mid O) = \max_l \frac{P(\lambda_l) P(O \mid \lambda_l)}{P(O)} \; , \tag{16.46}$$

where the complexity of determining $P(O \mid \lambda_l)$ is bounded by $O(N^2 T)$, presupposed the *forward–backward* algorithm [Hua90] is used. An obvious way of computing $P(O \mid \lambda_l)$ is to use the marginal density over all possible state sequences which might have produced the given observation, i.e.

$$P(O \mid \lambda_l) = \sum_s P(s, O \mid \lambda) = \sum_s \pi_{s_1} \prod_{t=1}^{T-1} a_{s_t, s_{t+1}} \prod_{t=1}^{T} b_{s_t}(o_t) \; . \tag{16.47}$$

Formula (16.47) leads to an exponential run time behavior. A relatively simple but tricky algorithm reduces this complexity: we define the *forward variable*

$$\alpha_{t,i} = P(o_1, o_2, \ldots, o_t, s_t = S_i \mid \lambda_l) \tag{16.48}$$

to be the probability of observing the first t symbols and being in state S_i after these t steps. The value of the forward variable in the first step is

input: $\boldsymbol{O} = (\boldsymbol{o}_1, \boldsymbol{o}_2, \ldots, \boldsymbol{o}_T)$
FOR i=1 to N
$\alpha_{1,i} = \pi_i b_i(\boldsymbol{o}_1)$
FOR t=2 to T
FOR j=1 to N
compute $\alpha_{t+1,j} = \left(\sum_{i=1}^{N} \alpha_{t,i} a_{i,j} \right) b_j(\boldsymbol{o}_l)$
output: $\sum_{j=1}^{N} \alpha_{T,j}$

Figure 16.10 Forward algorithm

$$\alpha_{1,i} = \pi_i b_i(\boldsymbol{o}_1) \quad , \tag{16.49}$$

i.e. the probability of starting at S_i and producing the output symbol $\boldsymbol{o}_1$. The probability for observing at time $t + 1$ the symbol $\boldsymbol{o}_{t+1}$ and being in state S_j can be defined recursively by:

$$\alpha_{t+1,j} = \left(\sum_{i=1}^{N} \alpha_{t,i} a_{i,j} \right) b_j(\boldsymbol{o}_l) \quad . \tag{16.50}$$

Here, $\sum_{i=1}^{N} \alpha_{t,i} a_{i,j}$ is the probability of being in any state S_i after t steps, having produced the sequence $\boldsymbol{o}_1, \boldsymbol{o}_2, \ldots, \boldsymbol{o}_t$, and turning into S_j.

Finally, the probability of producing a sequence of observations $P(\boldsymbol{O} \,|\, \boldsymbol{\lambda}_l)$ can be written as the marginal density over all admissible end states:

$$P(\boldsymbol{O} \,|\, \boldsymbol{\lambda}_l) = \sum_{j=1}^{N} \alpha_{T,j} \quad . \tag{16.51}$$

Figure 16.10 summarizes the forward algorithm.

The optimal state sequence for an observation $\boldsymbol{O}$ is computed using the Viterbi algorithm [Rab88].

We define the highest probability for a partial path ending up in state S_i:

$$\delta_{t,i} = \max_{s_1, s_2, \ldots, s_{t-1}} P(s_1, s_2, \ldots, s_t = S_i, \boldsymbol{o}_1, \boldsymbol{o}_2, \ldots, \boldsymbol{o}_t | \boldsymbol{\lambda}_l) \quad . \tag{16.52}$$

A recursive computation of the measure can be done based on the following observation: the highest probability of being after $t + 1$ steps in the state S_j only depends on the transition probabilities $a_{i,j}$, $(1 \le i \le N)$, and the probabilities for pathes through the model of length t. By multiplying the output probability of the $t + 1$ observation we get:

$$\delta_{t+1,j} = \max_i \left\{\delta_{t,i} a_{i,j}\right\} \cdot b_j(o_{t+1}) \quad . \tag{16.53}$$

These considerations show that the principle of optimality is valid and the dynamic programming technique can be applied to solve this problem. The above described optimization task is similar to (16.39) and (16.40).

Since we are looking for a path which maximizes (16.53) we have to store the actual state of each step. For that purpose we define the array $\Phi_{t,i}$ for tracing back the optimal path in following algorithm:

1. Initialization: for $1 \leq i \leq N$:

$$
\begin{aligned}
\delta_{1i} &= \pi_i b_i(o_1) \\
\Phi_{1i} &= 0
\end{aligned}
$$

2. Compute recursively: for $2 \leq t \leq T$ and $1 \leq j \leq N$:

$$
\begin{aligned}
\delta_{t,j} &= \max_{1 \leq i \leq N}\left\{\delta_{t-1,i} a_{i,j}\right\} b_j(o_t) \\
\Phi_{t,j} &= \arg\max_{1 \leq i \leq N}\left\{\delta_{t-1,i} a_{i,j}\right\}
\end{aligned}
$$

3. Terminate:

$$
\begin{aligned}
P^* &= \max_{1 \leq i \leq N}\left\{\delta_{Ti}\right\} \\
s_T^* &= \arg\max_{1 \leq i \leq N}\left\{\delta_{Ti}\right\}
\end{aligned}
$$

4. Computation of the optimal path: for $t = T-1, T-2, \ldots, 1$:

$$s_t^* = \Phi_{t+1,s_{t+1}^*} .$$

16.9   Different Types of Hidden Markov Modells

HMMs can be classified with respect to their topological structure and the statistical properties of their output probability functions.

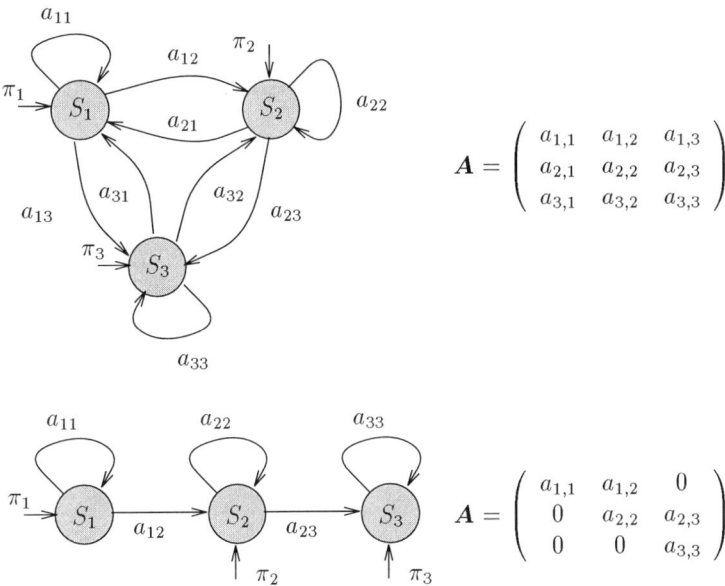

$$A = \begin{pmatrix} a_{1,1} & a_{1,2} & a_{1,3} \\ a_{2,1} & a_{2,2} & a_{2,3} \\ a_{3,1} & a_{3,2} & a_{3,3} \end{pmatrix}$$

$$A = \begin{pmatrix} a_{1,1} & a_{1,2} & 0 \\ 0 & a_{2,2} & a_{2,3} \\ 0 & 0 & a_{3,3} \end{pmatrix}$$

Figure 16.11 Examples for different topologies

Ergodic and *left right* HMMs are the most important topologies for pattern recognition applications. An HMM is called ergodic, if the graph of the stochastic automaton is complete, i.e. for all transitions $a_{i,j}$, $(1 \leq i,j \leq N)$, we have $a_{i,j} \neq 0$. Analogous, the left right HMMs are characterized by the transition probabilities $a_{i,j} = 0$ for $i < j$. Figure 16.11 shows an ergodic and a left right HMM with the corresponding transition matrices.

An HMM is called *discrete*, if the emission probabilities of all states are discrete. For continuous emission density functions we call the HMM *continuous*. For example, the parametric Gaussian density function (7.4) can be used for modeling the output densities.

Exercises

1. Compute the discrete Fourier transform of the following binary image:

$$\begin{pmatrix} 1 & 1 & 1 & 1 \\ 0 & 1 & 1 & 0 \\ 0 & 1 & 1 & 0 \\ 0 & 0 & 0 & 0 \end{pmatrix}$$

2. Find arguments as to why it is not advantageous to implement the two–dimensional Fourier transform as two subsequent 1D Fourier transforms.

3. Typical features of a speech signal are the zero crossings and the slopes in those points. Write a program which computes all zero crossings of a given speech signal. Implement the computation of the slope for a zero crossing. For that purpose define a neighborhood of discrete sample values and use linear regression for determination of the slope.

4. Implement a function which computes the LPC prediction coefficients for each sample of a given speech signal. Use the Gauss elimination procedure for solving the occurring system of linear equations.

5. Extend exercise 4 in Chapter 8.

6. A one–dimensional signal is defined by

t	0	1	2	3	4	5
f_t	2	6	1	-4	-3	0

Compute the coefficients a_1 and a_2 of the linear prediction and use the result for the determination of f_6.

7. Implement the dynamic time warping algorithm using different types of neighborhoods and distance measures. Use dynamic linking and inheritance (see also example 6 of Chapter 17)!

8. Define a class for discrete Hidden Markov Models. Which member variables are needed? Implement methods for learning the parameters of a Hidden Markov Model given a set of observation sequences. Use the cited literature and define methods for computing the probability that a given HMM has generated an observed sequence of features.

9. Work out a concept for a C++ class hierarchy useful for speech processing.

Part III
Pattern Recognition Algorithms

Edge orientation computed on on the image on page 3.

In this part of the book we implement a simple image segmentation system using most of the object–oriented ideas introduced in Part I and Part II.

17 An Image Analysis System

In this chapter we introduce the design of an image analysis system ANIMALS (AN IMage AnaLysis System, [Pau92b]). It is composed of the same classes introduced in the previous sections, especially of those found in Chapter 15. The various image processing algorithms implemented in ANIMALS will be described in following chapters. The C++ function call operator (Sect. 17.7) for classes unifies object–oriented programming and functional syntax. We present a top level program for image segmentation as well.

17.1 Data Flow

Image segmentation was described and presented as a series of steps from the image signal to an initial symbolic description (Sect. 5.5, Figure 5.5). Every step has its own typical algorithms. The implementation of these algorithms as separate processes introduces the problem of how to connect the results. Figuratively speaking, some algorithms skip over a step in Figure 5.5, some introduce intermediate data structures and require other processes before the next step on the staircase can be reached. Through this approach, the image segmentation problem can be seen as one in data flow analysis. A top view of this data flow is shown in Figure 17.1; the dotted lines in this Figure represent the feedback in a closed control loop for active computer vision (Sect. 5.8). Among several alternatives, algorithms suitable for the present task have to be chosen in the segmentation and analysis stage; they have to be connected in a way that will eventually lead to the symbolic description.

The path from images to segmentation objects will be further described in the following section.

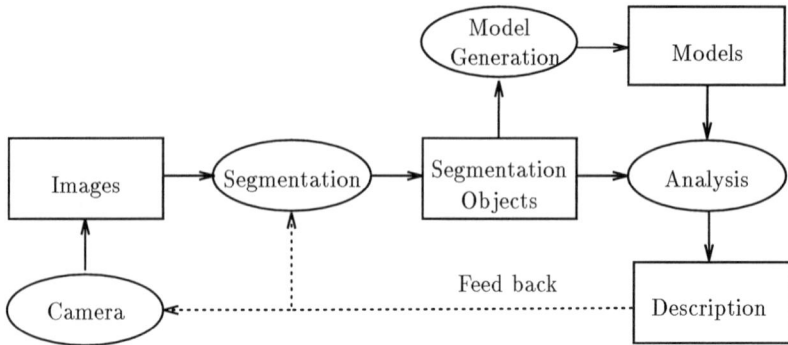

Figure 17.1 Data flow in an image analysis systems

17.2 Design of ANIMALS

The ANIMALS system is designed in an object oriented way according to the data flow in Figure 17.1. Data and algorithms for image processing are organized into hierarchies. Representation of the data uses ἵππος (Chapter 15). Image analysis is mainly seen as a problem of transforming information to other levels of abstraction. Naturally, the transformations are implemented as separate processes.

In this chapter we introduce the basic idea of a hierarchical ordering of algorithms which results in a hierarchy of image processing operators. We concentrate on line–based segmentation and exclude region based methods. In Sect. 17.7 we show how the functional and object–oriented view can be combined.

Figure 17.2 shows the various paths from images to line segments [Pau92c]. On level A, images are created; on level B, images are transformed; in C, edge images are transformed; in D, segmentation objects are processed. The major data classes appearing in this scheme are the intensity images, edge images, chain codes, lines, and segmentation objects which have been introduced in previous chapters. Edge detection leads from intensity images (gray or color) to edge images (arrow 8). The reverse direction (arrow 9) is used for the visualization of edge images (e.g.Figure 13.7). Line detection (Chapter 22) leads from edge images to segmentation objects containing chain codes (arrow 11). Visualization of segmentation objects can be done using raster images (arrow 14) or after conversion to a graphics format (arrow 13). Often, textual descriptions of the objects are desired (arrows 16–18). Some of the other transitions will be mentioned in the next chapters.

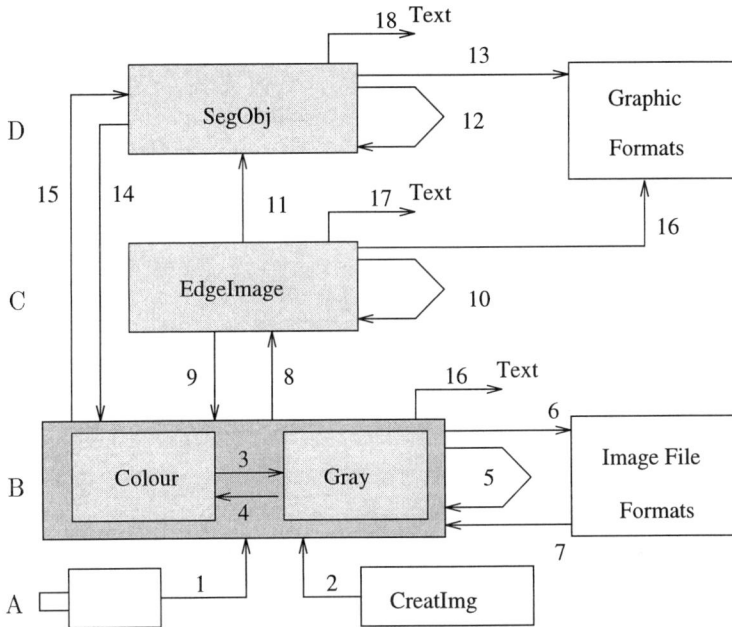

Figure 17.2 Data flow for line–based image segmentation. The arrows indicate processes that transform from one representation to another (cmp. Figure 5.5); they are explained in the text and in Table 17.1.

These transitions from one block to another can be implemented as functions, processes, or operator classes.

Arrow in Figure 17.2	Description	References
1	Sampling theorem	Figure 1.8
2	Synthetic images	Chapter 18
3,4	Color transformation	Eq. 11.3
5	Filters	Chapter 19
6,7	File formats	Sect. 11.4
8	Edge detection	Sect. 13
9	Visualization	Sect. 1.9
10	Edge image transform	Exercise 6
11	Line detection	Chapter 22
12	Line enhancement	Sect. 23
13	Data conversion	—
14	Visualization	Sect. 1.9
15	Segmentation	—
16,17,18	Information	—

Table 17.1   Data flow for line segmentation (refer to Figure 17.2)

17.3   XDR

As indicated in Sect. 15.9, all external representation of objects is done via
XDR. The interfaces between different processing stages can thus be reduced
to the objects passed from one process to another. Since the representation
is machine independent, the processes can run on different architectures.

In an evolving programming environment, changes in classes are common.
Often this requires a change, e.g. an addition, in the external representation.
It is unacceptable that old external data would then have to be discarded as a
result of this change. One possibility is to provide conversion routines which
convert old data to the new format. A more elegant way is to extend the
routines for storage and reading to handle different versions. This way, new
programs will both write new data formats as well as recognize and decode
old formats during read operations. Old programs will of course not be able
to read the new format. Normally, those old programs will either have to
be re–compiled or simply re–linked, depending on the extent of the changes

made. These mechanisms were incorporated into the class XDR without any
changes to the underlying nihcl mechanisms. [1]

17.4   Display and Capture

Naturally, image processing objects will have to be displayed on a raster
display. However, many different hardware solutions exist for image display.
Many of them are encapsulated by the X11 window system. However, display
using dedicated frame grabber cards or external monitors is a common application which is not covered by X11. If every ἵππος–object had an interface
to X11 (e.g. by a virtual method for Display in the class HipposObj, Example 137), programs would have to be linked with X11, even if no display is
actually done in the program. This is due to the fact that the compiler and
linker can generally not decide which virtual function will be actually called.
The linker thus has to include *all* virtual functions for classes which occur in
the source file, including all the virtual functions of all derived classes.

Even if shared libraries, i.e. dynamic linkage at run time of the program, are
used, the inclusion of X11 would be overhead.

The solution in ἵππος can be seen in Example 137 on page 199. A class
is provided for display called a "virtual frame buffer". All display methods
direct their requests to a frame grabber object. This object in turn passes the
display information via remote procedure calls to a *display server*.[2] Different
servers can now act as an interface to either X11 or special frame buffer
hardware.

Similar to image display, image capturing requires interfaces to dedicated
hardware which decreases portability when not handled properly. ANIMALS
has a general class Camera which is specialized to the actual frame grabbing
device and the connected camera. Typical parameters include the actual resolution, the image size, the input timing (PAL, NTSC) and the color space
(Sect. 11.3).

---

[1]It is however not possible to deal with all kinds of changes in a class. For example,
changes in the inheritance scheme can not be easily masked out.

[2]The SUN remote procedure call is used which is also based on XDR, however this
amounts to only a small storage overhead.

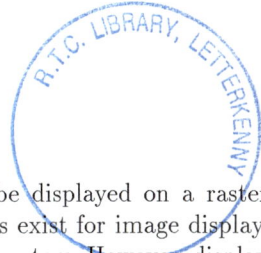

17.5   Graphical User Interfaces

Providing a comfortable user interface with graphical tools for image analysis is a complicated matter. The system Khoros[3] has solved this problem in a brilliant way [Ras92] and further research in the image understanding environment pursues this task (see for example [Har92] and the various articles in the proceedings of the *Image Understanding Workshop*, e.g. [Mun92]).

Real-time image analysis and active vision usually has to be performed without continuous user interaction. Also, graphical interfaces are more useful for program development. In ANIMALS, we can use the X11 tool tcl/tk [Ous94]. A graphical shell is put around the program which is used for argument processing in a text window and may display input and results in separate windows.

17.6   Geometric Distortions

We now interest ourselves in another feature of C++ classes which can simplify the interfaces for image operations. We use a low–level image operation as an example for an object–oriented implementation of operators.

A typical preprocessing step is the inversion of geometric distortions of an input image (arrow 5 in Figure 17.2). Examples may be found in [Nie90a]. An ideal (undistorted) image $s(x,y)$ is observed as $f(u,v)$, whereby the coordinates are distorted by

$$u = \Phi_1(x,y), \qquad v = \Phi_2(x,y) \quad . \tag{17.1}$$

The ideal image can be computed by

$$s(x,y) = f(\Phi_1(x,y), \Phi_2(x,y)) \quad . \tag{17.2}$$

The distortion functions Φ_1, Φ_2 are taken from a parametric family of functions. Typical classes are polynomial, affine, or projective transformations. Φ_1 and Φ_2 may belong to the same class and differ only in the parameters. For example, Φ_1 may be an affine transformation $u = a_{11}x + a_{12}y + a_{13}$ and Φ_2 may be $v = a_{21}x + a_{22}y + a_{23}$.

---

[3]Khoros is in the public domain, see Sect. C.1.

It is convenient, if we can code (17.2) directly into the programming language:

$$s[i,j] = f[Phi1(i,j),Phi2(i,j)]; \qquad (17.3)$$

We would like doing so, since the problem of reconstructing the ideal image is inherently independent of the actual distortion functions. A change in these functions should not affect the algorithm.

Using conventional programming languages, geometric distortions can be implemented as functions. The implementation of (17.2) will call the distortion functions via function pointers (Sect. 8.9).

Now, imagine that Φ_1 and Φ_2 belong to the same class of parametric functions, e.g. 2D affine distortions, and differ only in their coefficients. The major problem then is to combine the function pointers with their parameter sets without duplicating code.

One might attach the parameters as a vector argument to the functions:

$$f[Phi1(i,j,a1),Phi2(i,j,a2)]; \qquad (17.4)$$

However, the number of parameters for the different transformation classes are different (e.g. three parameters for the affine, six for the projective transformation). We can also find examples where the parameters differ not only in number but also in type.

Another similar problem can be formulated when you think of a resolution hierarchy. Imagine that you want to Fourier–transform each image level (Sect. 16.3). Each DFT will need different internal tables for precomputed sine and cosine values, depending on the image size. The algorithm and the function code will be the same for each DFT, however.

17.7 Polymorphic image processing

Section 17.6 showed how mathematicians write down algorithms using functional syntax. The functions Φ_i (resp. Phi1 and Phi2) exhibit *polymorphic* behavior. At the time of the actual computation, they may be either affine transformations or polynomials or perspective transformations, or both affine functions with different parameter sets.

This kind of semantics can be expressed by the syntax of object–oriented programming languages. It greatly simplifies programming and guarantees safe extensibility. If another programmer has to add radial distortions to the above mentioned transformations, the basic idea (and of course, the formula 17.2) would not change. Neither would the (object–oriented) program.

The great advantage of polymorphic functions over conventional function pointers will now be outlined. An abstract super–class provides the general interface to geometric distortions. Special classes inherit the interface and redefine the details.

The following is a simplified piece of C++ code for the declaration of three classes. The class Dist defines the abstract interface which is inherited by the derived classes for polynomial and affine distortion. The virtual constant operator declares an object interface in *functional syntax*. Example 155 shows the declaration of a functional interface using geometric correction classes; the missing parts are left as exercise 1.

```
class Dist {  // abstract class
 public:
    virtual int operator() (int,int) const;
};
class PolyDist: public Dist {
 public:
    virtual int operator()(int,int) const;
};
class AffineDist : public PolyDist {
    double a,b,c;
 public:
    AffineDist(int,int,int); // set a,b,c
    virtual int operator()(int,int) const;
};
```

(155)

The special operator() can be used to address objects like function calls without the need of specifying a method name.

Using the code fragment, a geometric correction mapping function can be written without actually knowing which kind of transformation will be applied. We assume a class for images which provides access mechanisms similar to the mathematical notation above. Distorted image f, corrected image object s, and the two transformation objects Phi1 and Phi2 are passed to the function as arguments (Example 156).

```
void corr(Dist& const Phi1, Dist& const Phi2,
  Image& s, Image& const f)
{
  for(int i = 0; i < s.vsize(); ++i)
    for(int j = 0; j < s.hsize(); ++j)
      s(i,j) = f(Phi1(i,j),Phi2(i,j));
}
```

(156)

Of course, a complete algorithm will have to take care of re–sampling, interpolation, and filtering, etc.

The classes declare a hierarchy of *operations*; instances of these classes (objects) represent the actual (mathematical) parametric function with a fixed set of parameters. For example, an affine transformation $u = 1.1x + 0.9y$ will be an object of class **AffineDist**.

Two distortion objects for affine transformations *share* the code for the computation. They differ in the coefficients (a, b, c) which are bound to the object.

A conventional implementation using function pointers would either have to use a complicated mechanism for linking the coefficients to the computation, or duplicate code in order to provide two functions Phi1 and Phi2, which are textually identical, except for the coefficients of the polynomial. This may be acceptable in this (simple) case; but in general — again, think of a DFT, or of even more complex functions — this will decrease the maintainability of programs. In typical image processing programs *many* simple functions are used; code duplication in several simple functions imposes the same problems on maintainability as duplications in a few complex parts.

If at a later stage, someone decides that radial distortions are required, the function corr in the previous source code fragment will *not* have to be modified. A new class for radial distortions redefining the **operator()(int,int)** will simply be derived from the abstract base class.

An arbitrary number of transformation–objects can be created (and destroyed) during runtime. If, in the conventional solution using duplicated code, three instead of two functions are needed, the code has to be copied again, compiled, linked, etc.

17.8 Efficiency

Sometimes people argue that object–oriented programming adds administrational overhead to the programs thereby causing a slow down in execution speed. This is not always the case, especially not in C++. Efficient image class access was described in Chapter 11. The ANIMALS system is designed to be efficient, both in storage requirements and computation time.

For example, a comparison of the execution times for a geometric distortion in an conventional implementation and the C++ implementation showed *no* measurable differences for affine distortions. The times were measured with `inline` virtual operators and `inline` image access operators. The conventional program used indirect function calls (via function pointer arguments) or direct function calls. In either case, the floating point arithmetic required for the evaluation of the transformation — i.e. the *real* work of the programs — by far exceeded the access and calling mechanisms. The execution times for a geometric correction using the function `corr` were 250 and 251 seconds resp. for a 256^2 image on an IBM PC (Intel SX 386/25 using DJ's GNU g++). On an HP 735 (99 MHz, AT&T C++ 3.1) Unix workstation the times were around 0.2 seconds.

17.9 Image Segmentation Program

In this section we illustrate a top down design of a program for image segmentation. The classes introduced in Part II are used for data representation. Operator classes (Sect. 17.7) are declared for the computation of this information. The actual implementation of these operators will be described in the following chapters and in the appendix.

Example 157 shows the static declarations for the main module. We use pointers to operator objects which can vary upon the actual command line arguments.

```
#include "ipop.h"
static char * inp, *outp, *prog;      // strings
static LowPass * filter = NULL;       // filter object
static EdgeDet * edgdet = NULL;       // edge detection object
static LineDet * lindet = NULL;       // line detection object
static void processArgs(int, char**); // argument processing (157)
```

Example 158 shows the main program. After processing the command line, an image object is read from an XDR stream. Images for intermediate results are created with the same dimension. The input image is filtered with a filter operator object. Algorithms for filters will be described in Chapter 19; operator classes are left as exercise 4 on p. 274.

```
#include "OIOxdr.h"
main(int argc, char **argv)
{
    processArgs(argc,argv);      // command line interpretation
        // read and create images
    printf("%s in: %s out: %s\n", prog, inp, outp);
    GrayLevelImage * f = GrayLevelImage::readFrom(OIOxdrin(inp));
    GrayLevelImage  g (f->getxsize(),f->getysize());
    EdgeImage       h (f->getxsize(),f->getysize());

    (*filter)(*f,g);             // low pass filter on input
    (*edgdet)(g,h);              // detect edge elements
    SegObj s;                    // to hold the results
    (*lindet)(h,s);              // connect edge elements
    s.storeOn(OIOxdrout(outp));  // store on stream
    exit(0);                     // close files, clean up, exit
}                                                           (158)
```

As in Example 156, we do not exactly specify which operator will actually be used; we use a pointer to an operator class which during run time can point to some object of its derived classes.

Edges detected in the filtered image are stored in an edge image. An edge
detection object can be implemented using the algorithms in Chapter 13 and
the exercises on classes on page 298. Edge elements are combined to lines and
stored in a segmentation object. The operator object for this purpose may be
based on the algorithms in Chapter 13 and Example 163. The implementation
of the file animals.h which can be used to compile the program is left as an
exercise.

We now define the functions for argument processing in Example 158. The
function usage is used to report errors or missing arguments (see also Exercises of Chapter 6). This function should be replaced by a more elaborate
version.

```
static void usage(const char * prog, const char * msg)
{
    fprintf(stderr,"%s: error %s\n", prog, msg);
    fprintf(stderr,"%s: usage is %s input output\n", prog, prog);
    exit(1);
}

static void defaultArgs()
{
    if (filter == NULL) filter = new Mean(3,5); // 3 x 5 median
    if (edgdet == NULL) edgdet = new Roberts;
    if (lindet == NULL) lindet = new Hystline;
}
```
(159)

The function processArgs in Example 160 actually interprets the command
line strings and should also be replaced with a comfortable routine. This
routine creates the edge detection object with the use of new.

```
static void processArgs(int argc, char** argv)
{
  prog = *argv++; // save program name
  while (--argc && (argv[0][0] == '-')) {
      if      (strcmp(*argv,"-sobel")==0) edgdet = new Sobel();
      else if (strcmp(*argv,"-gauss")==0) filter = new Gauss();
      else    usage(prog, "unknown option");
      ++argv;
  }
  if (--argc < 0) usage(prog, "missing input file");
  inp  = *argv++;
  if (--argc < 0) usage(prog, "missing output file");
  outp = *argv;
  defaultArgs();
}                                                              (160)
```

The program fragments in Example 157–160 can be combined to a nice image segmentation program. The missing function definitions are left as exercises.

Exercises

1. . The following essential parts are missing in Example 155:

   - the parameters for the polynomial mapping,
   - constructors (setting the parameters),
   - definition of the virtual functions (basically straightforward).

   Complete the example!

2. Extend Example 156 to handle interpolation.

3. Implement a hierarchy of operators and use the function call operator. Use a virtual operator and use pointers to objects. Test which operator is actually called for different assignments to these pointers.

   Write a header file **animals.h** for the declarations of this hierarchy.

4. Write a method *storeOn* which handles revision numbers. Extend your class by one new member and increment the revision. Decode the revision upon reading the data and enable your new program to read old data, for which the new member will be initialized with a default value.

5. Implement a class for image input from your frame grabber card. This should hide all hardware details — as in the case of speech input in Example 32.

6. Apply the technique of polymorphic operators introduced in Sect. 17.7 to the dynamic time warping (Sect. 16.7).

18 Synthetic Signals and Images

When testing new algorithms it is often useful to start experiments using synthetic data. Simple images can for example be generated by a nice interactive facility called popi [Hol88] (see Sect. C).

Many algorithms in the field of low level image and speech processing are concerned with noise reduction in data (see Chapter 19). These techniques are often based on assumptions about special noise distributions. For experimental evaluation of algorithms it is useful to have synthetic image generators for different noise effects, i.e. special distributions of noisy pixels.

In the following sections we describe some programming projects including algorithms for the generation synthetic images and synthetic sound. We describe how to create "magic 3D" images and conclude the chapter with a special case of synthetic images created from speech data.

18.1 Synthetic Sound

For evaluation of the correctness of programs, it is often useful to have an undisturbed input signal with well known features. In Example 31 we already saw a simple version of a sound generating program. This should now be extended to allow for various tests. In addition to the frequency, we need to set the loudness of the sound. Also, rectangular and triangular signals can be generated.[1]

If we want to create a sound signal consisting of several overlayed components, we have several choices. We can either create a program with lots of arguments for the various parameters; or, we can interactively ask for the signals to be generated; or, we can create a set of tools for the composition of sound files.

The last choice has several advantages. Imagine you want to test your large program and need some sound pattern in order to verify correct behavior of

---

[1]Listen to them on your sound device!

your code. You simply write a sequence of sound generation commands in your makefile, compose the outputs, and then run your program on them. This way you will not even have to record which signal is in which file, since this can easily be seen from your makefile.

The required tools are the programs for sound generation, a program which takes an arbitrary number of input files and creates an output signal which contains an addition of the input files,[2] and a program which modifies the amplitude of a given input signal.

18.2   Geometric Patterns

Similar to periodic sound signals, images of two–dimensional geometric objects with known position and shape are often used to test image processing objects. In contrast to computer graphics, usually no realistic imaged is desired. Instead, lines, points, circles, and rectangles — either filled or the contour only — have to be positioned in the synthetic image. Lattices of variable width or chess board patterns are also frequently used.

As in Sect. 18.1, these objects as simply created by a set of tools. Additional tools exist for the combination of images to a new one. Common combinations are image addition, exclusive "or", bit wise and logical "and" and "or", and multiplication of an image with a factor to reduce intensity. Also, combination of three gray level images to a color image can be a nice tool.

18.3   Pixel Noise

Many disturbances in real images are often based on pixel noise. Let us assume that statistically every n–th pixel is disturbed by noise, i.e. every pixel will be disturbed by noise with probability $1/n$.

Write a program which generates a homogeneous black or white gray–level image. Use this image and add in average to each n–th pixel an uniformly

---

[2]The input signals do not have to be combined with addition; there exist cases where a convolution of one with the other makes sense. Also, multiplication can be used in some cases.

distributed gray–level out of the interval $[a, b]$ using modulo arithmetics (see also below, Exercise 2). The parameters n, a and b are initialized by default and the user should have the possibility to adjust these parameters within the function call. In Figure 18.1 some examples are shown for a different choice of parameters.

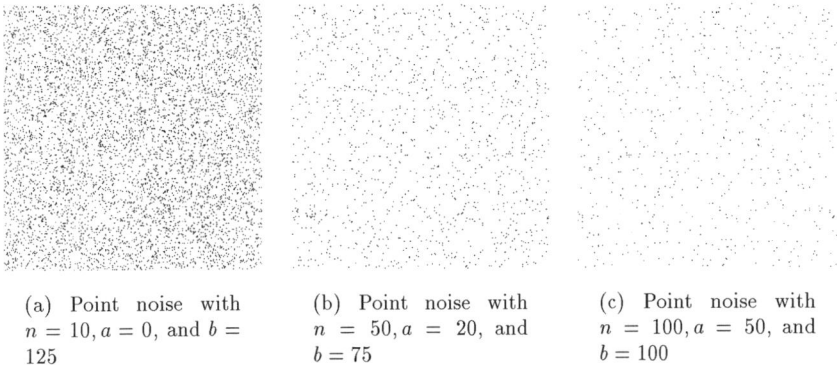

(a) Point noise with $n = 10, a = 0$, and $b = 125$

(b) Point noise with $n = 50, a = 20$, and $b = 75$

(c) Point noise with $n = 100, a = 50$, and $b = 100$

Figure 18.1   Examples for point noise

18.4   Gaussian Noise

Gaussian noise is often assumed to be an adequate modeling of real noise effects occurring in images recorded by CCD cameras or other sensors. For generating normally distributed gray–levels with the mean zero and a variance of one, the famous and fairly tricky algorithm of G. E. P. Box, M. E. Muller and G. Marsglia can be used [Knu73, Joh87]. The described method is based on two $[0, 1]$–uniform distributed random numbers u_1 and u_2. Using both numbers we compute $v_1 = 2u_1 - 1$, $v_2 = 2u_2 - 1$ and $s = v_1^2 + v_2^2$. If the value of s is greater or equal to one, the algorithm starts again with the computation of both uniformly distributed random numbers u_1 and u_2. Otherwise one can proof that the random variable

$$X = v_1 \sqrt{\frac{-2ln\ s}{s}}$$

underlies a normal distribution.

Use the textual description of the algorithm for an implementation of a random number generator for normally distributed numbers with mean zero and variance one. Use this function to generate a Gaussian image where the mean gray–level is determined by the parameter m. The variance can be modified by choosing different discretization steps of the continuous density function.

Figure 18.2 Examples for Gaussian (left) and salt–and–pepper (right)

The same idea can be used to create a sound signal of Gaussian noise.

18.5   Salt–and–Pepper Noise

A special kind of noise is the *salt–and–pepper noise*. Each pixel in the gray–level image has one value out of the set $\{a, b\}$. These values appear with the same probability of $1/2$ (see Figure 18.2). Implement a function for generating salt–and–pepper noise, where the gray–levels a and b are parameters of the function call.

Put the common parts of the implementation of this algorithm the one in Sect. 18.4, and the one in Sect. 18.3 in a separate module used by both image generators. Apply the same ideas to sound signals and use the same random generators for both areas.

18.6 Different Views of a 3D Polyhedral Object

In this section, a program should be written for generating different views of an object. Figure 18.3 shows different views of a polyhedral object. We proceed in three steps.

First, write a program which creates a synthetic white image including black points at specified locations. The coordinates of these points and their gray–level should be parameters of the function call.

Then, develop a program which creates an image with digital lines. The program takes as input a set of points. Each line is determined by a pair of coordinates.

For the generation of two dimensional images of three dimensional objects a procedure is needed, which has the set of three dimensional corners or vertices of the object as input data. The computed gray–level image should be synthetisized out of the given rotations and translations and the projection of the image points into the image plane. Whether the program will use orthographic or perspective projection (see Sect. cam:model:abs) should be an option of your program.

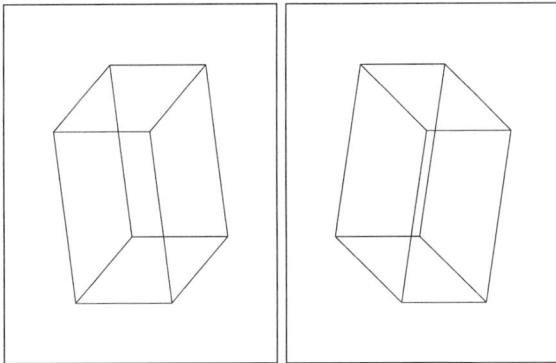

Figure 18.3 Different views of a polyhedral object

18.7   Digits and Letters

Sometimes it is required to annotate an image by inserting text into the image directly. Implement a general program which results in a small image including one letter or digit. Background and foreground colors should be parameters of the function call.

Write a program which has as input parameter an image, a sequence of digits and letters and spots the string in the image. The coordinates where the upper left corner of the string starts in the image should also be a parameter of the implemented function.

Figure 18.4   Inserted text in a subimage of Figure 11.2 (right)

You should keep in mind however that the TEX– and Postscript–people have done such things for ages. One of the principal jobs for computer typesetting is to provide fonts, i.e. descriptions of characters in different sizes. Keep your project small and simple; use the bitmaps for characters on the screen of a personal computer!

18.8   Single Stereo Images

Recently, single stereo images (SIS) became very popular. They look very mysterious on the first glance. Nevertheless, the idea those images are based on is fairly easy. Human have two eyes. If someone looks at a point in the three–dimensional space, this point can be seen by each eye. The projection of

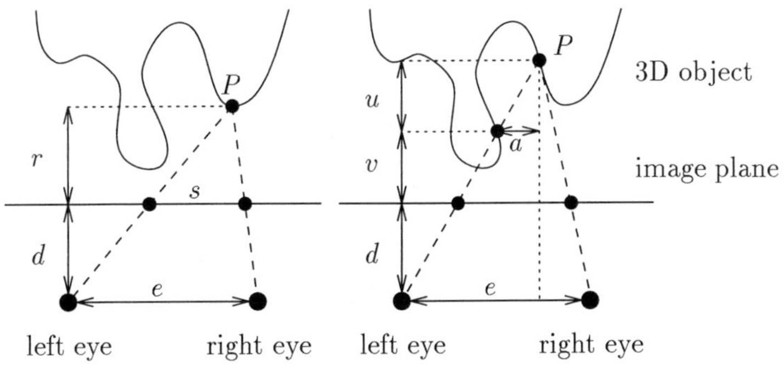

Figure 18.5 One 3D point gets two points in the image plane (left); hidden point removal (right)

this point on an image plane along the eye's ray causes for each eye a separate two–dimensional point. In autostereograms these corresponding points are elements of *one* image and get the same gray–level. Figure 18.5 shows the geometrical relations. Since we have similar triangles, the distance between both projected points is

$$s = \frac{r \cdot e}{r + d} .$$

(18.1)

If a range image is used as input data, formula (18.1) yields for each 3D surface point the corresponding coordinates of the two–dimensional image points.

Technically, it is incorrect to plot a stereo pair into the image plane which corresponds to a 3D point on the object being visible to one eye only. If we do so, we will get ambiguities near depth steps in range values. Let (x_l, y_l) and (x_p, y_p) the 2D coordinates of the left eye and the object point P. The distance u is computed by

$$u = \frac{a \cdot (d + r)}{|x_p - x_l|} ,$$

(18.2)

where $r = u + v$ is the depth value known from the range image. This equation can be used to decide, whether a point visible by both eyes by comparing u and the corresponding range value for all admissible values of a. If the range value exceeds or is equal to $v = r - u$, the ray is intercepted and thus the point is not visible.

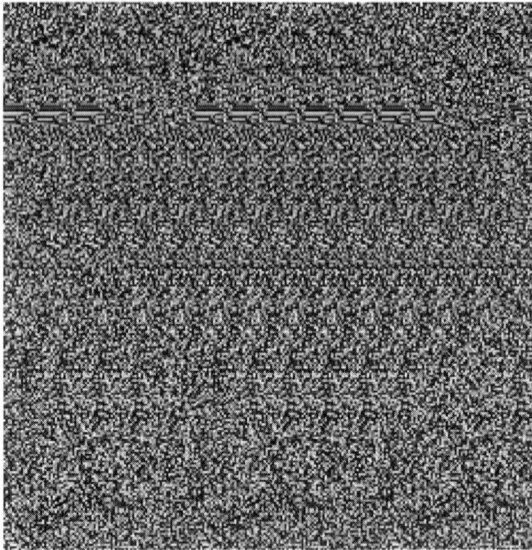

Figure 18.6   Example of a single stereo image

Now, we can compute corresponding points for each range values. These correspondences are visualized by the assignment of identical gray–levels to each pair of pixels. The gray–levels necessary for coloring can be taken from a random image (see Sect.18.3). Figure 18.6 shows an example for an automatically generated SIS for Figure 11.3 by applying the introduced algorithm.

18.9   Spectrogram

In this section we close one gap between speech processing and image processing. Image generation methods are required for speech analysis for *spectrograms* which are introduced now. A spectrogram is a pictorial visualization of the frequencies in a sound signal. Every pixel in the spectrogram image corresponds to a certain frequency and a moment in time. The intensity corresponds to the energy of the related frequency in the sound signal.

Usually, a frequency analysis of each individual frame in the speech signal is done using a Fourier transform. In order to use the FFT (Sect. 16.2), it is useful to have a frame length which is a power of two (e.g. 256 samples). The frames can of course overlap in time and overlapping parts can be weighted (e.g. by the Hamming window). Now, compute 256 Fourier coefficients from 256 sample values and scale the resulting floating point numbers to 256 gray values. These 256 values now correspond to a column in the image. An example of a spectrogram is shown in Figure 18.7.

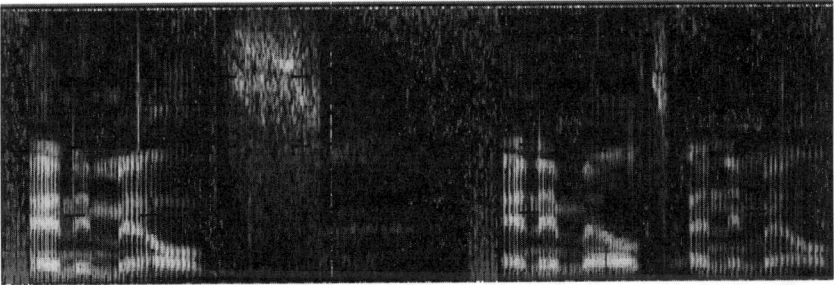

Figure 18.7 Spectogram of the utterance "animals animals"

Use the signals created in Sect. 18.1. Overlay them with noise created in Sect. 18.4 using a tool as described in Sect. 18.1. Create an image object of appropriate size and compute the spectrum. Colored spectrograms can be created as well when the Fourier coefficients are mapped onto RGB values.

Exercises

1. Use the functions in Sect. 18.3 and build a program `CreateImage` where options admit the generation of different noisy images.

2. In Example 138 we have seen an implementation of the class `GrayLevelImage`. Add a new method which allows the addition of two images, where corresponding pixels are added modulo 256.

3. Write a program which reads a range image, a noise image and computes an autostereogram.

4. Implement a class which admits the generation of speech signals describing parameterized trigonometrical functions. The class should also provide methods for addition and other operations on these speech signals.

19 Filtering and Smoothing Signals

Filters and operators used for smoothing signals are fundamental parts of the preprocessing stage of many pattern analysis systems.

In chapter 18 we have implemented some algorithms for generating noisy images. Noise in images or other signals used for pattern recognition purposes is an undesirable effect and has to be reduced or eliminated, if possible. The reduction of noise can be realized by the smoothing of patterns. In the literature there are many different approaches for smoothing and filtering signals. The following sections will briefly introduce some basic algorithms, which should be implemented by the reader using the techniques introduced in the first part of this book.

Beside the elimination of noise, digital filters are also used for emphasizing interesting parts in an image, such as regions or edges. For getting higher continuity in digital signals, smoothing operators are used.

Filters can be designed for two different domains: the frequency and the spatial–domain. In the following chapter we will avoid treating filters in the frequency domain, because the mathematical background, i.e. the Fourier–transform and its characteristics, [1] needed for those techniques would exceed the scope of the book. The following subsections are confined to methods in the spatial–domain.

The first chapter introduces the problems of how digital images can be computed using analog signals. The quantization of the gray–levels has noise effects which can be measured by the signal to noise ratio (see Chapter 7). The following projects describe filters which should reduce noise and smooth an image. Another project is dedicated to the problem of how to magnify an image to double size using linear reconstruction techniques.

---

[1]See Chapter 16 for first introductions to Fourier–Transform

19.1   Mean–Filter and Gaussian–Filter

Mean-filtering is a very simple and obvious linear smoothing technique. A current pixel gray–level or value in a time–ordered signal is set to the mean of neighbored sample data. In image processing applications the neighborhood is usually defined by a quadratic 3×3 or 5×5 mask. For time ordered signals the mean is computed using some predecessors or successors of the current position.

It should be mentioned that this filter smears the signal values. Images will blur and edge detection is made more difficult as a result of its use. That is the reason why we warn against mean–filtering. Nevertheless, mean–filters are easily implemented and the runtime depends on the image size and grows linearly in proportion to this measure. The runtime of an efficient implementation is approximately independent of the size of a given neighborhood.

Figure 19.1   Mean–Filter

Each gray–level in the defined neighborhood is weighted with 1 in the case of the mean–filter. It is a reasonable assumption that increasing the distance should imply a decrease in weights. In the case of Gaussian–Filters these weights are defined using the Gaussian density function. A digitized version for a 3×3 neighborhood is, for example,

$$\frac{1}{16} \begin{bmatrix} 1 & 2 & 1 \\ 2 & 4 & 2 \\ 1 & 2 & 1 \end{bmatrix}. \tag{19.1}$$

Figure 19.2 Gaussian–Filter on quadratic subimage

19.2 Median–Filter

The edge preserving character of the median–filter justifies its popularity. If a high signal–to–noise ratio is given, it is recommended to give median–filters priority over other filters (see [Mac81, Tab84]). A lot of research is being done to weight the advantages and disadvantages of this nonlinear filter [Bov87, Chi83]. In [Yam81] it is shown that in images with the presence of convex or concave ramp edges and impulsive noise median filtering will improve edge detection results.

The algorithm for median–filters first requires the definition of a neighborhood of the current pixel. In general, we use masks of quadratic size. All gray–levels of the neighbored pixels $p_1, p_2, \ldots, p_N$ are ordered using the „leq"–relation of real numbers. The new pixel value is the gray–level of the pixel in the middle of this ordering.

Beside its smoothing capabilities the median filter is fairly easy to implement. The runtime of the algorithm depends linearly on the image size.

If we take the minimum of these ordered values, we get the erosion–filter. Dilatation is the filter which results from the maximum values. In general, filters which use ordered sequences of its neighbored signal values are elements of the class of morphological operations.

Figure 19.3 Median–Filter

19.3 Smoothed Median–Filter

In [Luo94] the median–filter is extended to a corner preserving filter operation.
The basic idea of this algorithm is a graduated application of median filtering.
The 5×5 mask is divided up into four differing stripes (see Figure 19.4). For
each subset of included pixels (1–4) the classical median is computed. The
final pixel value of the center of the 5×5 mask is received by the median of
the four resulting values of the prior median operations. It can be shown that
the described smoothed median filter also suppresses Gaussian noise.

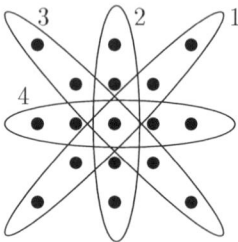

Figure 19.4 Four elliptic masks (1–4) where the median is separately applied
(left); result of smoothed–median filtering (right).

19.4   Edge Preserving Smoothing

Another method which is also based on computing the mean of neighbored pixels for smoothing purposes is explained in this section. Nevertheless, the selection of the pixels for averaging is done by the use of a special technique based on statistical principles. The algorithm suggested in [Nag79] uses for each pixel P eight different 5×5–masks which generators are shown in Figure 19.6. The pixels in the environment of P with a distinguishing mark are used for the following computations. The symmetrical use of 19.6 (a) and (b) results in eight different masks. Each of these masks include seven points for the calculation of the new gray–level. In contrast mask (c) includes nine elements for the following computations. For each mask we compute the variance. The mask with the lowest variance is selected. The central pixel P gets the mean value of all points marked in this mask. An example of the result of this filter is shown in 19.5.

Figure 19.5   Edge Preserving Filtering

19.5 K–Nearest Neighbor Averaging

The filter of „K-Nearest-Neighbor-Averaging" [Dav78] is an additional edge preserving filter which can be used iteratively. Let P be a pixel out of an array with N points. Take K points out of this array which are closest to the gray–value of the image point P. Assign the mean of these points to the pixel P. With a growing value of K, this filter converges to the mean–filter, the reduction of noise grows and the complete image blurs.

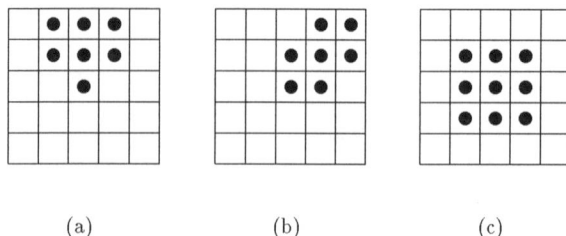

(a)   (b)   (c)

Figure 19.6   Masks for Smoothing

It is suggested to use $N = 9$ and $K = 6$ (see [Dav78]). In this case you take the eight neighbors of P and determine the five nearest gray–levels. The mean of the gray–levels of P and the five additional points is assigned to the intensity of P.

In [Brü90] it is shown that this filter is very powerful. The computation time and the result of smoothing depends on the number of iterations. In average the runtime for a 256×256–image is about 30 seconds and increases linearly with the image size. From previous experience it is known that three iterations yield satisfiable results.

Figure 19.7   Examples for K–nearest neighbor filtering with $K = 2, 5, 9$

19.6 Conditional Average Filter

Another iteratively applicable filter is suggested in [Pra80] and is called „Conditional Average Filter". In a 5×5 mask around the central pixel P we compute the mean of all pixels whose difference in the gray–level with the intensity of P is lower or equal to a given threshold θ. The gray–level of P is assigned to this value. The problem of this algorithm is obviously the selection of the threshold θ. In [Brü90] the computation of θ is correlated with the maximum gray–level of the given image. The threshold θ is computed by $\theta = \alpha \cdot G_{max}$, where $\alpha \in [0, 1]$. The best results were made choosing $\alpha = 0.1$. The advantage of conditional averaging is that edges, where the change in gray–levels exceeds θ, are not blurred. Regions, where gray–levels differ with a difference lower or equal to θ, are smoothed. In practice, this filter eliminates weak edges. Therefore, even the adaptive selection of the threshold should be used with caution.

The sorting of gray–levels is not necessary, therefore the runtime of conditional average filters is in general lower than of K nearest neighbor filters.

Figure 19.8 Conditional average for different thresholds ($\theta = 100, 150, 200$)

19.7 Linear Reconstruction

In this project we have to implement an algorithm for the magnification of images. One common technique is to use linear reconstruction, i.e. the gray–levels of new pixels are linear combinations of gray–levels of neighbored image points.

To get double size of the image we successively decompose the image into 2×2 squares

$$
\begin{array}{cc}
f_{i,j} & f_{i,j+1} \\
f_{i+1,j} & f_{i+1,j+1}
\end{array}
$$

and compute the gray–levels of five additional points a, b, c, d, and e using linear interpolation between the gray–levels.

$$
\begin{array}{ccc}
f_{i,j} & a & f_{i,j+1} \\
b & c & d \\
f_{i+1,j} & e & f_{i+1,j+1}
\end{array}
$$

Implement a function doubleSize which magnifies the input image using the sketched technique. Discuss different strategies for the computation of the non–unique gray–level c.

Use your program and magnify an arbitrary image iteratively. Which effects are observable? Is it possible that the images in Figure 19.9 are computed using the above method? Give reasons for your answer!

Figure 19.9 Examples for enlargements

19.8 Elimination of Noisy Image Rows

Most CCD cameras do not record scenes line by line, but sample first the odd and finally the even lines of the image. If we have moving objects in the scene we can observe the so called *interlace effect*, which is based on the sampling of the camera. Assume the sampling of each line takes t_s ms time. When we start at time t at the first line of the image, the record of the second line will be $n t_s$ ms later, where $2n$ represents the number of lines of the CCD chip. Consequently, a moving object can change its position in $n t_s$ ms, and the odd and even image rows are shifted. This shift can be computed analytically, if the technical data of the CCD chip and the speed of the moving object are known. In practice, there is nothing known a priori about the moving object. Therefore, we have to find another – more convenient – approach to remove interlace effects. Unimaginative – but in practice sometimes sufficient – is to cancel rows with even numbers and to double each odd numbered row. If rows of the image do not include the moving object we have no interlace and therefore nothing to change. One possible approach to locate and remove interlace effects in the image is the use of statistical methods. Based on the experience that the transition of one row to its successor does not include high rapidity of gray–levels, using a correlation coefficient we can decide whether one row is corrupted by interlacing or some other kind of noise. If the test is positive, we have to reduce this disturbance. Let $f_{i,j}$ ($0 \leq i < M$, and $0 \leq j < N$) be the gray–levels of the given image. We take the covariance $\sigma_{r,r+1}$ of two successive rows r and $r+1$

$$\sigma_{r,r+1} \quad = \quad \frac{1}{N} \sum_{k=0}^{N-1} (f_{r,k} - \mu_r)(f_{r+1,k} - \mu_{r+1}), \tag{19.2}$$

where μ_r and μ_{r+1} are the means of gray–levels of the actual rows. The correlation coefficient

$$\rho_{r,r+1} \quad = \quad \frac{\sigma_{r,r+1}}{\sqrt{\sigma_{r,r}\sigma_{r+1,r+1}}} \tag{19.3}$$

yields the following decision rule for two rows: If $|\rho_{r,r+1}| > \theta$, where θ is a threshold value, we will do no changes. Otherwise we say both rows are not similar, consequently we have to smooth the transition from row r to $r+1$. This can be done by copying r to $r+1$. Implement this suggested algorithm and discuss its use for interlace elimination!

19.9   Resolution Hierarchies

The runtime behavior of many algorithms, for example filtering, edge detection, or region segmentation, depends on the size of the processed image. On the one hand, for some applications one does not need maximal image resolution. In a new paradigm, named *active vision* (see Sect. 5.8), one of the main principles is selectivity of the algorithms in resolution. This can lead to a lower computation time, needed for example in real time image processing. On the other hand some edge detection algorithms first search for edges on a low resolution image, and take these edges as an initial edge estimation for another search at a higher resolution. In this way, stepwise a more precise result can be obtained.

The representation of an image at several resolutions leads to *image pyramids* (see Figure 19.10). An image pyramid is a series of images $f_j(x, y)$, where $0 < j < n$, and $0 \leq x, y < 2^n$. Herein, n is given by the size of the original image. The pyramid is created by a bottom up approach. Formally, the image $f_k(x, y)$ is computed from $f_{k+1}(x, y)$:

$$f_k(x, y) = reduce\ (f_{k+1}(x, y))\quad .\qquad\qquad (19.4)$$

The function $reduce(\cdot)$ is called the *generating function*. For each reduced image both the resolution and the sample density decreased. One simple form of the function $reduce(\cdot)$ is:

$$reduce(f_{k+1}(x, y)) = \sum_{m=a}^{b} \sum_{n=c}^{d} w(m, n) f_{k+1}(2x + m, 2y + n)\qquad (19.5)$$

where $w(m, n) \in \mathbb{R}$ is a weighting function and a, b, c, d are integers. A simple version of $w(m, n)$ is given by $w(m, n) = \frac{1}{4}$. In this case, the pyramid is generated by an averaging process.

There exist many variations in the way, the next lower resolution has to be computed. One possible approach is to use another weighting function or another type of function $reduce(\cdot)$, for example a local maximum, minimum or morphological function.

One special case of a pyramid is the so called *Gaussian pyramid* [Bur83]:

$$f_k(x, y) = \sum_{m=-2}^{2} \sum_{n=-2}^{2} w(m, n) f_{k+1}(2x + m, 2y + n)\qquad (19.6)$$

with

$$w(m,n) = \hat{w}(m)\hat{w}(n) \tag{19.7}$$

and

$$\hat{w}(0) = \alpha \tag{19.8}$$

$$\hat{w}(-1) = \hat{w}(1) = \frac{1}{4} \tag{19.9}$$

$$\hat{w}(-2) = \hat{w}(2) = \frac{1}{4} - \frac{\alpha}{2} \ . \tag{19.10}$$

The Gaussian pyramid results in a sequence of images. Each computed image represents a low–pass filtered copy of its predecessor in the given hierarchy. In [Bur83] it is shown that the Gaussian pyramid construction generates images with a band limit one octave lower than their predecessors. Thus, the pre–conditions of the sampling theorem are valid.

In this project a class image pyramid for images has to be implemented. Start with an abstract base class, which contains methods for computing a weighting function, a generating function and methods to select special resolutions of the pyramid elements. Take into consideration that several image types are possible, for example binary images, gray–level images, or edge images. Derive a concrete class and then implement the special form of a Gaussian pyramid for a ἵππος GrayLevelImage (see Figure19.10). An object of a pyramid should also be used as a normal GrayLevelImage, so a suitable method should be provided.

Exercises

1. In Chapter 18 several noise generators were described. Write a program which admits the addition of noise of a special type to a given image. Verify by experiments the characteristics of introduced filter operations – like the suppression of Gaussian noise by the use of smoothed median filtering.

2. Write a program which visualizes the difference of two filtered images. Explain the observation if you use the difference image of erosion and dilatation.

3. The idea of smoothed median filtering is a subsequent application of the median filter to different sets of pixels. Use this idea to develop other hybrid filters using other types than median operations. Which object–oriented programming techniques provide useful tools for realizing this kind of *polymorphism*? Do as many experiments as you like and formalize the observed results of your filters. Additionally, apply the line detection algorithms introduced in Chapter 22 to filtered images and describe the resulting images.

4. Implement a class hierarchy for filters. A scheme is given in Example 161.

5. Show that the total number M of pixels of a Gaussian pyramid is bounded by

$$M \; < \; \frac{4}{3}N^2 \; , \tag{19.11}$$

where the first image has a resolution of $N \times N$ and a decreasing factor of two per stage.

```
#include <GrayLevelImage.h>
#include <EdgeImage.h>
#include <SegObj.h>

class IP_OP : public Object { };
class Filter: public IP_OP {
 public:
   virtual int operator()
     (GrayLevelImage&,GrayLevelImage&) const = 0;
};
```

$\left(161\right)$

Example 162 declares the interface to filter operations which transform one gray–level image into another.

```
class LowPass : public Filter {
 public:
   virtual int operator()
     (GrayLevelImage&,GrayLevelImage&) const = 0;
};
class Mean: public LowPass {
   int xs, ys;
 public:
   Mean(int sizeh, int sizev) : xs(sizeh/2), ys(sizev/2) {}
   virtual int operator()
     (GrayLevelImage&,GrayLevelImage&) const;
};
class Gauss: public LowPass {
 public:
   virtual int operator()
     (GrayLevelImage&,GrayLevelImage&) const;
};
```

(162)

Examples 163–165 declare the interface to edge detection operations which transform a gray–level image into an edge image.

```
class EdgeDet: public IP_OP {
 public:
   virtual int operator()
     (GrayLevelImage&,EdgeImage&) const = 0;
};
```

(163)

```
class Sobel: public EdgeDet {
 public:
   virtual int operator()
     (GrayLevelImage&,EdgeImage&) const;
};
```

(164)

```
class Roberts: public EdgeDet {
 public:
   virtual int operator()
     (GrayLevelImage&,EdgeImage&) const;
};
class LineDet : public IP_OP {
 public:
   virtual int operator() (EdgeImage&, SegObj&) const = 0;
};
\begin{progexample}{edgedet5:obj:ex}
class Hystline : public LineDet {
 public:
   virtual int operator() (EdgeImage&, SegObj&) const;
};
```
(165)

6. Extend the filter classes of exercise 4 on page 274.

A simple implementation of a mean filter is given in Example 166.

```
int Mean::operator()
  (GrayLevelImage& in ,GrayLevelImage& out) const {
  fprintf(stderr,"Apply Mean %dx%d\n", 1+2*xs, 1+2*ys);
  for (int i = 0 ; i < in.getysize(); ++i)
    for (int j = 0 ; j < in.getxsize(); ++j) {
      int r = 0, c = 0;
      for (int k = -1* ys ; k <= ys ; ++k) {
        for (int l = -1 * xs ; l <= xs; ++l) {
          if ((i + k < 0) || (i + k >= in.getysize()) ||
              (j + l < 0) || (j + l >= in.getxsize()))
            continue;
          ++c; r += in[i][j]; }
      }
      out [i][j] = r / c;  // c >= 1
    }
  return 0;
}
```
(166)

Figure 19.10 Examples for images of different resolutions ($\alpha = 0.4$)

20 Histogram Algorithms

Histograms were generally introduced in Chapter7. In the following sections we will define several useful preprocessing steps using histograms. Each algorithm can easily be implemented and tested. This chapter concludes with the implementation of a class *histogram* written in C++.

20.1 Discriminant and Least Squares Threshold

Histograms are conventionally used for computing a binary image of a given gray–level image. Binary images produce a reduction of input data and often applied for separating an object from its background. A suitable value for binarization can be found by creating a gray–level histogram. If the background and the observed object have strongly different gray–levels, then both regions easily can be separated by searching for the relative frequencies found in the histogram. This distinguishing of an object from its background produces what is known as a *bimodal histogram*. The threshold lies between the maxima found within the histogram.

For many gray–level images this technique is not applicable because foregrounds and backgrounds usually have more than just the two extrema expected in the histogram. Figure 20.1 shows an example of binarization. The threshold was computed using the minimum between the two maxima of gray–levels in the bimodal histogram.

As this example demonstrates, methods other than valley–seeking are required. A promising approach to solve this problem is to use some statistical information about the gray–levels and formalizing an optimization problem.

As mentioned above, to aid data reduction and to simplify the successive processing steps it is sometimes useful to partition the set of different gray–levels into two classes. This can be done by computing a threshold θ: each gray–level which is greater or equal to this value falls into the first, the others in the

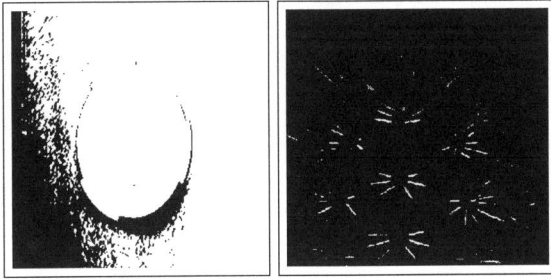

Figure 20.1 Binary image created from Figure 13.2 (left) and from Figure 11.2 (right) with bimodal histogram analysis

second class. The threshold is determined by solving an optimization problem. For that, we define the values of admissible gray–levels by $g_1, g_2, \ldots, g_L$. The discrete probability for each gray–level in a given image can be easily determined by a gray level histogram. Let $f_{i,j}$ be the gray–level at the image point (i, j). The probability p_ν that the image point (i, j) has the gray–level g_ν is

$$p(f_{i,j} = g_\nu) = p_\nu := \frac{|\text{image points with gray–level } g_\nu|}{|\text{image points}|}. \tag{20.1}$$

The bipartition of all gray–levels is done using a threshold $\theta = g_l$. Let Ω_1^l and Ω_2^l be the disjoint sets of gray–levels induced by a given threshold value g_l, i.e.

$$\Omega_1^l = \{f_{i,j} \; ; \; f_{i,j} \leq \theta\} \tag{20.2}$$
$$\Omega_2^l = \{f_{i,j} \; ; \; f_{i,j} > \theta\}. \tag{20.3}$$

Using this notation, the probability that an image points lies in one of the above classes is:

$$p(\Omega_1^l) = \sum_{\nu=1}^{l} p_\nu \quad \text{resp.} \quad p(\Omega_2^l) = 1 - p(\Omega_1^l) \tag{20.4}$$

The threshold is expected to satisfy the following properties:

1. $p(\Omega_1^l)$ and $p(\Omega_2^l)$ should not be equal to zero

2. the absolute difference of means for the gray–levels appearing in Ω_1 and Ω_2 should be as large as possible.

A criterion which considers this requirements is the following product:

$$J_l = p(\Omega_1^l)p(\Omega_2^l) \cdot \left(\sum_{\nu=1}^{l} \frac{p_\nu g_\nu}{p(\Omega_1^l)} - \sum_{\nu=l+1}^{L} \frac{p_\nu g_\nu}{p(\Omega_2^l)} \right)^2 \qquad (20.5)$$

which has to be maximized with respect to the gray–level index l.

$$l \quad = \quad \operatorname*{argmax}_{l'} \ J_{l'} \qquad (20.6)$$

Thus, the computation of $\theta = b_l$ is bounded by L evaluations of J_l.

An example for a binary image computed using the threshold (20.6) is shown in Figure 20.2. More details concerning this technique can be found in [Nie83].

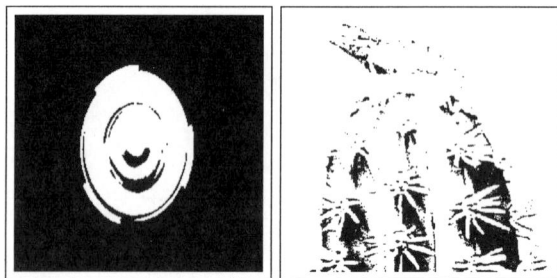

Figure 20.2 Binary image created from Figure 13.2 (left) and from Figure 11.2 (right) with discriminant analysis

20.2   Histogram Entropy Thresholding

In this section we will define an alternative algorithm for threshold determination using the entropy concept (see Chapter 7). Let p_ν $(0 \le \nu < L)$, the discrete probabilities for observing the gray–level g_ν. Now, we search for a bipartition (see 20.2,20.3) of the set of gray levels. Let θ be the threshold value g_l and let us assume that this threshold induces two distributions for the following sets of formal random variables

$$A_l = \left\{ \frac{p_1}{\sum_{\nu=1}^{l} p_\nu}, \frac{p_2}{\sum_{\nu=1}^{l} p_\nu}, \cdots, \frac{p_l}{\sum_{\nu=1}^{l} p_\nu} \right\}, \qquad (20.7)$$

$$B_l = \left\{ \frac{p_{l+1}}{1 - \sum_{\nu=1}^{l} p_\nu}, \frac{p_{l+2}}{1 - \sum_{\nu=1}^{l} p_\nu}, \cdots, \frac{p_L}{1 - \sum_{\nu=1}^{l} p_\nu} \right\}. \qquad (20.8)$$

For each set the entropy (7.18) can be computed as

$$H(A_l) = -\sum_{\mu=1}^{l} \frac{p_\mu}{\sum_{\nu=1}^{l} p_\nu} \log \frac{p_\mu}{\sum_{\nu=1}^{l} p_\nu} \qquad (20.9)$$

and

$$H(B_l) = -\sum_{\mu=l+1}^{L} \frac{p_\mu}{1 - \sum_{\nu=1}^{l} p_\nu} \log \frac{p_\mu}{1 - \sum_{\nu=1}^{l} p_\nu}. \qquad (20.10)$$

Here again, the complexity for computing θ is bounded by the number of gray–levels L.

The optimal threshold for binarization results from the maximization of the entropy of the complete image, i.e. the sum of the entropy of the distributions A_l and B_l

$$l = \underset{l'}{\operatorname{argmax}} \left(H(A_{l'}) + H(B_{l'}) \right). \qquad (20.11)$$

An application of this threshold for binarization is visualized in Figure 20.3.

Figure 20.3 Binary image created from Figure 13.2 (left) and from Figure 11.2 (right) with entropy analysis

20.3   Multithresholding

If more than one object is superimposed on a homogeneous background so that the gray–level histogram has multiple maxima, i.e. multimodal, the image can be decomposed into regions with different gray–levels. Each object and the background get uniform gray–levels.

A straightforward approach for the computation of the set of thresholds can be done by the optimization of the following multivariate function which is an obvious generalization of the entropy method of the previous section.

$$
\Psi(l_1, l_2, \ldots, l_k) = \log\left(\sum_{\nu=1}^{l_1} p_\nu\right) + \log\left(\sum_{\nu=l_1+1}^{l_2} p_\nu\right) + \ldots + \log\left(\sum_{\nu=l_{k+1}+1}^{L} p_\nu\right)
$$
$$
- \frac{\sum_{\nu=1}^{l_1} p_\nu \log p_\nu}{\sum_{\nu=1}^{l_1} p_\nu} - \frac{\sum_{\nu=l_1+1}^{l_2} p_\nu \log p_\nu}{\sum_{\nu=l_1+1}^{l_2} p_\nu} - \ldots - \frac{\sum_{\nu=l_{k+1}+1}^{L} p_\nu \log p_\nu}{\sum_{\nu=l_{k+1}+1}^{L} p_\nu} \qquad (20.12)
$$

where the number k of different gray–levels must be known a priori. The set of thresholds is computed by solving the following optimization problem:

$$
(l_1, l_2, \ldots, l_k) = \underset{(l'_1, l'_2, \ldots, l'_k)}{\arg\max} \Psi(l'_1, l'_2, \ldots, l'_k). \qquad (20.13)
$$

20.4   Local Histogram Equalization

The principle of local histogram linearization is to use a window of size $M \times M$. The transformation of the central pixel in the window is found by equalizing the histogram of the local window. The discrete density function $p(g_\nu) := p_\nu$ is defined by the relative frequencies of each gray–level g_ν in the mask. The discrete distribution function is given by

$$
P(g_l) = \sum_{\nu=0}^{l} p(g_\nu). \qquad (20.14)
$$

The histogram equalization transformation over the given window is now defined as

$$
T(f_{i,j}) = g_{\max} P(f_{i,j}) \qquad (20.15)
$$

for the central pixel at the point (i, j), where g_{max} is the maximal gray–level of the actual window and $f_{i,j}$ represents the gray–level of the image point (i, j).

In Figure 20.4 you can find an example for local histogram equalization. The window size is 5.

Figure 20.4 Result of local histogram equalization on Figure 13.2 (left) and Figure 11.2 (right)

20.5   Lookup Table Transformation

The transformation of gray–levels is an often used preprocessing step. Two functions in Figure 20.5 describe the assignment of each gray–level of the original image (t–axis) to the new value (y–axis). The distortion is based on a polygon or a third order polynomial, which is determined by four points $(0, a), (b, c), (d, e)$, and $(255, f)$.

The general form of third order polynomials is:

$$f(t) \quad = \quad a_0 + a_1 t + a_2 t^2 + a_3 t^3.$$

The computation of the coefficients can be done by solving the system of linear equations:

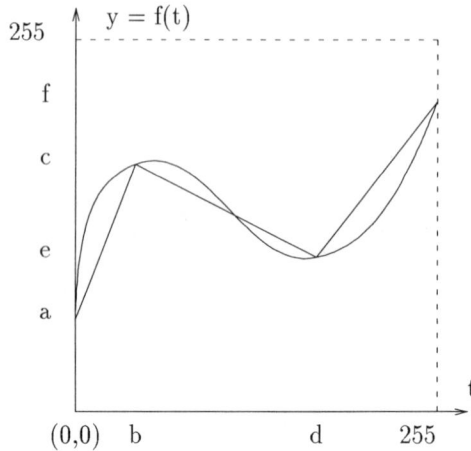

Figure 20.5   Correction of gray–levels

$$a = a_0, \tag{20.16}$$
$$c = a_0 + a_1 b + a_2 b^2 + a_3 b^3, \tag{20.17}$$
$$e = a_0 + a_1 d + a_2 d^2 + a_3 d^3, \quad \text{and} \tag{20.18}$$
$$f = a_0 + a_1 255 + a_2 255^2 + a_3 255^3. \tag{20.19}$$

$$a_0 = a, \tag{20.20}$$

$$a_1 = -\frac{1}{K}(-255^3 b^2 e + 255^3 b^2 a + 255^3 d^2 c - 255^3 d^2 a - b^3 d^2 f + 255^2 b^3 e$$
$$-255^2 b^3 a - 255^2 d^3 c + b^3 d^2 a + b^2 d^3 f - b^2 d^3 a + 255^2 d^3 a \tag{20.21}$$

$$a_2 = \frac{1}{K}(255 b^3 e + b^3 da - 255 b^3 a - b^3 df - 255^3 be - d^3 ab + bd^3 f +$$
$$255^3 ba + 255^3 dc + 255 d^3 a - 255^3 da - 255 d^3 c), \tag{20.22}$$

$$a_3 = -\frac{1}{K}(255 b^2 e - 255 b^2 a + 255^2 dc - b^2 df + b^2 da$$
$$-255 d^2 c - 255^2 be + 255^2 ba \tag{20.23}$$
$$+d^2 bf - d^2 ba + 255 d^2 a - 255^2 da),$$

where

$$K = 255bd \left(-d^2b + 255^2b + 255d^2 + b^2d - 255^2d - 255b^2 \right). \quad (20.24)$$

An application of this technique is shown in Figure 20.6.

Figure 20.6 Result of a lookup table transform ($a = 50, b = 70, c = 90, d = 144, e = 200, f = 100$) on Figure 13.2 (left) and Figure 11.2 (right)

20.6 A Class for Histograms

Previous sections show that there are a lot of operations on histograms. These methods should be provided by a C++ class. We call this class `Histogram`. The concrete representation and computation of historgrams is hidden for its users. A suitable header file for this class is given below (Example 167). The detailed implementation of each method is easily done by applying the explainations given so far. The internal representation of a histogram is based on a vector of integers, i.e. `Matrix<int>`. The index represents the current gray–level and the associated entry the number of occuring in the given image.

```
class Histogram {
 private:
  Matrix<int> histogram;
 public:
  Histogram(const GrayLevelImage &);
  Histogram(const Histogram &);

  void smooth(void);              // smooth the histogram
  int bimodal_threshold(void);    // computes the minimum
                                  // between two maxima
  int least_square_threshold(void); // compute the threshold
                                  // by the least square
                                  // method
  int max_entropy_threshold(void); // compute the threshold
                                  // by the entropy method
};
```

(167)

Exercises

1. Implement a class histogram. The methods should include all algorithms described so far, i.e. smoothing, global histogram linearization, and local histogram equalization.

2. Write utilities for the visualization of histograms and the discrete distribution function of gray–levels.

3. Proof that (20.5) is equivalent to

$$J_l = \frac{p(\Omega_1^l)\sum_{\nu=1}^{L} g_\nu p_\nu - \sum_{\nu=1}^{l} g_\nu p_\nu}{p(\Omega_1^l)(1 - p(\Omega_1^l))}. \tag{20.25}$$

4. Generalize the least square threshold technique (Sect. 20.1) for solving the multithreshold problem (Sect. 20.3).

5. Show that the multithreshold computation is bounded by $\binom{L+k-1}{k}$ evaluations of $\Psi(l_1, l_2, \ldots, l_k)$.

21 Edge Images

Various principles for edge detection which create edge images from gray level images could be seen in Chapter 13. As already outlined in Sect. 13.2, further algorithms exist. Some of them will be introduced in this chapter. The algorithm best suited for a given edge image actually depends upon the image data itself.

21.1 Robert's Cross

Edge detection using the first derivation was motivated by the central differences in Eq. 13.2. An implementation using this idea will make use of the four neighbors of a given pixel (see also Sect. 11.9). Even simpler than (13.2) is the so called *Robert's Cross* operator which also uses only four pixels (Eq. 21.1).

$$f_1(i,j) = f(i,j) - f(i+1,j+1) \quad \text{and} \quad f_2(i,j) = f(i,j+1) - f(i+1,j) \ (21.1)$$

Since the differences are computed diagonally (as a "cross"), the values f_1 and f_2 are not the horizontal or vertical derivations, but instead are the approximations of directional derivations. The results of the application of this operator are shown in Figure 21.1.

21.2 Second Derivative

Instead of searching for maximal edge strength in the first derivative of an intensity image, the zero crossings of the second derivative can also be used. Figure 13.3 already showed this idea for continuous one–dimensional functions.

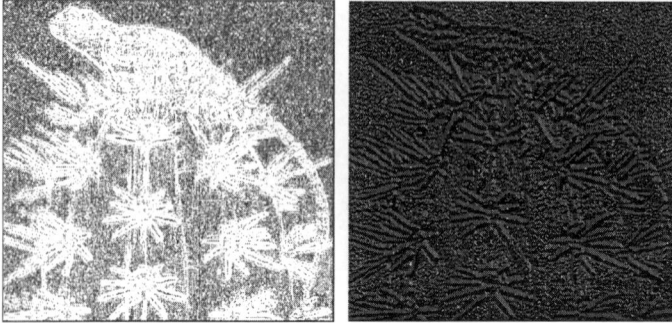

Figure 21.1 Robert's image: strength and orientation

The second derivative can be computed by the *Laplace–Operator* for discrete images. Three implementations of this operator are shown in Figure 21.2. Another possible definition uses larger neighborhoods as in Eq. 21.2.

$$g(i,j) = \sum_{\mu,\nu}(f(\mu,\nu) - f(i,j)) \tag{21.2}$$

Figure 21.2 Mask definition for the discrete approximation of the second derivation (Laplace–Operator).

A major disadvantage of this operator is its sensitivity to noise. Usually, the Laplace operator will detect amongst the correct edges various scattered edge points. Additionally, the definitions in Figure 21.2 and Eq. 21.2 will compute no edge direction. By a simple modification, however, a directed version of the Laplace operator can be defined, as shown in Eq. 21.3.

$$
\begin{array}{rcl}
f_{xx}(i,j) & = & 2f(i,j) - f(i-1,j) - f(i+1,j) \\
f_{yy}(i,j) & = & 2f(i,j) - f(i,j-1) - f(i,j+1) \\
g(i,j) & = & f_{xx}(i,j) + f_{yy}(i,j)
\end{array}
\tag{21.3}
$$

Various edge operators are based on Laplace operators (Marr/Hildreth [Mar80], Haralick [Har82]). Usually, the intensity image is filtered with a Gauss–filter (Sect. 19.1) in order to reduce the sensitivity of the operator to noise. The results of directed Laplace edge detection on the un–filtered intensity image are shown in Figure 21.3.

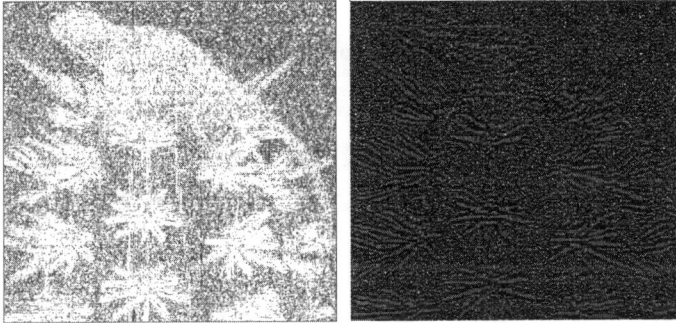

Figure 21.3 Laplace image (directed version): strength and orientation

21.3 Edge Model Masks

The masks in Sect. 13.4 and 21.2 were used to compute derivations of the intensity function by a convolution of the image function with the mask.

Another approach to edge detection are the application of edge masks. These masks represent typical shapes of edges; a convolution of the image function with these masks will yield a large response if an edge of the expected form and direction is present at the actual position in the image. Usually, several masks are applied which represent different directions of an edge. Figure 21.4 shows four simple masks of size 3×3 called the *Robinson–Operator* [Rob77]. For every position in the image, all four masks are applied; the greatest response is used as the edge strength. The four masks represent edge directions of 0, 45, 90, and 135 degrees. The sign of the response can be used to extend the directions to the range $180 \ldots 360$ degrees. Figure 21.5 shows the result of this operator.

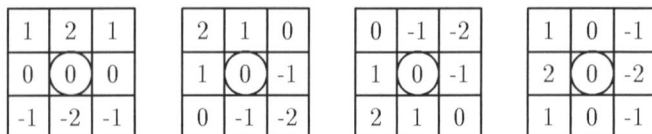

1	2	1
0	(0)	0
-1	-2	-1

2	1	0
1	(0)	-1
0	-1	-2

0	-1	-2
1	(0)	-1
2	1	0

1	0	-1
2	(0)	-2
1	0	-1

Figure 21.4   Mask definition for the Robinson–Operator.

Figure 21.5   Robinson image: strength and orientation

Another operator of this class is introduced in [Nev80]. It uses 6 masks of size 5×5 which detect 12 orientations; they are shown in Figure 21.6. The relatively large masks will smooth the image implicitly; the operator is thus less sensitive to small changes than for example the Robinson–operator. Further operators of this type are for example by Kirsch [Kir71], Prewitt [Pre70] and Ritter [Rit86]. The result of the Nevatia/Babu operator is shown in Figure 21.7.

100	100	100	100	100
100	100	100	100	100
0	0	0	0	0
-100	-100	-100	-100	-100
-100	-100	-100	-100	-100

100	100	100	100	100
100	100	100	78	-32
100	92	0	-92	100
32	-78	-100	-100	-100
-100	-100	-100	-100	-100

100	100	100	-32	-100
100	100	92	-78	-100
100	100	0	-100	-100
100	78	-92	-100	-100
100	32	-100	-100	-100

100	100	0	-100	100
100	100	0	-100	100
100	100	0	-100	100
100	100	0	-100	100
100	100	0	-100	100

100	-32	-100	-100	-100
100	78	-92	-100	-100
100	100	0	-100	-100
100	100	92	-78	-100
100	100	100	32	-100

-100	-100	-100	-100	-100
32	-78	-100	-100	-100
100	92	0	-92	-100
100	100	100	78	-32
100	100	100	100	100

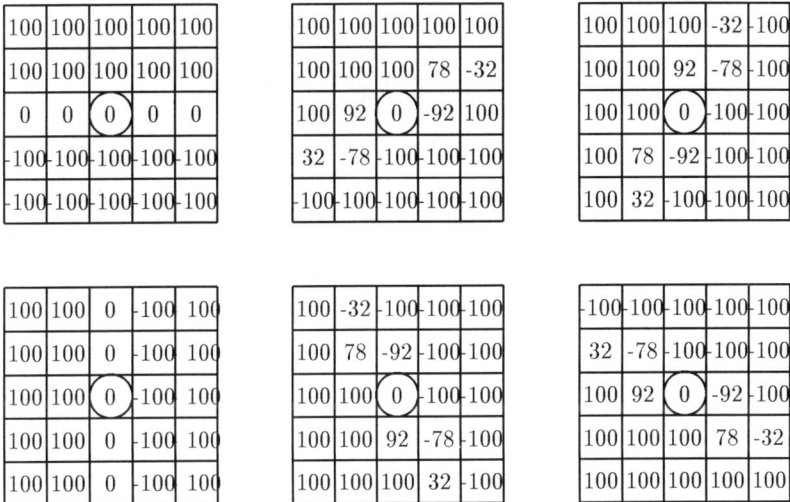

Figure 21.6 Mask definition according to Nevatia and Babu [Nev80].

21.4 Alternative Methods

Another type of edge detection algorithms uses parametric models for edges. The image intensity function is compared to the model function and the parameters are tuned to an optimal fit according to an error criterion.

The classical algorithm of this type was published by Hückel in [Hue73]. The model function is adjusted in a circular neighborhood of the actual image position. A simplified version uses a rectangular window.

Several other ideas for edge detection have been published and tested, all of which cannot be described here. Among them are those operating in the spatial frequency domain (cmp. Chapter 16.3), where high frequencies correspond to sharp edges in the spatial domain. Edges can be found using a high–pass filter [Ros82].

Statistical classification principles can also be used for edge detection (e.g. in [Kun87, Hau84, Hua88, Har88]). So called "Multi-Scale-Algorithms" use

Figure 21.7 Nevatia and Babu image: strength and orientation

different spatial resolutions (e.g. the method of Marr and Hildreth, see above, and [Ros71, Ekl82, Ber86, Ber87]).

21.5 Thinning of Edge Images

Due to possible noise in an image, most edge detectors will erroneously indicate a possible edge at many points. In addition, edges in the images are not normally ideal step edges (Figure 13.1) or roof edges (i.e. edge profiles looking like the roof of a house) but instead are blurred or disturbed due to sensor and quantization noise. Edge operators will thus localize edges additionally in the neighborhood of a real edge. The edges appear smeared.

Edge operators like the Sobel operator (Sect. 13.4) will create two edges in the edge image — even for an ideal step edge in the intensity image. Small changes in the lighting conditions may also result in large differences in the edge strength along a real edge. Changes in the surface and reflectance characteristics of the objects can yield the same effects.

In order to facilitate the connection of edge points to lines, it is useful to eliminate some edge point after edge detection. Three algorithms will be presented in the following sections. They transform an edge image into a new edge image (arrow 10 in Figure 17.2). For the description of the algorithms we use the following notation. The actual position (i, j) in the edge image will be called the point P. We compute the following values which can be directly mapped to the fields in the class `Edge` and `EdgeImage`:

- $f(P)$ the gray value in point P,

- $s(P)$ the edge–strength in point P,

- $r(P)$ the edge–orientation in point P,

- $S_{max} = \max_P S(P)$ the maximal edge–strength in the image

We will also need this notation in Chapter 22.

21.6   Edge Thresholding

Edge images may be further enhanced or modified still yielding edge images (arrow x in Figure 17.2). The simplest method for reduction of weak edge elements is to use a global threshold. All edges with strength below the threshold will be removed, i. e. their edge strength will be set to zero. Usually, this method is too simple. Thresholds have to be chosen differently for every image in order to get reasonably good results.

A better technique is to use a threshold relative to maximum edge strength in the image (Eq. 21.4).

$$s'(P) := \begin{cases} s(P) & , \quad \text{if } s(P) > \gamma * S_{max} \\ 0 & , \quad \text{otherwise} \end{cases} \qquad (21.4)$$

The parameter γ can be set globally for an image. Since this method uses the maximal edge strength, it can be applied to an edge image no matter which edge operator was used to create it.[1] The result of this operation is shown in Figure 21.8.

---

[1]Remember, the edge strength in an edge image is not normalized. Different operators will have completely different ranges of the edge strength!

Figure 21.8 Thresholded image of Figure 11.2. On the left: threshold of 10 %, on the right: threshold of 20 %

21.7 Non Maxima Suppression

The algorithms for **N**on-**M**axima-**S**uppression (NMS) use the local context of an edge position for edge thinning. Preferably those edge points are taken into consideration which are close to the edge gradient, i. e. in an orthogonal direction to the edge orientation. If these neighbors have the same orientation as the actual point, they will most likely belong to the same edge in the intensity image. The goal is now to select the "best" among these points and to suppress the others. An edge point is simply removed if its strength is smaller than those of its neighbors having the same orientation.

A two–phase implementation is proposed in [Nev80]: The edge image is scanned an internal label image is created with the same dimensions. For every edge element P the neighbors N_L and N_R (Figure 21.9) are located.

The following conditions are tested:

- $s(P) \geq s(N_L)$ and $s(P) \geq s(N_R)$;

- $|r(P) - r(N_L)| < 30°$ and $|r(P) - r(N_R)| < 30°$;

- $s(P) > S_{th}$.

If all three conditions are true, P is marked in a label field of the same size as the input image, and N_L and N_R are marked as "excluded".

The label image is then scanned; a new edge image is created; all edge elements marked in the label image which are not simultaneously excluded will be included in the output image.

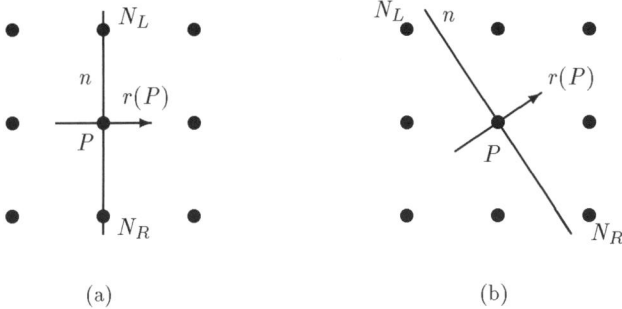

(a)   (b)

Figure 21.9   Edge thinning according to Nevatia/Babu

The result of NMS is shown in Figure 21.10.

Figure 21.10   NMU image Figure 11.2. Left: threshold 10%, right: threshold 20%

21.8   Non Maxima Absorption

The **Non–Maxima–A**bsorption (NMA) is also an interative edge thinning
method. Rather than eliminating some edge elements — as in the previous
methods — the idea here is to shift edge strength from the smaller edge
elements to the bigger ones.

As in the previous section, the neighbors N_L and N_R of an actual point P are
used (Figure 21.9). Then P and its two neighbors are inspected.

- If the edge strength in P is the biggest of the three, $\alpha \cdot s(N_L)$ resp.
  $\alpha \cdot s(N_R)$ of the strength of its neighbors is added to P.

- If the edge strength in P is the smallest of the three, it will be reduced
  by $2 \cdot \alpha \cdot s(P)$.

- If P has one neighbor P^+ with a larger strength, and one P^- with a
  smaller one, its strength will be reduced by $\alpha \cdot s(P^-)$ and increased by
  $\alpha \cdot s(P^+)$. This will be done only if the orientations are similar.

A difference in edge orientation of ≤ 30 degrees turns out to be a feasible
value. The result of this method is shown in Figure 21.11.

Figure 21.11   NMA image Figure 11.2. Left: threshold 10%, right: threshold 20%

21.9 Class Edge Revisited

The implementation of the class Edge was done efficiently with respect to storage and computation time (Example 141). Some bits the storage layout were unused; proposals for use of the remaining bits were made in Example 121. In Table 21.1 we list several flag values which can be associated with an edge element and which can be stored in the remaining storage space of an Edge object.

is closed	if start is equal to end
is start	starts a line
is end	ends a line
has succ	the successor field is valid
is edge	is an edge (no matter whether strength is high)
is vertex	several lines meet here

Table 21.1 Flags for structure edge

These new features will be used in the next chapter. Example 168 shows how they are incorporated in the class for edges (Example 121). Special care has to be taken for the external representation of edge objects. The order of bit fields is machine dependent; thus, the value of all may not be used for external storage.[2]

---

[2]That means that the method storeOn has to code the flags into a long integer value using bit operations; then, xdr_long can be used, cmp. 15.9.

```
struct Edge {
    static const int onum;              // constants in class-scope
    static const float odunit, const float orunit;
    union {
      unsigned int all;
      struct {
        unsigned int f_strength : 16;
        unsigned int f_orient   : 8;
        unsigned int successor  : 3; // chain code
        unsigned int is_closed  : 1; // see table
        unsigned int is_start   : 1; // see table
        unsigned int is_end     : 1; // see table
        unsigned int has_succ   : 1; // see table
        unsigned int is_edge    : 1; // see table
        unsigned int is_vertex  : 1; // see table
      } fields ;
    };
    Edge() { all = 0; }    // clear
    // etc.
};
```

$\left(168\right)$

Exercises

1. How can edge strength and edge orientation consistently be derived from the Robert's Cross definition?

2. Which discrete values for the orientation (Sect. 13.5) will be appropriate for the masks in Sect. 21.3?

3. Find a derivation of the Laplace operator (Sect. 21.2) from twofold application of the simple differential operator in Eq. 13.2.

4. Estimate minimal, maximal, and "normal" edge strength for the various edge operators.

5. Implement a fast and machine independent storage routine for the edge elements (Example 168).

6. Convert an edge image to a gray level image using the edge strength. Normalize it to 256 gray values.

7. Extend the filter classes of exercise 4 on page 299.

A simple implementation of the sobel operator (Sect. 13.4) is given in Example 169.

```
const int Edge::ONUM = 144;

static int geto(int fx, int fy)
{
 return (((fx==0) && (fy==0)) ? Edge::ONUM+1 :
          int((M_PI+ atan2(fy,fx)) / Edge::ONUM));
}

int Sobel::operator() (GrayLevelImage& in,EdgeImage& out) const
{
  printf("Apply Sobel %dx%d\n",in.getxsize(),in.getysize());
  for (int i = 1 ; i < in.getysize()-1; ++i) {
    for (int j = 1 ; j < in.getxsize()-1; ++j) {
      int fx= -in[i-1][j-1] - 2*in[i][j-1] - in[i+1][j-1]
            + in[i-1][j+1] + 2*in[i][j+1] + in[i+1][j+1];
      int fy= -in[i-1][j-1] - 2*in[i-1][j] - in[i-1][j+1]
            + in[i+1][j-1] + 2*in[i+1][j] + in[i+1][j+1];
      out [i][j].strength = int(sqrt(fx*fx + fy*fy));
      out [i][j].orient  = geto(fy,fx);
    }
  }
  return 0;
};
```

(169)

22 Line Detection Algorithms

The edge elements detected by the algorithms in Chapter 13 and Chapter 21 will now be connected to lines. This is called *contour* or *line following*.

22.1 Line Detection

After edge detection with one of the various operators defined in the previous chapters, and after an optional line thinning (Sect. 21.5), edge elements may still be isolated or scattered in space. In order to detect continuous lines, these edge elements have to be connected and gaps have to be closed. Groups of edge elements are connected to lines.

The input to line detection algorithms is an edge image (`EdgeImage`); the output is a set of lines which is represented by a segmentation object. Different line detection algorithms create different line representations. The most basic result is a segmentation object (`SegObj`) consisting of lines represented as chain codes (`Chain`). Some algorithms (e.g. the Hough Transform, Sect. 22.6) will compute straight line segments without going through the chain code representation. Other algorithms combine edge detection — as described for the edge operators — with line following, e.g. the Canny operator (Sect. 22.7) and the Shen operator (Sect. 22.8).

For a simple line detection based on edge images we now compute three additional values for every element of the edge image. The edge class was already extended for this purpose (Sect. 21.9).

- We number all the lines found in the image. The first number is a label for the line which the edge element belongs to. A temporary label field is needed for this purpose (an `int` matrix, Sect. 11.2).

- The second value is a chain code number pointing from the actual edge element to the potential successor.

- The flag field in the edge class will contain information about features of the edge as indicated in Table 21.1.

We now turn to algorithms for the computation and use of these values.

22.2 Local Connectivity

The so called *local connectivity analysis* can be used to connect edge elements to lines. The neighborhood of an edge element is searched for potential line elements.

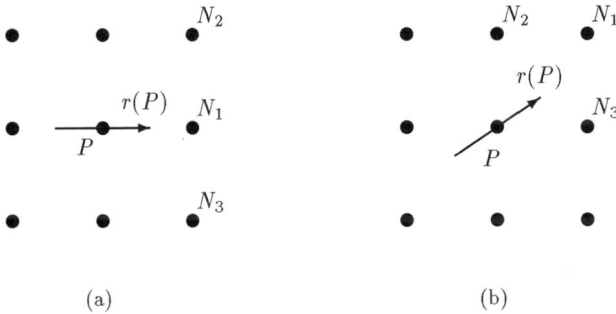

Figure 22.1 Neighborhood for line following [Nev80].

Nevatia and Babu [Nev80] propose a parallel and a sequential component for the algorithm. In the parallel part we inspect a 8–neighborhood (Sect. 11.9) of each edge point. As shown in Figure 22.1, three points N_1, N_2 and N_3 will be used, which are closest to the inspected edge direction $r(P)$ of the actual point P. The successor of P is selected from these points based on the most similar edge direction $r(P)$. If more than one point has similar direction, the one with the higher edge strength is chosen. If all three neighbors have similar direction and strength, the point closest to the edge direction — in Figure 22.1 this is always called N_1 — in P is chosen. This direction is recorded as a chain code in the field `successor` (Example 168).

In the next (serial) step, all marked edge points will be grouped to lines. The image is scanned line by line to find potential start points for lines. If the edge strength at the actual position exceeds a given threshold and if the actual point does not yet belong to another line, it is marked as a start point of a new line; a new line label is created. Using the successor field created in the first part of the algorithm, the line is then tracked through the image until the path reaches a position with an edge strength which is too low, or a position which belongs to another line already. All these points are marked with the same line label. The tracking tries to jump over small gaps, where the edge strength is too low, in order to eliminate small interruptions due to noise. The lines are represented as chain code objects. These objects are added to a segmentation object which is the final result of the line detection algorithm. Figure 22.2 and 22.3 show this algorithm symbolically.

Since this algorithm tries to combine *all* edge points to lines, it is essential to apply line thinning before line tracking.

22.3 Hysteresis Thresholds

The use of larger contexts for edge localization may enhance the recognition. Instead of a small neighborhood for edge detection, the whole context along the line can be important for line detection.

Two thresholds for the edge strength are used in the so called "hysteresis–algorithm": an upper limit Σ_o and a lower threshold Σ_l. These parameters are coupled by a factor β according to Eq. 22.1. Good results can be obtained with β in the range of 0.3 to 0.5. Experimental evaluation in [Brü90] showed that the choice of β is not critical for the result. A default value of $\beta = 0.33$ is reasonable.

$$\Sigma_l = \beta \Sigma_o \qquad\qquad (22.1)$$

After an edge thinning step, all those positions in the edge image which have an edge strength higher than Σ_o are chosen as candidates for a start of a line. Each start point is tracked in both directions — along the edge orientation and in the opposite direction. Candidates for successors are selected as illustrated in Figure 22.1.

Search for edge point P_{act} which does not belong to any segment.				
Assign to P_{act}: new number $SegNum$ and label "has no predecessor".				
IF	P_{act} has a successor $c(P_{act})$			
THEN	Choose point P_N which is successor of P_{act} reachable by $c(P_{akt})$.			
ELSE	**Try to jump over gaps of one pixel**			
	Compute potential succesors $N_i \in \{N_1, N_2, N_3\}$ of P_{akt}, and for all N_i the potential successors N_{i1}, N_{i2} and N_{i3} (Figure 22.1).			
	Search for the first point N_{ij}, where $i, j \in \{1, 2, 3\}$ and: $|r(N_i) - r(P_{akt})| < 30$ degrees $\wedge$ $|r(N_{ij}) - r(N_i)| < 30$ degrees $\wedge$ chain code element $c(N_{ij})$ (i.e. there exists a successor of N_{ij}).			
	IF	N_{ij} is found (i.e. closing of gaps succeeded)		
	THEN	Connect (P_{act}) and N_i. Let next point P_N be N_{ij}.		
	ELSE	No successor P_N of P_{act} is found (end of segment).		
IF	Successor P_N of P_{act} is found			
THEN	IF	P_N has already a segment number S_N		
	THEN	IF	S_N is equal to $SegNum$	
		THEN	P_{act} is labeled by "end cycle". Label P_N "start cycle".	
		End of segment is reached.		
	ELSE	P_N gets actual segment number $SegNum$.		
		Let P_N be the new actual point P_{act}.		
UNTIL End of segment is reached..				
UNTIL Each edge point has a segment number (i.e. all image points are traversed).				
Label segments with new numbers (Figure 22.3).				

Figure 22.2 Serial part of line following algorithm according to [Nev80].

In order to be accepted as an line element, a candidate has to fulfill three conditions:

- The edge strength has to be greater than the lower threshold Σ_l.

- The orientation in the actual position P must be similar to the candidate's orientation.

- The candidate may not be member of another line.

New number for each segment:
Let new segment number *NewSegNum* = 0.
FOR All points P_a with the label "has no predecessor" or "start cycle"
Increment *NewSegNum*.
Choose successor of P_a as next point P_N reachable by $c(P_a)$.
Set the segment number of P_N to *NewSegNum*.
Let P_N be the new actual point P_a.
UNTIL There exists no successor of P_a (i.e. $c(P_a)$ has no value $\quad\lor\quad P_a$ is labeled by "end cycle").

Figure 22.3   Serial part of line following algorithm according to [Nev80] cont.

If more than one candidate fulfill all three conditions, the one with the biggest edge strength is chosen. This can happen only in two cases. Either these candidates belong to the same line and have not been eliminated by the edge thinning phase; it should thus be avoided to use these points for another line; in order to do so, their edge strength is reduced to a value below the lower limit Σ_o. If on the other hand these candidates belong to different lines, their edge strength will be increased to $\Sigma_l*(1+\epsilon)$, where ϵ is 0.01. This is illustrated in Figure 22.4–22.6.

Search for one edge point P without a segment number, where the edge strength $s(P)$ is greater than the upper threshold Σ_u. Call this point P_{act} and assign to this point the not yet used segment number *SegNum*.
Search forward
Set the actual point P_{act} to the start point P.
Search backward
UNTIL All edge points are processed (i.e., traverse the whole image).

Figure 22.4   Line following with the hysteresis algorithm (1) [Brü90]

Search forward		
Compute possible successors $N_i \in \{N_1, N_2, N_3\}$ of P_{act} of the direction $r(P_{act})$ gemäß Figure 22.1.		
Compute successor N_i, where: $s(N_i) > \Sigma_l \quad \wedge \quad \|r(N_i) - r(P_{act})\| < 30$ degrees $\quad \wedge \quad \{N_i$ has no segment number $\vee \ N_i = P \ (=$ start point of the segment$)\}$.		
IF	Successor N_i was found	
THEN	IF	one point is P (start point of the line)
	THEN	A cyclic period is found. Connect P_{act} and P. The start and end of the segment is reached.
	ELSE	Let N be the candiate with maximum $s(N_i)$. Connect N and P_{act}. Let N be the actual point P_{act}. Let N be the temporary end point P_e.
	Reduce the set of non processed candidates $s(N_i)$ to $\Sigma_l + \epsilon$.	
ELSE	End of segment is reached.	
UNTIL End of segment is reached.		

Figure 22.5   Line following with the hysteresis algorithm (2) [Brü90]

22.4   Closing of Gaps

After the lines have been followed as outlined above, an attempt can be made to close small gaps which result from errors in the edge image. The goal of this step is to combine lines which are separated by few (here: up to two) pixels.

For each line found in the image, the end is inspected and the points shown in Figure 22.7 are searched for possible start or end points of another line. Similar neighbor masks can be used for other directions.

Usually, small segments are discarded in a final processing step, e.g. all those chain codes shorter than three pixels.

Search backward		
Determine potential predecessors $V_i \in \{V_1, V_2, V_3\}$ of P_{act} with the orientation $r(P_{act}) + 180$ degrees according to Figure 22.1.		
Compute the predecessor V_i, where: $s(V_i) > \Sigma_l \quad \wedge \quad |r(V_i) - r(P_{act})| < 30$ degrees $\wedge \quad \{V_i$ has no segment number $\vee \; V_i = P_e$ (= end point of the segment)$\}$.		
IF	Predecessor V_i is found	
THEN	IF	One of the candidates is P_e (end point of the line)
	THEN	Cyclic period is found. Connect P and P_{act}. The start point of the segment is reached.
	ELSE	Let V be the candidate with maximum $s(V_i)$. Connect V and P_{act}. Let V be the actual point P_{act}.
	Reduce the set of non processed points $s(V_i)$ to $\Sigma_l + \epsilon$.	
ELSE	Start of the segment is reached.	
UNTIL Start of the segment is reached.		

Figure 22.6 Line following with the hysteresis algorithm (3) [Brü90]

22.5 Zero crossings in Laplace–Images

The Laplace operator (Sect. 21.2) will generate an edge image with zero crossings corresponding to lines in the intensity image. These have to be located. Since we have to deal with images, zero crossings of a two–dimensional curve have to be found.

Figure 22.8 shows a ideal diagonal edge and the corresponding response of the operator (using Figure 21.2 left). A simple algorithm is to locate horizontal and vertical zero crossings and to mark these points as edges. A heuristic search for tracking these points and generating lines is described in [Mar76].

22.6 Hough Transform

One example of an algorithm which generates straight line segments directly from the edge image, is an application of the Hough–Transform [Pit93]. The idea behind the Hough–Transform is to express the features in the image in a

(a)   (b)

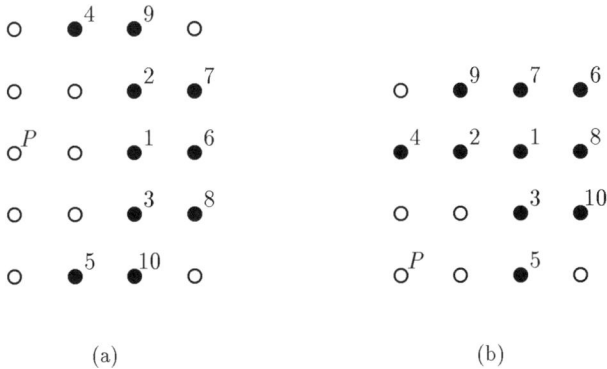

Figure 22.7 Points which will be inspected for gap closing. The positions will be visited in the order given by the numbers. The points are shown for an edge orientation of $r(P) = 0$ degrees (a) and $r(P) = 45°$ (b).

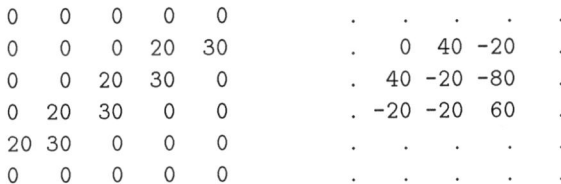

```
0   0   0   0   0          .    .    .    .    .
0   0   0  20  30          .    0   40  -20   .
0   0  20  30   0          .   40  -20  -80   .
0  20  30   0   0          .  -20  -20   60   .
20 30   0   0   0          .    .    .    .    .
0   0   0   0   0          .    .    .    .    .
```

Figure 22.8 Image and Laplacian image

parametrized form. The image is then transformed to a *parameter space*. The parameter space is digitized and quantized and called an *accumulator array*. Occurrences of these features are recorded in accumulator. Local maxima in the accumulator are used as an indication of the feature in the image.

This rather theoretical idea can be applied to the detection of straight lines. The lines are expressed in a two–dimensional parameter space by their orientation and the distance of the line to the origin (see Figure 22.9). We use an edge image (EdgeImage) as input and create a segmentation object (SegObj) as output containing straight lines (which have to be represented as objects; in ἵππος this is done in a class StrLineSeg[1]).

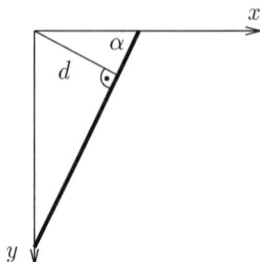

Figure 22.9 A straight line and its parmaters d and α of the accumulator array

```
typedef Array2d<int> accu;
inline int dist(int y, int x, int o)
{
    // sin_tab and cos_tab are arrays including the
    // associated values of sine and cosine functions
    return (int)(x*sin_tab[o]+y*cos_tab[o]);
}
void hough(Edge** edges, int sizex, int sizey)
{
    accu a(int(1+sqrt(sizex*sizex+sizey*sizey)),Edge::OrientNumb);
    for(int i = sizey-1; i >= 0; --i)
      for(int j = sizex-1; j >= 0; --j) {
        Edge* e = & edges[i][j];
        if (e->orient < Edge::OrientNumb)
            a[dist(i,j,e->orient)][e->orient] += e->strength;
      }
}
```
(170)

Assume an input edge image of size $a \times b$. An intermediate integer array of dimension $\sqrt{a^2 + b^2} \times 144$ — this is the maximum distance of a line in the

---
[1]The implementation is left as an exercise (1).

image to the origin and the quantized orientation — is initialized to zero. For each edge element in the edge image we calculate the assumed line from the element's position and the edge–orientation; we get two values which are used as index in the accumulator which is incremented by the edge strength. Maximal values in the accumulator are then used as indication of a straight line in the input image. Example 170 shows the core of the transformation algorithm in C++.

Some problems in the implementation are the difficulty to find maxima in the accumulator and the fact, that interrupted straight lines in the input image create *one* value resp. cluster in the accumulator. An example is shown in Figure 22.10.

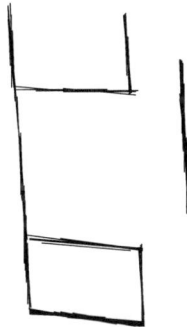

Figure 22.10   Result of straight line detection with the Hough–Transform of Figure 11.2

The idea of the Hough transform can be used to detect objects which can be described as parametric curves with more than two parameters. Some restrictions have to be imposed on the parameter space in order to reduce the effort for searching in the accumulator. This way, circles or ellipses [Bal82, Hor93] can be detected.

22.7   Canny Line Detection

An algorithm for line detection was introduced in [Can86] which optimizes
the following criteria:

- *Detection,*

- *Localization* and

- *Uniqueness.*

This algorithm combines Gaussian–filtering, edge detection, thresholding, and
line detection to an optimal solution for a given type of edges. A complete
mathematical description of this idea would be beyond the scope of this book,
see [Can86, Nie90b] for details.

One principle result of this work is the fact that we can not maximize these
criteria simultaneously. The better the detection is, the worse the localization
will be.

Various implementations of this operator can be found in the public domain
software (see Sect. C.2). In most cases a shell has to be built around these
routines in order to incorporate them into the object–oriented framework. A
result of the Canny edge detection is shown in Figure 22.11.

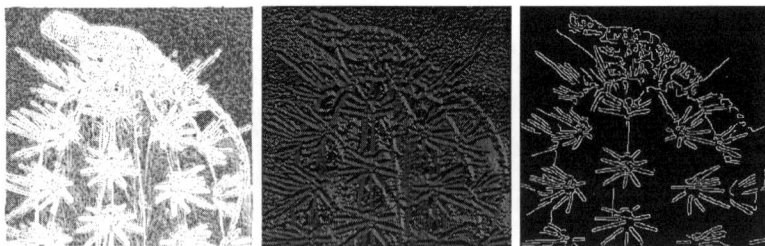

Figure 22.11 Canny image: strength and orientation and final result

22.8 Shen and Castan

Although Canny showed the principally optimal solution for edge detection (under certain assumptions), the research still continued. The Deriche–Filter [Der87, Der90] and the *Operator of Shen and Castan* [She86, She88, Cas90] also use Gaussian–filters and combined edge detection; the major advantage in comparison to the Canny operator is the more efficient implementation. Intermediate results of the Shen operator are shown in Figure 22.12.

Figure 22.12 Shen image: strength and orientation

22.9 Representation as Segmentation Objects

Segmentation objects are used as common interface data structures representing all possible results of image segmentation. No matter whether the line segmentation algorithms compute straight line segments — as in the Hough transformation —, or chain codes, as in the algorithm of Sect. 22.3, the representation should still look similar in order to facilitate further processing (e.g. post–processing of chain codes in Chapter 23).

Segmentation objects form a shell around Sets of nihcl and guarantee that no inconsistencies occur in the representation (Sect. 15.8). The sets in nihcl will not only record *references* to the objects in the set, i.e. they will not create a copy of them. It is thus essential to allocate a new line object for each line detected and to add this to the segmentation object. A code fragment is shown in Figure 171.

```
Chain * follow(Edge ** ei, int i, int j)
{
    Chain * cp = new Chain(j,i);   // (x,y) coordinates
    // follow the edge, append to cp
    return cp;
}
void segment(SegObj& s, EdgeImage& ei)
{
    for(int i = ei.getsizey()-1; i >= 0; --i)
      for(int j = ei.getsizey()-1; j >= 0; --j) {
        Edge* e = & ei[i][j];
        if (e->strength > threshold) // allocate and add
            s.add(*new AtomLine(follow(ei,i,j)));
      }
}
```

$$\boxed{171}$$

Exercises

1. Implement a class for straight line segments. Derive it from the class LineRep2D.

2. Get public domain versions of various edge detectors and adapt them to your object–oriented system. Use external C functions (Sect. 8.5) and encapsulate the functions without modifying them (if possible).

3. Proof the correctness of distance computation in Example 170!

4. Extend the filter classes of exercise 4 on page 299.

   Parameters and a helper function are shown in Example 172.

   A simple implementation of a line detection operator is given in Example 173.

```
#include "SegObj.h"
#include "AtomLine.h"
#include "Chain.h"
// this fcn converts direction vectors to chain code directions
static int direction(int x, int y)
{
  static short d[3][3] = {{5,6,7}, {4,8,0}, {3,2,1}};
  return d[y+1][x+1];
}
static const int threshold = 50;      // for edge strength
static const int strength_diff = 25; // similarity
static const int orient_diff   = 30; // similarity
static const int minimum_length= 20; // minimum length
```

(172)

```
void Hystline::operator() (EdgeImage&edge, SegObj&sego) const
{
  Matrix<int> element(edge.getxsize(),edge.getysize());
  for (int i=1; i<edge.getysize()-1; i++)
   for (int j=1; j<edge.getxsize()-1; j++)
     element[i][j]= 0;
  for (int y=1; y<edge.getysize()-1; y++)
   for (int x=1; x<edge.getxsize()-1; x++)
    if ((element[y][x]==0)&&((edge[y][x]).strength>threshold)) {
      element[y][x]= 1;
      Chain * line= new Chain(*new PointXY(x,y));
      int xpos= x, ypos= y, success= 1;
      while (success){
          int stop= 0;
          for (int yn=-1; yn<2; yn++)
           for (int xn=-1; xn<2; xn++) {
            if (!stop && (element[ypos+yn][xpos+xn]==0) &&
               (edge[ypos+yn][xpos+xn].strength > threshold) &&
               (abs((int)edge[ypos+yn][xpos+xn].orient-
                  (int)edge[ypos][xpos].orient)< orient_diff) &&
               (abs(edge[ypos+yn][xpos+xn].strength-
                edge[ypos][xpos].strength)<strength_diff)){
              xpos+= xn; ypos+= yn; stop= 1;
              element[ypos][xpos]= 1;
              line->append(direction(xn,yn));
            }
            if (!stop && (xn==1) && (yn==1)) success= 0;
          }
      }
    if (line->length()> minimum_length)
       sego.add(* new AtomLine(*new Chain(*line)));
    }
}
```

(173)

23 Chain Codes

A suitable and often used representation for lines are *chain codes*. The basic principles of chain codes were already introduced in section 15.4. In ἵππος a class for chain codes is implemented. Thus, an abstract data type Chain is available and can be used for applications and subsequent image recognition stages. In the following project some further methods have to be added to this elementary class. Some of the described algorithms were suggested in [Fre80, Zam91].

23.1 Length of a Chain

The length of a chain can be computed using the simple formula

$$l = a + b \cdot \sqrt{2} \quad , \tag{23.1}$$

where a is the number of even– and b the number of odd–valued links in the given chain.

23.2 Smoothing

Chain codes are often disturbed by noise and have indentations. We need a method in the class for chain codes which admits the smoothing of lines represented as chain codes.

Let S_1 and S_2 be two subsequent directions in the given chain code. In Table 23.1 rules are summarized which should be used for smoothing chain codes. For that purpose we define $m = \min(S_1, S_2)$ and $M = \max(S_1, S_2)$.

The arithmetic, i.e. summation, is done modulo 8. The smoothing procedure has to be done iteratively until there is no change of the chain code. Figure 23.1 shows an example.

$M - m$	m	new direction
0	—	no change
1	—	no change
2	odd	$m + 1, m + 1$
2	even	$m + 1$
3	odd	$m + 1$
3	even	$m + 1$
4	—	delete m and M
5	odd	$m - 1$
5	even	$m - 2$
6	odd	$m - 1, m - 1$
6	even	$m - 1$
7	—	no change

Table 23.1 Rules for smoothing chain codes ([Zam91], p. 21)

Give a proof that this algorithm terminates after a finite number of iterations and add this method to the actual implementation of chain codes. Write a program for the visualization of chain codes, i.e. generate a synthetic image which shows the (set of) chain codes. Describe the smoothing effects!

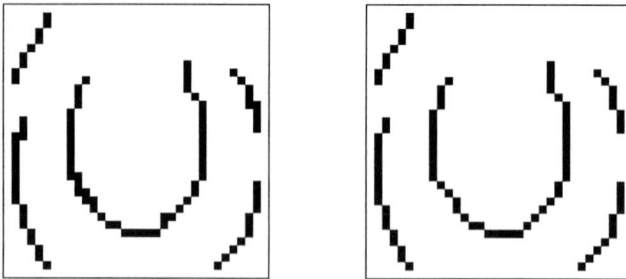

Figure 23.1 Original chain code (left) and smoothed line (right).

23.3 Digital Linear Lines

Due to the fact that chain codes have only eight discrete directions, straight lines in the image have to be approximated by these discrete steps. The process of drawing straight lines characterized by two points, i .e. the start and the end point, was already part of a project (see section 18.6). Use this function and implement a constructor for a chain code of a straight line, where the start and end points are given arguments. Furthermore, a boolean function has to be implemented which returns true if a given chain code represents a straight line and false otherwise. The decision criteria for a straight line are specified as follows:

(a) The whole chain code includes only two different directions, S_1 and S_2, where the following constraint has to be valid: $|S_1 - S_2| \equiv 1 \bmod 8$.

(b) The direction which is less often element of the chain code always has the other direction as predecessor and successor in the sequence of directions.

(c) S_1 and S_2 must be *homogeneously distributed* over the complete chain code.

The conditions (a) and (b) are easily checked. The homogeneity is computed using the following recursive procedure: Let the direction, which is more often part of the chain code, be denoted by S. Compute out of the given chain code a new formal chain code where the directions are the number of directly subsequent elements of the direction S. Check for this formal chain code conditions (a), (b), (c) until convergence.

Take the boolean function and check whether your straight lines generated by the implemented constructor are digital linear lines.

23.4 Similarity

For the classification of objects based on lines, like e.g. classification based on shapes, it is often necessary to match chain codes. Of course, the lines will not fit exactly, when real images are used. Therefore, we need a similarity measure for chain codes. For that purpose compute the absolute area A included by two lines. We assume that the area equals the number of enclosed pixels and the start and end points of each chain code are connected by virtual lines. Let l_1 and l_2 be the length of both lines. A measure for similarity is defined by

$$d = 2A\,(l_1 + l_2) \quad . \tag{23.2}$$

Implement this similarity measure as a method in your class. Test this distance function using several examples and discuss your results.

23.5   Intersections

A line can have intersections with itself. For example, the digit 8 is written with one intersected line. Extend the class for chain codes with a method which computes the set of intersections of one chain code. Additionally a synthetic image should be generated, where the enclosed areas of a chain code are colored. For filling areas in the plane when the shape is given there exist a lot of efficient algorithms in the field of computer graphics.

A method for the determination of intersections of two chains is also required. For that purpose, we determine the bounding rectangle for each chain. Obviously, any intersections of both chains will lie in the common area of these two bounding rectangles. If there exist no intersections, the two chains are disjunctive. For the intersection areas of the bounding boxes we proceed recursively as follows: we discard the portions of the chain codes lying outside, and for the remaining parts we compute the bounding rectangles, again. This process is repeated until all intersections are found or it is established that no intersection exists.

23.6   Rotation

Objects in real world can be translated and rotated. In this project two methods have to be implemented which admit the translation and rotation of chain codes. The translation is trivial. Even the rotation by a multiple of 90° is fairly easy. In general, arbitrary rotations will cause distortions. The chain must be treated as a curve and thus rotated, re–quantized an re–coded into the underlying image lattice (see Figure 23.2). What is the worst case difference in length of the chain code after rotation? Nevertheless, implement a function for chain code rotation. Let the center of rotation be the starting point of the actual chain. Show that arbitrary movements in the two–dimensional image plane can be decomposed into the implemented rotation and translation functions.

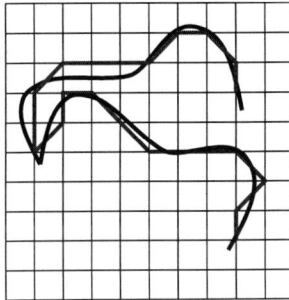

Figure 23.2 Illustration of a line, the rotation of the line (40°) and the corresponding chain codes

23.7   Conversion

A data reduction of chain code representations results from a polygonal approximation of chain codes by using straight line segments. The computation of the needed straight line segments can be formalized as an optimization problem: The approximation error should be below a given threshold; whereas, the number of line segments should be as minimal as possible.

For the judgment of the quality of the approximation a distance measure between straight lines and a chain code element is needed. One suitable measure was defined in Sect. 23.4. In the current case, we have the constraint that both the chain code and the polygonal approximation begin and end up in identical points.

Implement a simple polygonal approximation algorithm and check its complexity.

A more sophisticated solution of this problem is the so called *split algorithm*. The basic idea of this approach is due to a recursive division of the line segment into smaller segments. The decomposition of one segment stops, if the linear segment approximates the curved segment with an appropriate error.

Implement this technique and compare its complexity with the previously suggested algorithms for polygonal approximation. An example for polygonal approximations of line segments is shown in Figure 15.4.

Exercises

1. The animals shown in Figure 23.3 should be classified in gray–level images. Assume a homogeneous black background and let $\Omega_1, \Omega_2, \Omega_3$ and Ω_4 be the assiociated pattern classes.

   (a) Compute the closed contour–line for each object out of a given gray–level image.

   (b) Write programs for the determination of features like the area, length of the contour, or moments.

   (c) Define for each object a reference pattern r_λ and classify an observed object characterized by f using the decision rule

   $$\kappa \quad = \quad \min_\lambda \|r_\lambda - f\|, \tag{23.3}$$

   where κ is the computed class number and $\|.\|$ denotes the Euclidean distance of vectors.

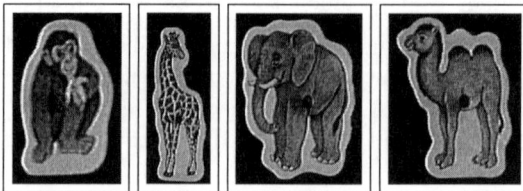

Figure 23.3 Animals

Part IV
Appendix

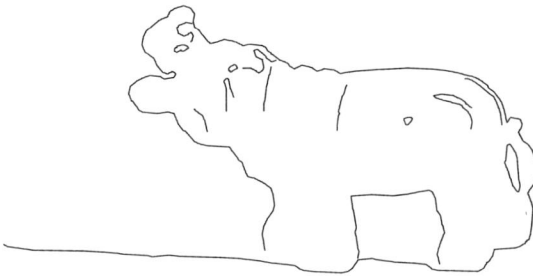

Lines extracted from the image on page 3.

In the appendix we list sources which can be used to complete the examples in the previous chapters. We describe how interested readers may access further information and request software via international computer networks. Basics of C, C++, and software development tools in Unix will be introduced.

A Basics of C++

In this appendix we briefly introduce the basic syntax of C++ for all those who do not already know C.

A.1 History

C and C++ are commonly used programming languages. C is derived from Algol [Ran67] and Pascal [Jen85] and was used for the Unix operating system. C++ is based on C and Simula [Bir83]. The language C is actually represented by two dialects: C due to Kernighan–Ritchie [Ker78] and ANSI-C.[1] For C++ there exists no international standard at the moment. We describe the actual version of C++ (3.1) as specified in the book [Str91a].

Most of all characteristics of ANSI-C are also valid for C++. A comparison of these languages can be found in [Sto90]. Like their ancestors, C and C++ are procedural programming languages. C++ incorporates some basic principles which are useful for object–oriented programming.

Programs written in C or C++ have their own typical appearance, which is characterized by many special characters. All characters of the ASCII code (23–126) are used except for @ and '. Special characters and sequences of them are often used as operators, which will be introduced in the subsequent chapters. Blanks and carriage return serve as separation. The input of programs is unformatted, except for preprocessor directives (see section 2.2).

---

[1] ANSI: American National Standards Institute

A.2   Identifier and Constants

Identifiers and numeric constants are similar to those found in other programming languages.

C++	Description	Example
identifier	letter [letter | digit*]	A, _A, A_2, a_2
character constant	'character'	'a'
octal number	'\mmm', m: 0–7	'\021'
special character	'\n' newline	
	'\r' return	
	'\b' back	
	'\t' tab	
	'\\' backslash	
string	string	"a\n\"a"

Table A.1   Basic constituents of the C++–syntax (1)

C++	Description	Example
block	{ [declaration]* [statement]* }	
function definition[2]	ID() block	main() {}
function call	ID(arguments);	puts("a");
preprocessor directive	# directive	#include
comment	// until end of line (only in C++)	
comment	/* comments */	
integer constant	[-]1-9+0-9*	-22, 1234
octal constant	0[0-7]*	007, 04711
hexadecimal constant	0x[0-9,A-F,a-f]+	0x7, 0xaf2F
double constant	[-][0-9]+.[0-9]+	0.33, .21, 1.

Table A.2   Basic constituents of the C++–syntax (2)

---

[2](Refer to Table A.2) This is only the simplest possibility.

Hexadecimal numbers may use upper or lower case. Long integers have a trailing character 'L'. All other definitions are case–sensitive. The backslash character is used to "escape" the meaning of the following character in various contexts (e.g. in strings and character constants). Strings in C++ and C are enclosed in double quotes. Characters are enclosed in single quotes; although they are *one* character by definition, they may use several keystrokes to be typed (see the examples for "newline", etc. in Tables A.1,A.2).

A.3 Basis Data Types in C and C++

Type	Explanation	Typical Size
[unsigned] char	character	8 Bit
[unsigned] short	integer	16 Bit
[unsigned] int	integer	32 Bit
[unsigned] long [int]	long integer	32 Bit
float	real	32 Bit
double	long real	64 Bit

Table A.3 Elementary data types

Table A.3 shows the list of basic data types in C and C++. The range of these data types indeed depends on the machine architecture. If integral variables are declared with unsigned, they are forced to have non–negative values. The precision of double variables is higher than for float declared objects, the range *may* be larger.[3] Characters are just tiny integers; their default sign depends on the implementation.

---

[3]There exist international standards for floating point numbers (IEEE).

B   Software Development Tools

In this appendix we describe some tools provided by the operating system Unix. First we introduce how teamwork is supported by file version and access control. Furthermore, some tools are explained for creation and management of huge program systems and the use of libraries.

B.1   Groups and ID's with Unix

Every user of a Unix system has a user name, which is a textual equivalent of a unique user number (user ID, uid) .[1] Users may be joint to groups, which also have a name and a number (group ID, gid). A user may be member of several groups; this is recorded in the file /etc/group. Upon login, the user is assigned to its uid and gid according to the file /etc/passwd.

Every file in the directory tree of the system is owned by a user. The uid is recorded with the file. The file is also assigned to a group[2]. Possibly different rights may be granted on a particular file for the owner, the group, and all other users. Read, write, and execute permissions may be set or refused independently to all of them (Figure B.1, see the manual entry for chmod). Defaults for the settings may be given (see the manual for umask). New files inherit the user and group ID of the user creating the file. The commands chown and chgrp allow change of these settings.[3]

On BSD systems, gid and uid are set according to the settings of the current directory. On SYS5 systems, the user may use the command newgrp.

---

[1] As usual: there are exceptions to this rule.

[2] Try ls -l to see the user and group assignments of the file.

[3] Permission to use these commands varies between Unix–flavors.

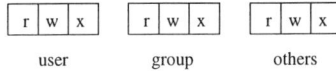

Figure B.1 Read (r), write (w), and execute (x) permissions with Unix

B.2   Program Building with make

In the programming phase of a system, interfaces often have to be modified. Necessarily, adaption of the other – dependent – modules should be done to preserve consistency. Unix provides the powerful program make[4] to detect and update those modules which are out of date after such a change. This program make is useful for the development of small programs; it is even more required for large modular programs. The subsequent description introduces syntax and functionality of this tool. Additional information can be found in Unix manuals (man make).

For example, you might have implemented a lot of modules which can be compiled separately into object code. In C/C++ those object files end in .o. In the linking stage several object files can be involved. Thus, the programmer has to make sure that a change of the object files will be followed by a new linkage of the program. The tool make supports the management of those dependencies. The implementor defines the file dependencies in a Makefile once, and describes the commands to be executed as well.

The file Makefile in the actual directory is read by the tool make. A Makefile can in general contain four different kinds of lines: target lines, shell command lines, macro definitions, and include lines. If something in the dependency graph has changed, i.e. the latest modification of a file is more recent than the modification time of files which depend on this target, the call of make will cause execution of all commands which are required for the update.

- dependencies:
  Dependencies describe how one file target depends on another file. The target specification starts on the first column of the Makefile and is followed by a colon. After the colon, a list of dependencies can be given.
  `target : list of files`

---

[4]Also included in all sorts of MS–DOS Compiler packages.

If a target does not have any dependents specified after the separator ":"
on the target line all commands associated with the actual are executed.

- shell commands:
  `<TAB> command`
  The lines including shell commands follow the target line and begin with
  a `<TAB>` symbol. The command lines can be continued across more than
  one line by ending each line with a backslash.

- Lines starting with a **#** are treated as comment lines.

We now give an example and explain the actions specified in the `Makefile`. We
deal with a program `prog.c`, the related object file `prog.o` and an executable
`prog`. These files are related as follows:

- If the program `prog` has to be generated, it is necessary to produce the
  object file `prog.o`.

- If the file `prog.c` will be changed, `prog.o` has to be generated again.

- If the file object file `prog.o` is younger than `prog`, `prog` has to be linked.

The syntactic representation of these dependencies in the `Makefile` is as
follows. Three basic types of entries can be observed:

- dependencies:
  Dependencies describe how one file target depends on another file. The
  target specification starts on the first column of the Makefile and is followed by a colon. After the colon, a list of dependencies can be given.
  `target : list of files`
  If a target does not have any dependents specified after the separator ":"
  on the target line all commands associated with the actual are executed.

- shell commands:
  `<TAB> command`
  The lines including shell commands follow the target line and begin with
  a `<TAB>` symbol. The command lines can be continued across more than
  one line by ending each line with a backslash.

- Lines starting with a **#** are treated as comment lines.

Target lines with their subsequent command lines are called *rules*. A typical simple `Makefile` is shown in Example 174.

```
# Simple make file for building prog
prog   : prog.o
         cc -o prog prog.o
prog.o : prog.c
         cc -c prog.c
```

(174)

The execution of the program **make** causes the first rule of the make file to be evaluated. By specifying the target of generation you can select special rules of the `Makefile`. For instance, the command **make prog** generates the executable program **prog**, assumed the actual version does not exist, yet. If you simply call **make prog.o**, only the compilation of **prog.o** is done. The command lines are normally printed before they are executed. Further options and facilities can be found in the Unix manual.

B.3   The Use of Libraries

Programs and modules developed by a team can result in many files which have to be written into an archive. For example, object files which have to be linked with other programs should be summarized. Unix provides a tool which allows the generation and the management of those archives. The tool `ar -r file lib` will add or replace the file `file` in the library `lib` and `ar -d file lib` for deleting the file `file` from the library. The table of contents of the archive file can be printed using the command `ar -t lib`.

B.4   Version and Access Control with `rcs`

RCS is very useful for teamwork. It allows easy sharing of code which is readable for all and writable for only one of the group at a time. The three basic programs for RCS are:

- `ci` (check in)

- `co` (check out)

- `rcs` (revision control system)

Their function is shown in Figure B.2. Common abbreviations in the diagram are `ci -u file` which is equivalent to the sequence

`ci file; co file;`

the command `ci -l file` stores the file and locks it. This is equivalent to

`ci file; co -l file.`

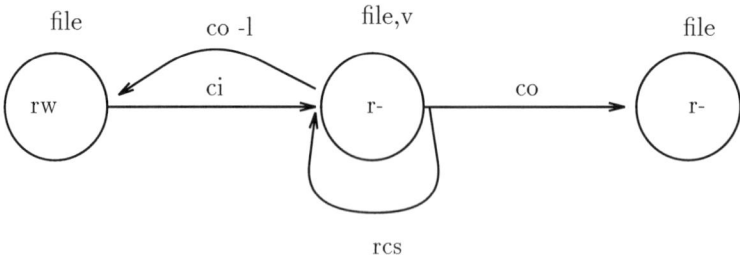

Figure B.2 RCS commands and file mode

Example 175 shows a combination of **Makefiles** and **rcs**. The strings `$@` and `$?` are handy shortcuts for the target and the dependent of the rule respectively. The version information in this makefile is again inserted by `rcs`[5]

---

[5]RCS will filled in the information about **this** file, i.e. the TEX–source file for this chapter!

```
# Makefile for use with rcs
# RCS will fill and update in the following strings
# $Revision: 3.6 $
# $Author: paulus $
prog   : prog.o
         cc -o $@ $?
prog.o : prog.c
         cc -c $?
prog.c : prog.c,v
         co $?
```
(175)

The following describes the strategy for teamwork using rcs under Unix. First, ask the system manager to establish a group for your team. This group will be permanent in the system.

Every time you want to do group work you have to perform the following steps:

- Join the group
  In BSD systems this will be done by changing the current directory to one which belongs to the group.
  In System V system you will have to do an explicit change by newgrp.

- Set default write permissions to the group (using umask).

- If you start with a new subject, create a subdirectory for the work with group ownership of the new group which has write permissions for the group.

- Use rcs for all files which are created or modified by the editor (i.e. source files, makefiles etc.).

In addition, rcs fills certain strings with values which can be used for documentation and information purposes. Further rcs tools inspect the version file; see the manuals for details on rcsdiff, rcsmerge, and rlog.

C Source Codes and Tools

Various tools were mentioned in the book which can assist programming or pattern processing. Many of them are in the public domain and can be copied freely.

C.1 List of Tools

A very nice interactive facility for image processing and segmentation is the Khoros system [Ras92]. The system is very large and requires a Unix workstation with X11. Programs for almost all image processing issues addressed in this book can be found in this system. The system is written in C and some parts are included in Fortran.

The nihcl system which was used in Part II of the book is also available in the public domain with full source code.

The GNU tools are available at many places under the so called "copyleft".

The TEX macros for structograms can be found in ftp sites for TEX, at least in Germany.

C.2 How to get the sources

The programs khoros, nihcl cdecl, xfig, etc. were mentioned in the text. They are all available for Unix only. In order to get them, connect to your nearest ftp site. Most of these programs should be available there. If not, try to find them with archie or xarchie.

All examples printed in this book are available by ftp as well from

`ftp.uni-erlangen.de`

They can be compiled and run on MS-DOS as well using DJ's g++ GNU compiler. If you have no access to ftp, send a 1.5'' disk to the authors of this book and include a stamped and addressed envelope.

C.3 X11

Various packages exist for the display and interactive manipulation of images on the screen. To list some of them which use the X11 windows system which is most common under Unix:

- xv
- ImageMagick
- Khoros

These programs can also be found on ftp sites.

C.4 Slides

If you want to use the book for teaching, you might want to get the program examples in source code (Sect. C.2). We also provide a postscript version of slides which we use for teaching. They include all examples, figures, tables, and explanatory text. They are available by ftp at the above noted address.

C.5 Addresses

Dr.–Ing. Dietrich W. R. Paulus & Dipl.–Inf. Joachim Hornegger

Lehrstuhl für Mustererkennung (Informatik 5)
Martensstr. 3
D–91058 Erlangen   Phone: + 49/9131/7775
Germany   Fax: + 49/9131/303811
email: paulus@informatik.uni-erlangen.de
email: hornegger@informatik.uni-erlangen.de

C.6   Headers and Source Files

When you want to build your own system from the exercises and examples, you should start with the source code provided by ftp. Then do a typedef byte in a file Object.h. The assignment of file names to the examples is shown in Table C.1.

PointXY.h	81
LineRep.h	142
Sobel.C	169 172 173 166
Chain.h	139 143
Edge.h	146
Chain.C	144 145
Matrix.h	99
Matrix.C	101
testprog.C	157 158 159 160
PointXY.C	82
SegObj.h	151
GeoObj.h	148
AtomObj.h	149
AtomLine.h	150
Object.h	126 127 129 130
Object.C	128
EdgeImage.h	123
GreyLevelImage.h	138
ipop.h	161 162 163 164 165 165
HipposObj.h	137

Table C.1   List of header files and corrseponding examples

C.7   Dummy Definitions

In order to get a complete system for the linker, the following dummy definitions have to be provided to the compiler. They are really dummies and should be replaced by useful code. They just allow that all examples can be compiled and linked. These definitions are included in the ftp package mentioned above.

C.7.1 Listing of animals/dummy/Dictionary.h

```
1  #ifndef DICT_H
2  #define DICT_H
3  #include "Set.h"
4  class Dictionary : public Set { public: Dictionary(); };
5  #endif
```

C.7.2 Listing of animals/dummy/OIOxdr.h

```
1   #ifndef OIOxdr_H
2   #define OIOxdr_H
3
4   #include <Object.h>
5
6   class OIOin  {  } ;
7   class OIOout {  } ;
8
9   class OIOxdrin : public OIOin {
10   public:
11      OIOxdrin(char*);
12  };
13  class OIOxdrout : public OIOout {
14   public:
15      OIOxdrout(char*);
16  };
17  #endif
```

C.7.3 Listing of animals/dummy/Represent.h

```
1  #ifndef REP_H
2  #define REP_H
3  #include <HipposObj.h>
4  class Represent : public HipposObj { public: Represent(); };
5  #endif
```

C.7.4 Listing of animals/dummy/SeqCltn.h

```
1  #ifndef SEQCLT_H
2  #define SEQCLTP_H
3  #include "Object.h"
4  class SeqCltn : public Object { };
5  #endif
```

C.7.5 Listing of animals/dummy/Set.h

```
1   #ifndef SET_H
2   #define SET_H
3   #include "Object.h"
4   class Set : public Object {
5   public:
6   Set();
7   Set(const Set &);
8   };
9   #endif
```

C.7.6 Listing of animals/dummy/dummies.C

```
1   #include <stdio.h>
2   #include <stdlib.h>
3   #include "math.h"
4   #include "ipop.h"
5
6   #include <Chain.h>
7   #include <AtomLine.h>
8   #include "LineRep.h"
9   #include "GreyLevelImage.h"
10  #include "SegObj.h"
11  #include "OIOxdr.h"
12  #include <LineRep.h>
13
14  /////////////////////////////////
15  // Dummies
16  /////////////////////////////////
17  OIOxdrin::OIOxdrin(char*) {}
18  OIOxdrout::OIOxdrout(char*) {}
19  SegObj::SegObj() {};
20  void SegObj::storeOn(OIOout&) {};
21  SegObj::Display(DisplObj&) { return 0; }
22  void SegObj::add(const GeoObj&) {}
23  GeoObj::GeoObj() {}
24
25  // simplified DEFINE CLASS macro
26  DEFINE_CLASS(SegObj,0)
27  DEFINE_CLASS(GeoObj,0)
28  DEFINE_CLASS(AtomLine,0)
29  DEFINE_CLASS(AtomObj,0)
30  DEFINE_CLASS(HipposObj,1)
31  DEFINE_CLASS(GrayLevelImage,0)
32  DEFINE_CLASS(LineRep,1)
33
34  void AtomLine::storeOn(OIOout&) {}
35  void AtomObj::storeOn(OIOout&) {}
36  GeoObj::Display(DisplObj&) { return 0;}
37  AtomObj::AtomObj(void) {}
```

```
38   AtomLine::addRep(const Represent&) { return 0; }
39   void GeoObj::storeOn(OIOout&) {}
40   Set::Set() {}
41   AtomLine::AtomLine(const Represent&) {}
42   ChainSeq::ChainSeq(const ChainSeq&) {}
43   void ChainSeq::append(byte)        {}
44   Chain::Display(DisplObj&) { return 0; }
45   LineRep::LineRep(const PointXY&)     {}
46   LineRep::LineRep()                   {}
47   static PointXY p;
48   const PointXY& LineRep::Start() const
49   { return start; }
50   double LineRep::length() const { return 0; }
51   PointXY LineRep::End() const { return p; }
52   Represent::Represent() {}
53   int Gauss::operator() (GrayLevelImage&,GrayLevelImage&) const
54   { return 0; };
55   int Roberts::operator() (GrayLevelImage&,EdgeImage&) const
56   { return 0; };
57   HipposObj::HipposObj(float f) { reliability = f; }
58   void HipposObj::storeOn(OIOout& o) { }
59   void Chain::storeOn(OIOout& o) { }
60   void LineRep::storeOn(OIOout& o) { }
61   GrayLevelImage::Display(DisplObj&) { return 0; }
62   EdgeImage::Display(DisplObj&) { return 0; }
63   Dictionary::Dictionary() {}
64   void Object::storeOn(OIOout&) {};
65   Class::Class(char *, int) {};
66   void GrayLevelImage::storeOn(OIOout&) {};
67
68   /////////////////////////////////
69   // real work
70   /////////////////////////////////
71   EdgeImage::EdgeImage(int x,int y) : Image(x,y), image(x,y) { };
72   Edge * EdgeImage::operator[] (int i) { return image[i]; }
```

Bibliography

[Arp92]   R. B. Arps, W. K. Pratt (Hrsg.): *Image Processing and Interchange: Implementation and Systems*, SPIE Proceedings 1659, San Jose, CA, 1992.

[Bal82]   D. Ballard, C. Brown: *Computer Vision*, Prentice-Hall, Englewood Cliffs, NJ, 1982.

[Bau67]   L. E. Baum, J. A. Eagon: *An Inequality with Applications to Statistical Prediction for Functions of Markov Processes and to a Model for Ecology*, Bull. Amer. Math. Soc., Bd. 73, 1967, S. 360–363.

[Ber86]   F. Bergholm: *Edge Focussing*, in *Proceedings 8th Int. Conf. on Pattern Recognition*, Paris, 1986, S. 597–600.

[Ber87]   F. Bergholm: *Edge Focussing*, *IEEE Trans. on Pattern Analysis and Machine Intelligence*, Bd. 9, Nr. 6, 1987, S. 726–741.

[Big89]   N. L. Biggs: *Discrete Mathematics*, Clarendon Press, Oxford, 1989.

[Bir83]   G. Birtwistle, O. Dahl, B. Myrhang, K. Nygaard: *Simula Begin*, Auerbach Publ. Inc., Philadelphia, PA, 1983.

[Boo91]   G. Booch: *Object Oriented Design*, Benjamin / Cummings, Redwood City, CA, 1991.

[Bov87]   A. Bovik, T. Huang, D. Munson: *The Effect of Median Filtering on Edge Detection*, *IEEE Trans. on Pattern Analysis and Machine Intelligence*, Bd. 9, Nr. 2, 1987, S. 181–194.

[Bra78]   W. S. Brainerd: *Fortran 77 Programming*, Harper and Row, New York, 1978.

[Bre88]   P. Bremaud: *An Introduction to Probabilistic Modeling*, Undergraduate Texts in Mathematics, Springer, Heidelberg, 1988.

[Bro85]   I. N. Bronstein, K. A. Semendjajew: *Taschenbuch der Mathematik*, Harri Deutsch, Thun, 1985.

[Brü90]   H. Brünig: *Konzeption und Realisierung einer flexiblen Bildsegmentierung*, Dissertation, IMMD 5 (Mustererkennung), Universität Erlangen–Nürnberg, Erlangen, 1990.

[Bun92]   H. Bunke (Hrsg.): *Advances in Structural and Syntactic Pattern Recognition*, Series in Machine Perception and Artificial Intelligence, World Scientific Publishing, Singapore, 1992.

[Bur83]   P. Burt, E. Adelson: *The Laplacian Pyramid as a Compact Image Code*, *IEEE Transactions on Communications*, Bd. 31, Nr. 4, 1983, S. 532–540.

[Bus92]   R. Busch: *Editorial, Informatik Spektrum*, Bd. 15, Nr. 5, 1992, S. 253–254.

[Can86] J. F. Canny: *A Computational Approach to Edge Detection, IEEE Trans. on Pattern Analysis and Machine Intelligence*, Bd. 8, Nr. 6, 1986, S. 679–698.

[Cas90] Castan: *Optimal Filter for Edge Detection Method and Results, Proc. of the First European Conf. on Comp. Vision, No 427*, 1990, S. 12–17.

[Chi83] R. Chien, C.-L. Yeh: *Quantitative Evaluation of some Edge Preserving Noise Smoothing Techniques, Computer Graphics and Image Processing (CGIP)*, Bd. 23, 1983, S. 67–91.

[Cla92] A. F. Clark: *Image Processing and Interchange — The Imaging Model*, in Arps und Pratt [Arp92], S. 106–116.

[Coa90] P. Coad, E. Yourdon: *Object-oriented analysis*, Prentice Hall, Englewood Cliffs, NJ, 1990.

[Dan90] P.-E. Danielsson, O. Seger: *Generalized and Separable Sobel Operators*, in H. Freemann (Hrsg.): *Machine Vision for Three-Dimensional Scenes*, Academic Press, San Diego, 1990, S. 347–380, With an Appendix by I. Sobel.

[Dav78] L. Davis, A. Rosenfeld: *Noise Cleaning by Iterated Local Averaging, IEEE Transactions on Systems, Man, and Cybernetics*, Bd. 8, Nr. 9, 1978, S. 705–710.

[Dem77] A. Dempster, N. Laird, D. Rubin: *Maximum Likelihood from Incomplete Data via the EM Algorithm, Journal of the Royal Statistical Society, Series B (Methodological)*, Bd. 39, Nr. 1, 1977, S. 1–38.

[DeM79] T. DeMarco: *Structured Analysis and System Specification*, Prentice-Hall, Englewood Cliffs, NJ, 1979.

[Den94] J. Denzler, H. Niemann: *A Two-Stage Real Time Object Tracking System*, in Pavešić et al. [Pav94].

[Der87] R. Deriche: *Optimal Edge Detection Using Recursive Filtering, Proc of the 1. Int. Conf. on Computer Vision, London*, 1987, S. 501–505.

[Der90] R. Deriche: *Fast Algorithms for Low-Level Vision, IEEE Transactions on Pattern Analysis and Machine Intelligence (PAMI)*, Bd. 12, 1990, S. 78–87.

[Dij75] E. Dijkstra: *Goto statement considered harmful, Commm. ACM*, Bd. 18, 1975, S. 147 f.

[Dud72] R. Duda, P. Hart: *Pattern Classification and Scene Analysis*, J. Wiley, New York, 1972.

[Dud73] R. Duda, P. Hart: *Pattern Classification and Scene Analysis*, John Wiley & Sons, Inc., New York, 1973.

[Ekl82] J.-O. Eklundh, T. Elfving, S. Nyberg: *Edge Detection Using the Marr/Hildreth Opeartor with Different Sizes*, in *Proceedings 6th Int. Conf. on Pattern Recognition*, Munich, 1982, S. 1109–1111.

[Fis88] A. S. Fisher: *CASE*, John Wiley & Sons Ltd, New York, 1988.

[Fre80] H. Freeman: *Analysis and manipulation of lineal map data*, in H. Freeman, G. G. Pieroni (Hrsg.): *Map Data Processing*, Academic Press, New York, 1980, S. 151–168.

[Gal91] D. L. Gall: *MPEG: A Video Compression Standard for Multimedia Applications*, *Communications of the Association for Computing Machinery*, Bd. 34, Nr. 4, April 1991, S. 47–58.

[Gog78] J. Goguen, J. Thatcher, E. Wagner: *An initial algebra approach to the specification, correctness a nd implementation of abstract data types*, *Current Trends in Programming Methodology IV*, 1978, S. 80–144.

[Gol83] A. Goldberg, D. Robson: *Smalltalk-80: The Language and its Implementation*, Addison-Wesley, Reading, MA, 1983.

[Goo69] N. Goodman: *Languages of Art. An Approach to a theory of symbols*, Oxford Univ. Press, New York, 1969.

[Gor90] K. E. Gorlen, S. Orlow, P. S. Plexico: *Data Abstraction and Object-Oriented Programming in C++*, John Wiley and Sons, Chichester, 1990.

[Gut78] J. Guttag, J. Horning: *The algebraic specification of abstract data types*, *Acta Informatica*, Vol. 10, 1978, S. 27–52.

[Har82] R. Haralick: *Zero Crossing of Second Directional Derivative Edge Operator*, *SPIE*, Bd. 336, 1982, S. 91–99.

[Har88] R. Haralick, J. Lee: *Context Dependent Edge Detection*, in *Proceedings 9th Int. Conf. on Pattern Recognition*, Rome, 1988, S. 203–207.

[Har92] R. M. Haralick, V. Ramesh: *Image Understanding Environment*, in Arps und Pratt [Arp92], S. 159–167.

[Hau84] R. Hauser: *A Stochastic Approach to Edge Detection*, in *Proceedings 7th Int. Conf. on Pattern Recognition*, Montreal, 1984, S. 52–54.

[Hol88] G. Holzmann: *Beyond Photography – the Digital Darkroom*, Prentice Hall, 1988.

[Hor93] J. Hornegger, D. W. R. Paulus: *Detecting Elliptic Objects Using Inverse Hough–Transform*, in *Image Processing: Theory and Applications*, Elsevier, Amsterdam, 1993, S. 155–158.

[Hua88] J. Huang, D. Tseng: *Statistical Theory of Edge Detection*, *Computer Vision, Graphics and Image Processing (CVGIP)*, Bd. 43, 1988, S. 337–346.

[Hua90] X. Huang, Y. Ariki, M. Jack: *Hidden Markov Models for Speech Recognition*, Nr. 7 in Information Technology Series, Edinburgh University Press, Edinburgh, 1990.

[Hue73] M. Hueckel: *A local visual operator which recognizes edges and lines*, *JACM*, Bd. 18, 1973, S. 634–647; erratum in Vol. 21, p. 350, 1974.

[Jen85] K. Jensen, N. Wirth: *Pascal User Manual and Report*, Springer, New York, 1985.

[Joh87] M. E. Johnson: *Multivariate Statistical Simulation*, Probability and Mathematical Statistics, John Wiley & Sons, Inc., New York, 1987.

[Ker78] B. W. Kernighan, D. M. Ritchie: *The C Programming Language*, Prentice-Hall Software Series, Englewood Cliffs, NJ, 1978.

[Kir71] R. Kirsch: *Computer determination of the constituent structure of biological images*, *Comput. Biomed. Res.*, Bd. 4, 1971, S. 315–328.

[Knu73] D. E. Knuth: *The Art of Computer Programming*, Bd. 2: Seminumerical Algorithms, Addison–Wesley, Reading, MA, 1973.

[Kro79] L. I. Kronsjö: *Algorithms: Their Complexity and Efficiency*, Wiley Series in Computing, John Wiley & Sons, Inc., Chichester, 1979.

[Kun87] A. Kundu, S. Mitra: *A New Algorithm for Image Edge Extraction Using a Statistical Classifier Approach*, *IEEE Trans. on Pattern Analysis and Machine Intelligence*, Bd. 9, Nr. 4, 1987, S. 569–577.

[Kun90] S. Kunzmann: *Die Worterkennung in einem Dialogsystem für kontinuierlich gesprochene Sprache. Dissertation*, Technische Fakultät der Universität Erlangen-Nürnberg, Erlangen, 1990.

[Luo94] A. Luo: *Helligkeitsbasiertes Rechnersehen zur direkten Ermittlung räumlicher Eigenschaften*, Verlag Shaker, Aachen, 1994.

[Mac81] R. Machuca, A. Gilbert: *Finding Edges in Noisy Scenes*, *IEEE Trans. on Pattern Analysis and Machine Intelligence*, Bd. 3, Nr. 1, 1981, S. 103–111.

[Mar76] A. Martelli: *An application of heuristic search methods to edge and contour detection*, *Comm. ACM*, Bd. 19, 1976, S. 335–345.

[Mar80] D. Marr, E. Hildreth: *Theory of Edge Detection*, Proceedings Royal Society London B, Bd. 207, 1980, S. 187–217.

[Mar82] D. Marr: *Vision: A Computational Investigation into the Human Representation and Processing of Visual Information*, W.H. Freeman and Company, San Francisco, 1982.

[Mun92] J. Mundy, T. Binford, T. Boult, A. Hanson, R. Veveridge, R. Haralick, V. Ramesh, C. Kohl, D. Lawton, D. Morgan, K. Price, T. Strat: *The Image Understanding Environments Program*, in *Proc. of the DARPA Image Understanding Workshop*, Hawaii, Jan. 1992, S. 185–214.

[Nag79] M. Nagao, T. Matsuyama: *Edge Preserving Smoothing, Computer Graphics and Image Processing (CGIP)*, Bd. 9, 1979, S. 394–407.

[Nev80] R. Nevatia, R. Babu: *Linear Feature Extraction and Description, Computer Graphics and Image Processing (CGIP)*, Bd. 13, 1980, S. 257–269.

[Nie83] H. Niemann: *Klassifikation von Mustern*, Springer, Heidelberg, 1983.

[Nie90a] H. Niemann: *Pattern Analysis and Understanding*, Springer, Berlin, 1990.

[Nie90b] H. Niemann: *Pattern Analysis and Understanding*, Springer, Heidelberg, 1990.

[Noe91] E. Noeth: *Prosodische Information in der automatischen Spracherkennung Berechnung und Anwendung*. Dissertation, Max Niemeyer Verlag, Tübingen, 1991, To appear.

[Ous94] J. Ousterhout: *Tcl and the Tk toolkit*, Addison-Wesley, Reading, Mass., 1994.

[Pau92a] D. W. R. Paulus: *Object Oriented Image Segmentation*, in *Proc. of the 4th Int. Conf. on Image Processing and its Applications*, Maastrich, Holland, 1992, S. 482–485.

[Pau92b] D. W. R. Paulus: *Objektorientierte und wissensbasierte Bildverarbeitung*, Vieweg, Braunschweig, 1992.

[Pau92c] D. W. R. Paulus, H. Niemann: *Iconic–Symbolic Interfaces*, in Arps und Pratt [Arp92], S. 204–214.

[Pau93] D. Paulus, H. Niemann, C. Lenz, L. Demling, C. Ell: *Fraktale Dimension der Kontur endoskopisch ermittelter Farbbilder von Geschwüren des Magens*, in S. J. Pöppl, H. Handels (Hrsg.): *Mustererkennung 1993*, Springer, Berlin, 1993, S. 448–491.

[Pau94] D. Paulus, A. Winzen, F. Gallwitz, H. Niemann: *Object–Oriented Knowledge Representation for Image Analysis*, in Pavešić et al. [Pav94], S. 37–54.

[Pav94] N. Pavešić, H. Niemann, D. Paulus, S. Kovačić (Hrsg.): *3–D Scene Acquisition, Modeling and Understanding, Proceedings of the Second German–Slovenian Workshop*, IEEE Slovenia Section, Ljubljana, Slovenia, June 1994.

[Pit93] I. Pitas: *Digital Image Processing Algorithms*, Prentice Hall, New York, 1993.

[PJ80] M. Page-Jones: *Practical Guide to Structured System Design*, Prentice-Hall, Englewood Cliffs, NJ, 1980.

[Poy92] C. A. Poynoton: *An Overview of TIFF 5.0*, in Arps und Pratt [Arp92], S. 150–158.

[Pra78] W. K. Pratt: *Digital Image Processing*, Wiley Interscience, New York, 1978.

[Pra80]   M. Prager: *Extracting and Labeling Boundary Segments in Natural Scenes, IEEE Trans. on Pattern Analysis and Machine Intelligence,* Bd. 2, Nr. 1, 1980, S. 16–27.

[Pre70]   J. Prewitt: *Object enhancement and extraction, Picture Processing and Psychopictorics,* 1970, S. 75–149.

[Pre88]   W. Press, B. Flannery, S. Teukolsky, W. Vetterling: *Numerical Recipes - the Art of Numerical Computing, C Version,* 35465-X, 1988.

[Rab88]   L. Rabiner: *Mathematical Foundations of Hidden Markov Models,* in H. Niemann, M. Lang, G. Sagerer (Hrsg.): *Recent Advances in Speech Understanding and Dialog Systems,* Bd. 46 von *NATO ASI Series F,* Springer, Heidelberg, 1988, S. 183–205.

[Ran67]   B. Randell: *ALGOL 60 Implementation,* Academic Press, 1967, 3. pr.

[Ras92]   J. R. Rasure, M. Young: *Open environment for image processing and software development,* in Arps und Pratt [Arp92], S. 300–310.

[Rit86]   X. Ritter, P. Gadev, J. Davidson: *Automated Bridge Detection in FLIR Images,* in *Proceedings 8th Int. Conf. on Pattern Recognition,* Paris, 1986, S. 862–864.

[Rob77]   G. Robinson: *Edge detection by compass gradient masks, Computer Graphics and Image Processing (CGIP),* Bd. 6, 1977, S. 492–501.

[Ros71]   A. Rosenfeld, M. Thurston: *Edge and Curve Detection for Visual Scene Analysis, IEEE Transactions on Computers,* Bd. 20, Nr. 5, 1971, S. 562–569.

[Ros82]   A. Rosenfeld, A. Kak: *Digital Picture Processing,* Academic Press, New York, 1982.

[Rum91]   J. Rumbaugh: *Object-oriented modeling and design,* Prentice-Hall, Englewood Cliffs, NJ, 1991.

[Sch90]   N. Schneider: *Kantenhervorhebung und Kantenverfolgung in der industriellen Bildverarbeitung,* Forschritte in der Robotik, 6, Vieweg, Braunschweig, 1990.

[She86]   Shen, Castan: *An optimal linear operator for edge detection, Computer Vision, Graphics and Image Processing (CVGIP),* Bd. 5, 1986, S. 109–114.

[She88]   Shen, Castan: *Further results on DRF Method of edge detection, Proc. Computer Vision, Graphics and Image Processing,* Miami, Bd. 6, 1988, S. 223–225.

[Shi87]   Y. Shirai: *Three–Dimensional Computer Vision,* Springer, Heidelberg, 1987.

[Shl88]   S. Shlaer, S. J. Mellor: *Object-oriented systems analysis,* Yourdon, Englewood Cliffs, NJ, 1988.

[ST95]   E. Schukat-Talamazzini: *Automatische Spracherkennung*, Vieweg, Wiesbaden, 1995.

[Sti82]   G. W. W. Stiles: *Color Science: Concepts and Methods, Quantiative Data and Formulae*, John Wiley & Sons Ltd, New York, 2. Ausg., 1982.

[Sto90]   C. Stockmayer: *Von Version zu Version, joop*, Bd. 12, 1990, S. 66–68.

[Str91a] B. Stroustrup: *The C++ Programming Language*, Addison-Wesley, Reading, Mass., 2nd. Ausg., 1991.

[Str91b] B. Stroustrup: *The C++ Programming Language,* 2nd, Addison-Wesley, Reading, MA, 1991.

[Tab84]   A. Tabatabai, R. Mitchell: *Edge Location to Subpixel Values in Digital Imagery, IEEE Trans. on Pattern Analysis and Machine Intelligence*, Bd. 6, Nr. 2, 1984, S. 188–201.

[Wal90]   G. Wallace: *Overview of the JPEG (ISO/CCITT) Still Image Compression Standard*, in *Electronic Image Science and Technology*, SPIE Proceedings 1244, Santa Clara, CA, Feb. 1990, S. 97–108.

[Weg87]   P. Wegner: *Dimensions of Object–Based Language Design, OOPSLA '87 Conference Proceedings, SIGPLAN*, Bd. 22, Nr. 12, 1987, S. 168–182.

[Wir83]   N. Wirth: *Programming in Modula 2*, Springer, Berlin, Heidelberg, New York, 1983.

[Wu83]   C. F. J. Wu: *On the Convergence Properties of the EM Algorithm, The Annals of Statistics*, Bd. 11, Nr. 1, 1983, S. 95–103.

[XDR88]   Sun Microsystems Inc., Stanford: *RFC External Data Representation Standard: Protocol Specifications*, sun os 4 manuals, network programming, part 2. Ausg., 1988.

[Yam81]   G. Yamg, T. Kuang: *The Effort of Median Filtering on Edge Location Estimation, Computer Graphics and Image Processing (CGIP)*, Bd. 15, 1981, S. 224–245.

[Zam91]   P. Zamperoni: *Methoden der digitalen Bildverarbeitung*, Vieweg-Verlag, Wiesbaden, 1991.

Index

List of Figures

List of Tables

Index for Exercises

Parallelism in Logic

von Franz Kurfeß

1991. xii, 299 pp. (Artificial Intelligence; edited by Wolfgang Bibel and Walther von Hahn) Softcover ISBN 3-528-05163-9

The potential of parallelism in logic reaches far beyond the exploitation of AND- and OR-parallelism usually found in attempts to parallelize PROLOG. This book discusses parallelism in logic and its exploitation on parallel architectures. A variety of categories of parallelism is discussed with respect to different levels of a logical formula and different ways to evaluate it. As an outcome of these investigations it is shown that modularity allows structuring of logic programs and meta-evaluation can be used to control the evaluation process on a parallel system. This combination yields a consistent programming framework with a wide scope. Finally, the suitability of a specific evaluation mechanism for parallel architectures is investigated.

Verlag Vieweg · Postfach 58 29 · 65048 Wiesbaden

vieweg

Modeling of Dynamic Object Systems

von Ralf Jungclaus

With a foreword by H.-D. Ehrich

1993. XVI, 231 Seiten (Vieweg Advanced Studies in Computer Science) Softcover
ISBN 3-528-05386-0

Aus dem Inhalt: Entwicklung von Informationssystemen: Grundlagen und Ziele – Grundbegriffe der Systemspezifikation und -modellierung – Semantische Begriffe – Die Sprache TROLL – Objekt- und Klassen-Spezifikation – Die Arbeitsweise – Verwandte Verfahren.

Das Buch gibt einen gut lesbaren und wohlfundierten Einblick in die objektorientierte formale Spezifikation von Datenbanksystemen. Leitend ist der Gesichtspunkt, daß Informationssysteme „reagierende" Systeme sind, deren Objekte sich parallel nebeneinander, ereignisabhängig und diskret verändern. Verwandte Verfahren dieses stark von logischen Aspekten geprägten Ansatzes werden aufgezeigt.

Über den Autor: Dr. Ralf Jungclaus ist Wissenschaftlicher Mitarbeiter am Institut für Informationsverarbeitende Systeme der TU Braunschweig (Leitung Prof. Ehrich).

Verlag Vieweg · Postfach 58 29 · 65048 Wiesbaden

vieweg

Fuzzy-Systems in Computer Science

Herausgegeben von Rudolf Kruse, Jörg Gebhardt und Rainer Palm

1994. x, 340 pp. (Artificial Intelligence; edited by Wolfgang Bibel and Walther von Hahn) Hardcover
ISBN 3-528-05456-5

Dieses Buch enthält ausgewählte und auf neuesten Stand gebrachte Fachaufsätze und „State of the Art"-Übersichtsartikel in englischer Sprache. Sie geben einen Überblick über aktuelle Trends sowie Zukunftsperspektiven der Fuzzy-Systeme. Besonderer Wert wird darauf gelegt, daß das Buch in einem ausgewogenen Verhältnis von Theorie und Praxis zur Fundierung von Konzepten, Methoden und Werkzeugen beiträgt. Hervorgegangen ist das Werk aus einem von der Gesellschaft für Informatik (GI), der Deutschen Informatik Akademie (DIA) und der TU Braunschweig gemeinsam veranstalteten GI-Workshop „Fuzzy-Systeme '93 – Management unsicherer Informationen" (Braunschweig, 21.-22.10.1993). Die Aufsätze wurden überarbeitet und um Überblicksartikel ergänzt, geschrieben von H. J. Zimmermann, H. Hellendorn, D. Nauck, C. Freksa, S. Gottwald und K. D. Meyer-Gramann.

Über die Herausgeber: Prof. Dr. Rudolf Kruse und Dr. Jörg Gebhardt arbeiten am Institut für Betriebssysteme und Rechnerverbund der TU Braunschweig.
Dr. Rainer Palm ist in der Zentralabteilung Forschung und Entwicklung der Siemens AG München tätig.

Verlag Vieweg · Postfach 58 29 · 65048 Wiesbaden

vieweg